TREKKING IN THE
WESTERN
ALPS

HILARY SHARP

Climbing consultant
VICTOR SAUNDERS

NEW HOLLAND

First published in 2002 by
New Holland Publishers (UK) Ltd
London · Cape Town · Sydney · Auckland

www.newhollandpublishers.com

Garfield House, 86–88 Edgware Road, London W2 2EA, United Kingdom

80 McKenzie Street, Cape Town 8001, South Africa

14 Aquatic Drive, Frenchs Forest, NSW 2086, Australia

218 Lake Road, Northcote, Auckland, New Zealand

2 4 6 8 10 9 7 5 3 1

ISBN 1 85974 453 2

Publishing Manager: Jo Hemmings
Series Editor: Kate Michell
Editorial Assistant: Anne Konopelski
Design concept: Alan Marshall
Designer: Hugh Adams
Cartography: William Smuts
Production: Joan Woodroffe

Reproduction by Modern Age Repro Co. Ltd, Hong Kong
Printed and bound in Singapore by
Kyodo Printing Co (Singapore) Pte Ltd

The author and publisher have made every effort to
ensure that the information in this book was correct
when the book went to press; they accept no responsi-
bility for any loss, injury or inconvenience sustained by
any person using this book.

Front cover: Approaching the Col du Bonhomme on the
Tour du Mont Blanc. *Back cover:* The author pictured on
the Tour du Mont Blanc. *Cover spine:* Snow-shoeing
appeals to all ages. *Title page:* Climber on the summit
of the Aiguille du Bionnassay. *This spread:* Approaching
the summit of the Weissmies. *Opposite contents page:*
The Aiguilles Charmoz, Blaitière and Plan, seen from
Vallorcine. *Contents page top:* The summit of Castor in
the Pennine Alps in winter; *middle top:* A traditional
Alpine house in Les Biolles, Vallorcine; *middle bottom:* A
snowy summer's day in the Aiguilles Rouges, above
Chamonix; *bottom:* The alpenrose in bloom in July.

Hilary Sharp runs Trekking in the Alps, a company that
organises guided treks in the European Alps, the
Pyrenees and on Mediterranean Islands, and snow-
shoeing holidays and treks. Trekking in the Alps,
Chemin des Biolles, Vallorcine 74660, France;
www.trekkinginthealps.com

CONTENTS

ABOUT THIS BOOK

The choice of treks and peaks for this book is inevitably subjective and arbitrary. I've chosen a sample to show what I think are some of the best aspects of the Western Alps. Some of these treks and peaks are very well known, regarded as classics, whereas others are personal favourites. This book does not aim to replace the maps you would normally use for such exploits, nor the detailed guidebook descriptions available for the peaks. My aim is to inspire you, to bring together in one book a selection of good walks for a large part of the Western Alps. Linked to those walks are summits that you'll see whilst doing these treks and may be tempted to climb during or after the trek.

Snow-shoe walks are also included as this is the best way to walk in the Alps in winter. On snow shoes you can get to many otherwise inaccessible cols and summits, allowing you to explore the superb winter alpine scenery.

All treks, peaks and snow-shoe walks are described using mountain huts for any overnights. This does not mean that camping isn't an option – it very often is, although camping anywhere other than on designated campsites should be done discreetly, and in the reserves and national parks camping is often forbidden.

Some of the treks in this book are circular – these are generally known as 'tours'. Others start and finish in different places, and for these it is usually possible to get local transport back to the start if you need to.

MAPS

Maps and strip maps are included to locate the treks and to show the general route. The strip maps and peak information give an idea of timings and distance, but **none of this is a substitute for your own personal navigation and adaptation of timings according to your walking pace and conditions**.

Details of further reference maps are given in the 'Essentials' factboxes that accompany the description of each trek, climb or snow-shoe walk. These can be bought locally or in large bookshops before arriving in the Alps.

LEGEND

Motorway		✗	International airport
Highway tunnel		✗	Airport/airstrip
Provincial road		▲	Mountain hut
Secondary road		▲	Campsite
Track/footpath	Col de Bise	)(	Mountain pass
Trek route alternative route	Mont Blanc ▲ 4807m (15772ft)		Peak in metres (feet)
Snow-shoe walk	Duwo Glacier		Glacier
International boundary	dam river		Water features
Railway			Altitude contour (3000m/9843ft on trek maps)
☐ GENÈVE Capital			Ridge
◉ Montreux City	MISCHABEL		Mountain range
◎ Zermatt Town	❼ ❼		Trek number
○ Champéry Village/building/ruin			Cable car/chairlift
Dinosaur ● tracks Place of interest			

Trek Essentials boxes summarize each trek, including approximate number of days required, means of access to the start and finish, highest elevations reached, trekking style involved and official restrictions, if any. Also mentioned are notable variations on the route.

Strip maps illustrate the elevation profile of each trek, including key passes and spot heights, as well as walking times. (NB Strip maps are illustrative and not designed for cross-reference between treks.)

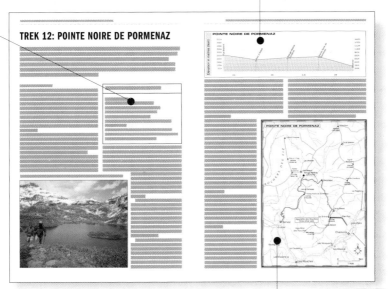

Top-class **mapping** pinpoints the route of each trek, with ridge lines, selected altitude contours, glaciers, passes and nearest roads included. Also illustrated in fainter blue lines are snow show walks.

Snow-shoe walk boxes provide route outlines and details of interesting features, including the grade of each walk and approximate timings.

Climb Essentials boxes summarize the characteristics of each climbing route, including summit height and grade of climb.

Specially sourced **topo photographs** show the general approach route to each climbing peak, with the route clearly marked in red.

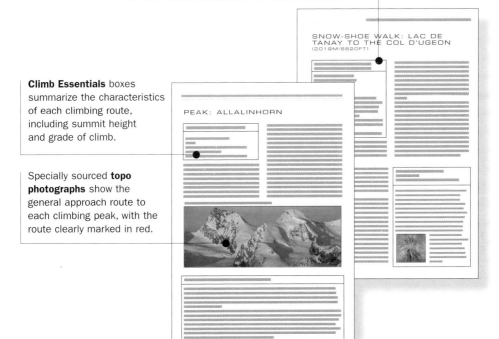

1

INTRODUCTION TO THE WESTERN ALPS

The Alps have fired the dreams of visitors, including walkers and climbers, for over two hundred years. Ever since the first foreign explorers ventured into the heart of the Chamonix mountains in the mid-18th century, people have been making the pilgrimage to the biggest mountains in Western Europe, either to discover the charms of the Alps by travelling on foot through the meadows and high passes, or to try their luck on an Alpine peak, or just to stand and stare.

Mont Blanc, the Matterhorn, Monte Rosa, the Gran Paradiso – all names that capture the imagination. More than sixty peaks reach the sought-after height of 4000m (13124ft) or more in the Alps, and the fact that these mountains are situated close together makes for awe-inspiring and immediate panoramas. Many of the best are to be seen from the smaller mountains set slightly apart from the main massifs. Impressive rocky passes, flower-filled meadows, lush valleys, charming old villages and perched Alpine huts complete the playground of the Alpine trekker.

Although part of modern Europe, traditional patterns of life still exist in the Alps, and on foot there are numerous opportunities to immerse yourself in this rugged, tough world, experiencing all that the Alps have to offer.

Mont Blanc's beautiful Brenva face.

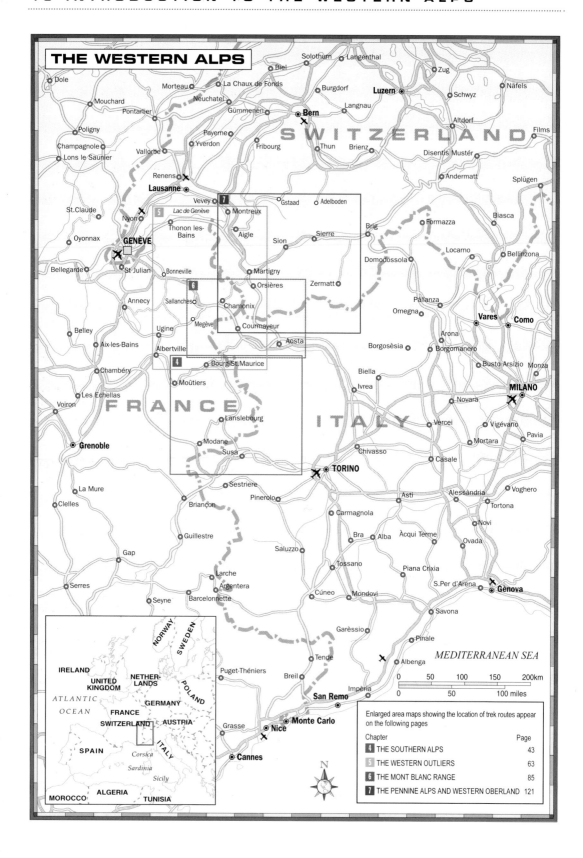

THE WESTERN ALPS

SWITZERLAND

FRANCE

ITALY

MEDITERRANEAN SEA

Lac de Genève

Enlarged area maps showing the location of trek routes appear on the following pages

Chapter		Page
4	THE SOUTHERN ALPS	43
5	THE WESTERN OUTLIERS	63
6	THE MONT BLANC RANGE	85
7	THE PENNINE ALPS AND WESTERN OBERLAND	121

0   50   100   150   200km
0   50   100 miles

NORWAY
SWEDEN
IRELAND
UNITED KINGDOM
NETHER-LANDS
POLAND
GERMANY
ATLANTIC OCEAN
FRANCE
SWITZERLAND
AUSTRIA
SPAIN
Corsica
ITALY
Sardinia
Sicily
ALGERIA
TUNISIA
MOROCCO

Solothurn, Langenthal, Biel, Zug, Näfels, Dole, Morteau, La Chaux de Fonds, Burgdorf, Luzern, Schwyz, Mouchard, Neuchatel, Langnau, Altdorf, Films, Pontarlier, Gümmenen, Bern, Poligny, Payerne, Thun, Brienz, Disentis Müster, Andermatt, Splügen, Champagnole, Yverdon, Fribourg, Vallorbe, Renens, Lausanne, Vevey, Gstaad, Adelboden, Brig, Formazza, Biasca, St.Claude, Nyon, Montreux, Sierre, Locarno, Bellinzona, Oyonnax, Thonon les-Bains, Aigle, Sion, Domodossola, Bellegarde, St Julian, Bonneville, Martigny, Zermatt, Pàllanza, Omegna, Vares, Como, Annecy, Sallanches, Orsières, Chamonix, Arona, Belley, Ugine, Megève, Courmayeur, Aosta, Borgosèsia, Borgomanero, Busto Arsizio, Monza, Aix-les-Bains, Albertville, Biella, MILANO, Chambéry, Moûtiers, Ivrea, Novara, Les Echellas, Voiron, Lanslebourg, Vercei, Vigévano, Pavia, Grenoble, Modane, Chivasso, Mortara, Susa, Casale, La Mure, Sestriere, TORINO, Asti, Alessàndria, Voghero, Clelles, Briançon, Pinerolo, Tortona, Carmagnola, Novi, Guillestre, Saluzzo, Bra, Alba, Àcqui Terme, Ovada, Gap, Tossano, Piana Crixia, S.Per d'Arena, Gènova, Larche, Serres, Argentera, Cúneo, Mondovi, Seyne, Barcelonnette, Savona, Garèssio, Pinale, Tende, Albenga, Puget-Théniers, Breil, Impèria, Grasse, Nice, Monte Carlo, San Remo, Cannes, N

THE ALPS

The highest chain of mountains in Western Europe, the Alps extend in a long convex arc from west to east. They are defined at their western extremity by the Rhône valley, and to the north by the Swiss plateau and the foothills of Germany and Austria. The eastern limit of the chain is the Hungarian plains, and the Italian Po valley forms the southern edge where the Alps lose height very suddenly all along their length.

Thus defined, the Alps are about 1200km (750 miles) long and 150–250km (90–155 miles) wide, their greatest extent being towards the east where the diverse mountain ranges fan out to the north and south. The Alps cover a total area of approximately 220,000km^2 (approximately 75,000 square miles); the average height is 1400m (4593ft), culminating in the highest summit, Mont Blanc, at 4807m (15772ft).

The Alps were formed by the gradual collision of the continental plates in the Tertiary period, which began about 65 million years ago. A former ocean bed, comprising many sedimentary layers, was pushed up and folded, creating the different rocks we know today. Consequently the mountains have varying geological formations at different altitudes, which can be astonishing and which are largely explained by the bulldozer effect of this slow collision.

Glaciers have covered the Alps at least four times: 1 million years ago, 500,000 years ago, 100,000 years ago and, most recently, 50,000 years ago, each Ice Age separated from the next by a warm period. Glaciers erode by their slow and powerful movement, taking with them silt and sand that they collect, which makes them more erosive. They also split and break softer rocks, by the freeze-thaw action in cracks and strata. Moraines are collections of boulders, stones and silt pushed to the sides and ends of glaciers as they move down. These moraines remain long after the disappearance of the glaciers, one of many testaments to their past presence.

During the last Ice Age the glaciers modified the form of the already-complex Alpine massifs. High up, deep valleys were created, the arêtes were accentuated, big U-shaped valleys developed and, later, powerful torrents gouged out precipitous gorges. After the glacial period, the climatic zones that we know today became established, with, for example, the Southern Alps enjoying an almost-Mediterranean climate.

Glacial cycles have existed throughout history and although at present the glaciers are in retreat

WHAT ARE THE WESTERN ALPS?

The Alps span an enormous area stretching across several countries from west to east. This book aims to provide a sample of treks in approximately half the region. There is no strict dividing line between east and west and one possibility would have been the border between French- and German-speaking Switzerland. However, several multi-day treks cross this line and to enable such treks to be included the region described as the Western Alps goes as far as Zermatt and the Pennine Alps. It extends south into the Ecrins massif, but doesn't include the Maritime Alps further south.

The bulk of the treks are centred around the main Alpine massifs of Mont Blanc and the Pennine Alps. This is a selection, and the exclusion of an area is due to lack of space, not because it doesn't merit attention. The treks and summits described here provide a sample of the vast range of possibilities in the Alps; they are certainly not the only worthwhile outings in the areas described.

this cycle is relatively normal. The 'Little Ice Age' from 1550 to 1820 saw the glaciers advance considerably, to the extent that villages in the valleys literally had the ice on their doorsteps. Since then the cycles have been shorter, and, for example, in 1955 the Bossons glacier in Chamonix had retreated very noticeably. In the 1970s and 1980s the glaciers briefly surged forward, to then retreat again quickly. The Bossons glacier in 1992 was at roughly the same level as it had been in 1955. It is not yet known whether the air pollution caused by man over the last century will affect the normal cyclic evolution of glaciers.

SIGNS OF WILDLIFE IN THE MOUNTAINS

Fortunately, this pollution has not yet had a severe effect on the Alps, and one of the joys of trekking in the Alps is the wildlife you can see or of which you may find signs. There are many different animals living in the mountains, each with its distinctive lifestyle. If you keep your eyes open you'll spot many indications of life, and with practice will be able to make an informed guess as to what creature left certain tracks, droppings or marks on trees, etc.

Different animals live at different altitudes and in varying types of terrain. In the forested valleys you'll find squirrels, deer, pine martens, foxes and badgers. Higher up, on the edge of the treeline and the meadows, blue hares and chamois are common. The area above the trees, up to around 3000m (9483ft), is home to marmots, ibex, chamois, foxes and ermines, whilst above that conditions are too barren and cold for any animal to want to live there permanently, although some will make forays to high altitude. For example, in August 1997 I found fox tracks on the summit of the Obergabelhorn at 4063m (13331ft).

When you find signs of animal life the first consideration is what creatures are possible candidates. Secondly, this list may immediately be reduced by studying the size, depth and distance between the tracks. These factors give a good idea of the size of the animal, and some animals will be

ALPAGES

For many years the main livelihood of Alpine people was their cattle. Hardy cows provided food and also products to trade. Today, mountain cheeses from areas such as the Abondance valley and Beaufortain are still famous and sold widely, but tourism has replaced agriculture as the main income nearly everywhere. Nevertheless, some farming remains, and the old traditions haven't completely died. The cattle spend the winters, which generally last at least six months, in the valleys, in stables, being fed on hay stored the previous autumn. In May, the cattle are put out to graze the lower fields, and as summer approaches they are taken up to the higher slopes. They graze ever higher as the summer progresses, usually reaching the highest grazing ground at the end of July. In September they descend and spend several weeks grazing in the valleys before being shut away again for the long, cold winter.

This process is called 'transhumance' and has been practised for centuries in the Alps. It is an important part of the Alpine calendar, and the departure and return of the cattle are celebrated in some villages. In September, as the cows return to the village they are often decked out in flowers and this is a fine excuse for a party.

Farmers or shepherds accompany their animals, and when they reach the higher grazing ground they stay up there for the summer. These areas are usually above the treeline, in the last really fertile land before the high-Alpine slopes of scree and minimal vegetation. The pastures often command spectacular views of the surrounding summits and give much pleasure to walkers. These summer farms (*alpages* in French) provide basic accommodation, or sell local products such as cheese. Throughout this book the word *alpage* is used for these places.

Often the *alpages* are owned jointly by a group of people or the *commune* (a *commune* is a town or group of towns with one mayor and local council). This came about because traditionally farmers weren't wealthy enough to own sufficient land to graze their animals so they joined together to be able to afford the meadows. Often *alpages* were blessed in a religious celebration, usually at the start of the summer season, hence the frequent presence of a cross.

Chamois are to be found throughout the Alps.

eliminated. Thirdly, a basic knowledge of the types of tracks produced by different animals is obviously essential to arrive at any sort of conclusion.

Tracks tell a story and it's quite fascinating to see, for example, the nightly comings and goings of hares or foxes. Similarly, you may well come across tracks emerging from holes in the snow, which could well belong to ptarmigan. Although clearly tracks are easier to find in winter in the snow, signs do exist in the summer, on wet ground; and also droppings and other signs of life are to be found everywhere if you know what to look for. For example, in the coniferous forests cones are abundant, and provide food for many birds as well as squirrels and mice. It doesn't take much experience to be able to distinguish the animal or bird that nibbled the cones you find. Tree trunks are often adorned with the work of the woodpecker, and holes excavated by these birds can then become home to other animals, such as martens, whilst ant hills provide nourishment for many forest dwellers, including the woodpecker and the badger. Bushes and tree branches may well have been nibbled, and it's interesting to be able to distinguish a hare's

ALPINE TREES

Photos of the Alpine valleys taken a hundred years ago show valleys that were cultivated as much as possible. The forests were cut back and the land prepared for crops and grazing. With the growth of tourism, agriculture has all but died out in most Alpine areas, with just cattle remaining. These are kept indoors in winter and graze the higher pastures in the summer months, so much of the forest has grown back.

Above 1000m (3281ft) Alpine forest consists largely of spruce and larch trees. These two trees have complementary requirements so they exist well together. The larch, recognisable for its needles which grow in a 'tuft', and which are pale green in spring, golden in the autumn, is able to survive in places where the water supply is irregular. By losing its needles in the winter it requires much less water during the winter months, enabling it to grow in exposed situations, such as on ridges, where in winter any water supply is frozen. The larch's deep roots give it good purchase in windy spots.

The spruce, which has dark-green needles growing regularly along the branch, has a shallower root system so it grows on more-protected slopes which tend to be wet even in winter. Hence it doesn't need to lose its needles. Spruce regularly grows to a height of 30m (98ft) and can live for more than 150 years. When spruce trees are blown over by the wind, larches tend to colonise the area, with the spruce only returning to benefit from the protection of the larch trees. The spruce thrive and finally grow tall, blocking out the light for the larch, which needs a maximum amount of sunlight for the short period (five months) when it has needles. The larches die, the spruce get blown over and the whole process starts over again.

The larch resists avalanches well. By losing its needles it presents less of an obstacle to the snow and wind of an avalanche. Its deep roots anchor it well to the slope, and you'll rarely see an uprooted larch; more likely it will be broken off at the trunk after a severe winter. High up, often at the limit of the treeline, is the Arolla pine, recognisable by its long needles and often stunted growth. Rather than be blown on the wind its heavy seeds are taken by the nutcracker bird, which stores them in cracks and crevices. Some of these inevitably germinate.

In areas regularly swept by avalanches only one tree always manages to consistently grow, and that's the alder. These small trees colonise slopes that are rocky and wet, or constantly running with water. They grow on ground that would otherwise be bare of vegetation, being too steep or unstable. Their roots can attach where everything else slips, and the tree can survive for months bent up under the snow. Without the alders these slopes would be bare and consequently more prone to erosion. The alders provide welcome shelter for other plants to grow and also for animals, such as chamois which frequent such slopes.

Many other trees are to be found in the Alps, according to the area, the soil type and the altitude. Birch, rowan, yew, hazel, juniper, oak, beech and willow are all common.

Larch trees turn a warm golden colour in the autumn.

signature from that of a deer, for example.

Once you begin to look for signs of life in the mountains, your walks may frequently be interrupted as you study the various trademarks left behind and your fellow walkers may become a little impatient with you. But it's important to remember that apart from the fabulous views in the Alps, there's another smaller-scale world co-existing with ours, which can be just as exciting. Numerous books are available on the subject.

The aptly-named spiniest thistle is particularly beautiful in the sun.

ALPINE FLOWERS

Walking in the Alps in the summer is a visual delight, not just because of the mountain views but also thanks to the plant life encountered along the way. This varies according to the altitude and geology and on a typical alpine trek you will see many different flowers and shrubs. Flowers are at their most abundant in early summer, but seasons arrive later at high altitude, so whilst in the valleys the plants are blooming from May onwards, at 2500m (8203ft) July will be the most common flowering time. Even late in the summer, towards the end of August or in early September, flowers are plentiful above 2000m (6562ft), but they tend to be smaller and you'll have to look for them a lot more than earlier in the season, when the meadows are carpeted with colour and the alpenrose tranforms the hillsides with its blazing pink flowers.

Knowing a few of the most common varieties of flowers is within the grasp of every walker. This is so regardless of whether you decide to try to learn the names of all the flowers you encounter, taking along a good guidebook and spending the evenings looking up the new species you've spotted that day, or whether you're quite happy just to enjoy the splendour of the Alpine flora. Many of the plants are miniature forms of plants that are grown in gardens at lower altitudes. Some plants, however, are peculiar to the Alps, and only grow in the most hostile places. They would not be at all happy in your garden, however much love and attention you lavished on them.

Whether the fine flora of the Alps will still be here in the future is questionable. Man is forever changing the Alpine landscape and the flowers consequently change too. Obviously picking flowers, especially by pulling out the roots, is to be avoided, even in a site where a certain flower is plentiful. But flower picking is not the biggest hazard to Alpine flora nowadays. The power-supply industry, tourism and agriculture all affect the original beauty of nature and the diversity of plant species in much more drastic ways. Areas are still being flooded as a result of dam construction, and some of these places are the only remaining sites of rare plant life.

Whilst natural slopes that are regularly skied seem to be little affected by the passage of skiers for several months of the year, bulldozed ski pistes irrevocably destroy ground flora. The humus accumulated over centuries is removed and the newly formed bare-scree surfaces are exposed to erosion. Should the construction of machine-graded ski runs be allowed to continue, certain Alpine areas risk losing their beautiful mountain landscapes, and consequently the basis of their summer tourism.

Agricultural practices have greatly changed in the Alps since the Second World War. Remote pastures are less used, and many wild hay meadows are no longer mown. These fields provided the most brightly coloured and spectacular meadows in the Alps, and nowadays they are often totally neglected, in which case they may well become forested again, or they are grazed by sheep or goats, which leave no flowers at all.

Whilst walking in the Alps you'll find that the hillsides can be divided into levels, where you'll find different plants at varying stages of development as you gain altitude. Below the treeline you'll find a rich variety of flora of mixed lowland and mountain species. Meadows and woods, lanes and banks are often very flowery, with large herbs, shrubs and trees. At the uppermost limit the trees, generally pine, spruce and larch, become dwarf and stunted and rather sparse. This is the sub-alpine zone. Above the treeline is the true alpine-plant zone, where conditions are too rigorous to support tree growth. Here the flora is highly specialised, with dwarf and carpeting shrubs replacing the trees, and all the flowers being adapted to the harsh climatic conditions encountered at this level. High on the barren screes you'll find ground- and rock-hugging plants, often with cushions or tufts, small leaves and brightly coloured flowers. All these features help them to survive as efficiently as possible, requiring a minimum of water, resisting high winds, extreme temperatures and attracting a maximum number of insects to achieve pollination.

A few of the most common or interesting alpine plants are described in this book, but anyone interested in knowing more about what they are seeing is recommended to buy an identification book (see Bibliography). Be prepared for hours of frustration when you can't quite find the flower you've seen, but also a great sense of satisfaction when you manage to recognise something or find a particularly rare flower.

Finally, a word about mushrooms. Many different types are to be found in the Alps, and you'll often see people collecting them. If you decide to do this, be very careful what you eat. To be sure that what you've found is edible take your mushrooms to the local pharmacy where the pharmacist will be able to identify the type and advise whether eating these is a good idea.

ARCHITECTURE

Beyond and within the mountains and meadows there are numerous signs of human life in the Alps – particularly in the form of buildings. Two main criteria tend to govern the design of houses in the Alps. Firstly, the building has to be able to withstand the harsh mountain winters, when several metres of snow can pile up on the roof and gale-force winds can batter the structure for days on end. Secondly, the house must be built of materials that are near at hand and plentiful; in the Alps there are lots of trees, and stone is also fairly easily obtained.

Many of the old chalets, and some of the new, are constructed from larch. This wood is superb for building since it is very durable and does not need to be treated. Most old chalets and barns are larch, easily recognisable by its grey discoloration on the faces exposed to the weather. It remains a deep red/brown on sheltered walls. The roofs are of various materials, but almost all have some sort of device to prevent the snow sliding off. Quite

Traditional stone house in Vallorcine.

churches of many Alpine villages and towns date from the 17th and 18th centuries, and are decorated in the 'Alpine baroque' style, less ornate than the mainstream baroque style. They have finely decorated towers topped by impressive bulbs. There is a fine example of the style in Argentière, and an even better one in the Saas valley, the Road-Kirche at Saas Balen. This church has a superb double rotunda. Rome was the original home of baroque and the style spread first to the north of Italy – Turin bearing witness to this. Numerous Alpine churches were the work of architects and builders from the Milanese valley of Val Sesia, who took their art to the mountain towns via the Tarentaise and Maurienne valleys. Some churches have retained their rich baroque interiors, whilst others have been restored. Many of these churches also lost their bells during the First and Second World Wars, but, fortunately, a few still remain or have been replaced.

impressive avalanches can be seen coming off roofs which are not equipped to hold snow and it can be dangerous for pedestrians.

The roofs in the Chamonix area tend to be made of wooden slates, or nowadays often metal. In the Aosta region, parts of the Vanoise and the Tarentaise, and Switzerland, slate is used. The Valdotain (Aosta) roofs are particularly characterised by the use of thick slabs of stone. In parts of the Swiss canton of Valais you can still see the old wooden slates, called *ancelles*.

Until relatively recent times, Alpine people used to share their houses with their livestock, partly for warmth, and partly because they just had one house. So, usually, the lower floor would house the cattle, and the family would live above.

Other buildings were used to store hay or grain. These were often small wooden structures, with few or no windows, known in France as *mazots*. These days such little houses are sought after as garden sheds or decorations. *Mazots* were typically built up on piles of stone, leaving a gap between the ground and the floor, with the stilts guarded by an overhang that generally proved to be unsurmountable to rats and mice that would otherwise eat the stores of grain. Those used to store hay had to have ventilation holes to keep the hay dry – if wet it can ferment and catch fire.

Churches were always a centrepoint of the village, but often built just aside from the main settlement. Strangely, they are frequently on the most avalanche-prone site, and have to be protected by avalanche-deflector walls and the like. The

The characteristic, bulb-shaped bell tower of Argentière church.

2

ARRIVING IN THE ALPS

By walking in the Alps you'll find yourselves drawn into another world. The Western Alps cover three countries – France, Switzerland and Italy – and each area has its own peculiarities and traditions.

The proximity of this mountain range to several European cities – Lyon, Geneva, Zurich – as well as to numerous large towns enables vistors to have a wide choice of means of access to their chosen area, be it by plane, train or automobile. And on reaching your chosen destination, you will discover that the rest of your trip should be equally well-catered for with locals who are keen to accommodate you and the vast majority of whom will also share your love of the Great Outdoors.

Nowadays most villages in the Alps have at least one hotel or *gîte* to accommodate walkers, and the mountains are well-supplied with wardened huts, so you can take off into the hills, lightly laden, and travel for days amongst the mountains, going as far as you wish each day before stopping for the night. And should your weary feet demand somewhere more comfortable at the end of your trip, you will find that you are never that far away from luxury hotels.

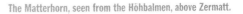

The Matterhorn, seen from the Höhbalmen, above Zermatt.

GETTING TO THE ALPS

By Air

The growth of cheap airlines serving Europe has made it a fairly inexpensive proposition to visit the Alps. For the Western Alps described here, the airports of Lyon, Geneva and Zurich are the most convenient. All are served by train routes into the Alps. Car hire is also reasonable from the airports, especially if booked beforehand on the Internet. Once in the area a car is not essential for the trekking and climbing. It's almost always possible to access the routes in this book by public transport or a short taxi ride.

By Rail

Renowned for its TGV (*Trains à Grande Vitesse*), France has an efficient rail network. This now links to the Eurostar service which comes from Britain through the Channel Tunnel. Many of the small Alpine towns are served by local trains.

In Switzerland the train service runs like clockwork, so don't expect to catch a train if you're a minute late – it will have left. The trains often operate in conjunction with the postbus system, which serves all villages with post offices.

The Italian trains and buses are a little more flexible, but the bus services in the Alpine valleys are reliable and an interesting social experience in high season.

By Road

The Alps are served by motorways which allow fast travel. French and Italian motorways have tolls, which are usually payable by credit card, though occasionally this is not possible in Italy. In Switzerland you must buy a sticker (*vignette*) to travel on the motorways.

In the winter you may well need snow chains on the higher roads in the Alps, and the passes above about 1800m (5906ft) are usually closed. You can ask the local tourist office or police for details. For more information see the Regional Directory at the end of each chapter.

ACCOMMODATION IN THE ALPS

There are lots of different ways to organise a trek in the Alps. Most of the walks in this book are multi-day trips and they are all possible making use

Boarding the Grand Saint Bernard Express at Sembrancher on the Chamonix–Zermatt trek; many Alpine areas are served by train.

The Col des Montets, near Chamonix, is a great place to discover the joys of snow shoeing.

of the extensive network of mountain huts for accommodation. Self-sufficient backpacking is also an option.

Camping

Camping obviously allows you to be more flexible on your trek, and you can have a wonderfully peaceful time, being out of sync with walkers using huts. However, a rucksack containing all you need to be self-sufficient for several days is a lot heavier than one with little more than your daily requirements in it. Camping in the national parks or nature reserves is generally forbidden or is allowed only a certain distance from the road, from sunset until sunrise. In these cases discretion is essential and you should certainly be very careful to leave no trace of your stay. Campfires are often not allowed in parks and reserves. If you choose to camp you should find out about local camping rules from tourist offices, guides bureaux or national park offices. There are plentiful campsites in the valleys, and most Alpine towns will have at least one site. Some get busy in the summer season, but there are some quiet places to be found, especially if you look for the basic sites with few facilities.

Some of the huts have areas designated as campsites, and often by paying a minimal fee you can use the hut facilities. However, you should

The Italian side of Mont Blanc as seen on the Tour du Mont Blanc.

working farms, with a refuge attached. They sometimes produce local specialities, such as cheese, which you will sample at dinner. The wardens of all huts are a source of information, and can also be very interesting, so if they don't seem too busy it's worth making conversation to find out more about the region you're walking through.

Most huts provide accommodation in dormitories, sometimes big, sometimes small. So you can expect it to be a bit noisier than your normal bedroom. The huts are equipped with blankets, so you do not need to take a sleeping bag, although a sheet bag is recommended, and is even required in some huts. In the summer all huts will, at the very least, have running cold water, and the ones below glacier level usually have better facilities than the high mountain huts. If a hut is wardened then meals will be available. This will generally be a set menu in the evening – good filling food is the norm, although if you're a vegetarian you may get more than your fill of omelettes! Breakfast is also provided – bread and jam traditionally. You are often able to buy chocolate and sometimes other snacks, and certainly drinks, both alcoholic and otherwise.

Many huts provide plastic clogs or similar hut shoes, which you can use during your stay, but this is not always the case. When you arrive at a hut you will usually be expected to remove your boots before going beyond the porch or entrance room. Then go and present yourself to the hut warden who will book you in and show you to your sleeping place. It's expected that you'll fold up blankets in the morning, and in some areas the way you fold is crucial so take good note on arrival!

You should tell the warden if you are taking half board (breakfast, dinner and bed) and he will tell you the times for the meals. Usually in huts it is expected that people will be in bed around 10pm, although that doesn't mean you won't come across the odd party. Going hut to hut gives a precious insight into the local life of the area. It's worth showing an interest in the local drinks for example, and often the wardens will be happy to introduce you to what their area offers. Huts do not always accept credit cards, so you need to be equipped with cash.

The other possible accommodation is *gîtes*. There are two types of *gîtes* in the French-speaking Alps. A *gîte d'étape* is a small hotel, usually in or near a village, which may also have dormitory accommodation. This is not to be confused with a *gîte* which is a property for rent.

On many treks there will be the possibility of

always check with the hut wardens before putting up your tent nearby. Camping near a hut and using their facilities without asking (and paying) is not regarded as good practice.

Mountain Huts

There is an impressive network of mountain huts in the Alps, ranging from the most basic to the really quite luxurious, with showers and small rooms. Many huts are owned by the relevant national Alpine Club, and run by a warden who takes on the management of the hut. The wardens make their money from the food and drinks they sell, whilst the nightly fee paid by guests goes to the Alpine Club. These huts will give a discount on the nightly fee if you're a member of an affiliated club, on presentation of your membership card.

Other huts are privately owned, and may even be

staying in hotels when you pass through small towns along the way. These can make a very pleasant break during a long hut-to-hut expedition, and provide the opportunity to look round town, and sample some local life.

For all accommodation, including campsites, it is recommended that you book ahead if you're going in high season, unless you have several options available and you don't mind being flexible. This is especially true for a group – two people are more likely to be accepted in a crowded hut than eight. The busiest time in the Alps is mid-July to mid-August. Telephone numbers change, so the best way to get reservation details is to contact the nearest tourist office, or the local 'section' of Alpine Clubs. The national Alpine Clubs all have Internet websites.

HEALTH AND HYGIENE

Whilst the Alps are a far cry from the more remote mountain regions of the world, health problems do sometimes occur during treks, usually as a result of poor hygiene – yours or someone else's. Let's face it, you're staying in mountain huts where the water supply is usually the nearest stream, the washing facilities may be a nearby trough, and the toilets are sometimes rather primitive.

Whilst many lower-mountain refuges have improved their facilities incredibly in the past few years, the fact remains that you're basically living on the move, and may not be able to be quite as clean as you would be at home. This is one of the experiences of doing a trek, to live differently, more simply, without all the complications of modern life,

A typical mountain house in northern Italy.

Discovering the village of Dolonne on the Tour du Mont Blanc.

but just occasionally your body may not quite have realised this and will complain. This is hardly ever a reason to panic. Anything you catch in the Alps can be dealt with easily by using pharmacy medicines, or just by taking care for a day or two.

Almost all Alpine villages have a fountain. This is always good drinking water unless there is a sign to say it isn't – in French *non potable*, in Italian *non potabile* and *Nicht trinkbar* or *Kein Trinkwasser* in German. It's a good idea to fill up water bottles from these fountains just in case you don't see any fast-running streams for a while. It is also pretty safe to drink water in the hotels or refuges, unless it says not to. Giardia and other similar nasties are extremely rare in the Alps and I've drunk from the streams without problems for years. Mountain water is usually the purest water you'll ever drink,

but obviously don't choose sluggish trickles or lakes, and look up first to see that there isn't an ibex peeing just above! The main hazard is at the huts, especially in winter, when people may not watch out where they relieve themselves and water supplies from snow can be contaminated.

Bouts of stomach problems are as often as not caused by dirty hands or cooking facilities as much as by the water supply. A couple of days of Immodium and lots of fluids usually clears these up. Don't hesitate to ask hut wardens for a simple dinner if you feel your stomach can't take another local speciality.

Basic hygiene is perfectly feasible, if you are prepared. You will, inevitably, make toilet stops outside some of the time. How you do this is up to you and your conscience (see 'Take Only Memories, Leave Only Footprints', p41), but try to always wash your hands afterwards, or in the winter carry wet wipes for this purpose (but be sure to carry them to a bin for disposal).

Sleeping with lots of other people in dormitories means you're potentially going to share lots of germs, so try to be sure the rooms don't get too stuffy. Leave a window open during the night, and put on another blanket if you're chilly – fresh air is the best way to avoid catching colds, and unventilated dormitories are most unpleasant by the morning. Some people react badly to insect bites and even the fibres on dormitory blankets; if that's you, be sure to come supplied with an antihistamine treatment that you can tolerate.

Finally, there's nothing worse than sleep deprivation, especially after several nights. Unless you regularly share your bedroom with up to twenty other people and are consequently used to the grunts, snuffles and snores that this inevitably involves, come equipped with earplugs or sleeping aids as people can't help the noises they make at night, and tired people snore even more than usual.

USEFUL TERMS

ENGLISH	FRENCH	ITALIAN	GERMAN
Weather terms			
weather	le temps	il tempo	Das Wetter
forecast	la prévision	il bollettino	Der Wetter-bericut
temperature	la température	la temperatura	Die Temperatur
hot	chaud	il caldo	heiss
cold	froid	il freddo	kalt
windy	venté	ventoso	windig
foggy	brouillard	nebbioso	neblig
sunny	ensoleillé	soleggiato	sonnig
rainy	pluvieux	piovoso	regnerisch
cloudy	nuageux	nuvoloso	bewölkt
stormy	orageux	temporalesco	stürmisch
snowy	enneigé	nevoso	schneereich, verschneit
thunder	le tonnère	il tuono	Der Donner
lightning	l'éclair	il fulmine	Das Blitzen
ice	la glace	il ghiaccio	Das Eis
gusts/gales	des rafales	le raffiche di vento	Die Bö, Der Windstoss
avalanche	une avalanche	la valanga	Die Lawine
verglace	le verglas	il ghiaccio vivo,la verglace	Das Glatteis
hail	la grêle	la grandine	Der Hagel
changeable	variable	variabile	veränderlich
freezing	glacial	il congelamento	eisig, eiskalt
white-out	un jour blanc	la luce abbagliante	Der Starkes Schnee-gestöber
starry	étoilé	stellato	sternklar
Emergency vocabulary			
help!	au secours!	aiuto!	hilfe
stop!	halte	stop (alt)	stop
quick	vite	presto	schnell
be careful!	faites attention	l'attenzione	achtung
emergency	une urgence	l'emergenza	Der Notfall
accident	un accident	l'incidente	Der Unfall
hospital	un hôpital	l'ospedale	Das Kranhenhaus
ambulance	une ambulance	l'ambulanza	Die Ambulanz
helicopter	un hélicoptère	l'elicottero	Der Hubschrauber
rescue	un secours	il soccorso	Die Rettung
SOS telephone	un téléphone d'urgence	il telefono di soccorso	Das Nottelefon
doctor	un médecin/docteur	il dottore, medico	Der Arzt
heart attack	une crise cardiaque	l'attacco di cuore,	Der Herzinfarkt
broken arm/leg	un bras/une jambe cassé(e)	il braccio rotto,	Der Armbruch, Beinbruch
asthma attack	une crise d'asthma	l'attacco d'asma	Der Asthmaanfall
stroke	une hémiplégie	l'attacco	Der Schlaganfall

3

TREKKING AND CLIMBING IN
THE ALPS

In 1760, Horace Bénédict de Saussure took in the splendour of the Mont Blanc massif from the vantage point of the Brévent and vowed one day to reach the top of the highest summit in western Europe.

Twenty-six years later Jacques Balmat and Dr Michel-Gabriel Paccard achieved this dream and thus began the history of mountaineering in the Alps. As peak after peak was climbed by determined climbers, so also explorers and nature lovers discovered the pleasures of walking in the Alps. Many pioneering Alpinists checked out their chosen summit from the *belvédères* (or viewing points) provided by the non-glaciated ranges, using paths over high passes, worn by centuries of travellers going from one valley to another for trade and cattle grazing.

The peaks have now become well known, their summits regularly adorned with mountaineers; but the paths, too, provide many avid hikers with superb multi-day treks, circumnavigating massifs, or travelling from one village to another by cols, summits and Alpine meadows. Established treks exist but there are also endless possibilities for variations, detours and totally new itineraries.

Heading up to the Col du Bonhomme on the Tour du Mont Blanc.

THE WEATHER IN THE ALPS

Until relatively recently, winter in the Alps was regarded as a time of endurance, certainly not pleasure. Life was very harsh, with several months of frequent snow, hence the old French description of the seasons as *la belle saison* – summer – and *la mauvaise saison* – winter. Nowadays there are as many visitors to the Alps in winter as in summer, if not more.

These two seasons are the times when it's usually possible to go up into the mountains. It's generally accepted that from late June to mid September, and from Christmas until Easter, there is likely to be more stable weather in the Alps than at other times. That said however, in the Alps the weather can be bad at any time of the year; that's why the mountains are green and verdant, not brown and dry. There is a saying that 'the calendar in Chamonix promises, three months of summer and nine months of winter'. This is a touch exaggerated, but it's true to say that autumn and spring don't exist in the Alps in the same manner as they do in the rest of Europe. Rather, May/June and October/November are change-over times between seasons when the weather can do anything.

'Stable' in the Alps means long periods (often weeks) of anticyclonic conditions, with hot and

High clouds can form suddenly, bringing bad weather.

generous sun in the daytime. In the winter these high- pressure systems often hold cold air down in the valleys, and frequently it will be cloudy and cold on the plains, but fine and sunny above, say, 1000m (3281ft). During the summer, high-pressure conditions give sun at all altitudes. Usually these stable periods give way to fronts coming either from the west, southwest or the northwest. In the summer bad weather doesn't generally last for long, but in the winter it can be rather more prolonged. Of course the vagaries of nature mean that it could rain on and off for weeks, and sometimes does, but this is the exception to the rule. The ground in the Alps is relatively permeable, which allows fast drainage of water, and this, added to the steepness of the slopes, means that wet ground doesn't last long.

In addition to being affected by general European weather systems, the mountains create their own anomalies, and these can be very localised. For example, take a frontal system approaching the Alps from the south-west, the air laden with moisture from the sea. When it arrives at the Alps the air is forced to rise to pass this barrier and in doing so cools, turning water vapour into droplets, resulting in precipitation on the slopes exposed to the south-westerly flow. The now-dry air sweeps down the north-easterly slopes, warming as it descends and, importantly, benefiting from a higher lapse rate (see p28) due to its dry nature, leaving this side of the Alps in a warm dry rain shadow. This is known as the 'foehn effect'. Although originally applied to a specific southerly wind, the term 'foehn' has now become the generic name for warm dry winds caused by this effect, irrespective of direction. Thus, a southerly foehn causes rain on the Italian side of the Alps, and a northerly foehn means that Italy will be largely dry, whilst France and parts of Switzerland get the bad weather.

A front can be accompanied by winds from a different direction, for example a westerly front is often accompanied by a southerly foehn, and frequently the wind changes direction after a front has passed. This means that if you're in the Alps and it's raining, it's worth a phone call to someone on the other side of the range, as fairly nearby you could be basking in the sun. Typically, for example, it can be raining in Chamonix on the northern side of the Mont Blanc massif and sunny in Courmayeur, on the southern side.

Afternoon storms are common in the summer in the Alps. These are the result of very warm air and they typically build up during the afternoon, with

High pressure can hold clouds in the valleys with sunny weather above.

huge anvil-shaped cumulus clouds forming over the mountains. The storms can be very violent, accompanied by impressive lightning and heavy precipitation, often hail and snow above 1500m (4922ft). These storms normally die out quickly and the night is usually clear, heralding a fine day to come.

As in all mountain areas, the weather in the Alps can change very rapidly. When heading off on a trek or a climb it's essential to try to get a weather forecast. Usually local forecasts are updated several times a day, and are often reasonably accurate. However, the forecasters can only work from the information they have – usually collated from local weather stations, and from computerised weather patterns. Sometimes fronts come in more quickly or more slowly than anticipated (maybe by up to six hours), an anticyclone can hold off a front for longer than expected, or a very localised change can affect the outcome. It is particularly difficult to forecast the weather in the spring and summer when storm fronts build up very quickly, and dissipate equally rapidly and unpredictably.

The long-term forecasts of five days should be treated with suspicion – only in very stable conditions can the outlook for the week be reliably given. The other problem you may face with the forecasts is that in general they are in the local language. A brief glossary of terms is included in 'Useful Terms' (see p23), but you can always ask at the local tourist offices, where usually somebody has at least a rudimentary knowledge of English.

The forecasters aren't gods and you should also use your own common sense. Just because they forecast 'grand beau', if you look out of your window and see menacing black clouds looming over the summits perhaps you have to assume they may be wrong and revise your objective for the day. Watch for bad-weather signs, such as high clouds and lenticular clouds. These are indications that there is a lot of air movement or moisture at altitude and often mean a front is coming. Every Alpine area probably has its own version of the Mont Blanc sayings: for example, 'if Mont Blanc's got a donkey's ears or is smoking a pipe the weather's going to change', or something to that effect. These are not just folklore, but are based on factual observations – always be ready to wait for better conditions if the weather is not good enough for your planned walk or climb. After all, the mountains will always be here, so don't fall into the trap of thinking it's now or never.

Typical Conditions and Temperatures
Winter
You can usually expect to find snow from at least 1000m (3281ft), if not lower. This snow generally arrives in November and doesn't start to disappear until April. Snow could well remain above 2000m

ACCLIMATISATION

When the human body goes to altitudes above about 2700m (8859ft), the relatively low amount of oxygen in the air starts to make itself felt, and the person begins to find it difficult to get enough oxygen to the brain and muscles with each breath taken. The normal result is fatigue and breathlessness.

Oxygen is transported round the body by red blood corpuscles, so it follows that if your blood contains a proportionately high percentage of red blood cells then you will be able to get oxygen to where it's needed more quickly. The extent to which people suffer from higher altitude varies, and as yet no reasons for this have been found. Athough you will probably acclimatise more rapidly if you're fit, you are not assured an easier passage than anyone else. It seems to be just the luck of the draw whether your body likes high altitudes or not.

By spending time above 3000m (9843ft), and working your body at these altitudes, you will encourage your blood to produce more red blood corpuscles. This helps the process of acclimatisation, and it is essential if you are to go higher in the mountains. If you come from sea level and go immediately to the summit of Mont Blanc at 4807m (15772ft) you will almost certainly experience headaches, dizziness, nausea and breathlessness. If, however, you come from sea level and do progressively higher treks and summits, beginning at about 2500m (8203ft), you will probably experience little if any high-mountain sickness. Slight breathlessness is normal on ascents for the first couple of days of a trek, and anyone walking uphill in the Alps can expect to feel at least a little weary.

Hydration is one important factor which will certainly help your body to adapt efficiently to higher altitudes. Be sure to drink plenty of water every day, morning and evening. Even in dry air when you may not have apparently been sweating, you lose a great deal of moisture through evaporation and this must be replaced or dehydration will occur.

Acute Mountain Sickness

Serious cases of altitude sickness (Acute Mountain Sickness) occur each year in the Alps - this is not exclusive to the higher ranges - and can lead to severe illness or death. Problems are basically due to the collection of fluid between the cells of the body, ie edema. There are principally two areas where edema occurs: in the lungs (high-altitude pulmonary edema or HAPE) and in the brain (high-altitude cerebral edema or HACE).

Initial symptoms may be mild: shortness of breath and a dry hacking cough are early signs of HAPE, whilst headaches (especially on waking in the morning) and loss of appetite and nausea are indicative of HACE. Less serious signs of inadequate acclimatisation are peripheral edema (swollen fingers and face) and erratic breathing at night. Alarm bells should also ring if you have reduced and dark urine. These symptoms should be taken seriously and dictate a change of plan.

It's important to give your body time to acclimatise before attempting any peak over 4000m (13124ft), and if in doubt it's better to turn back and try the summit another day rather than to press on and risk serious problems.

(6562ft) until June, and you should always be prepared for late snow to remain in shady spots even into the summer. Temperatures usually drop well below 0°C (32°F) at night, but in the day, in the sun, it can reach 15–20+°C (59–68+°F); but remember, as soon as the sun goes down the temperature plummets.

Summer

By July/August snow levels are usually above 3000m (9843ft) where permanent snow exists year-round. However, storms can produce surprising depths of snow as low as 1800m (5902ft) sometimes. Temperatures usually attain 25–30°C (77–86°F), but the air is rarely humid so the heat is comfortable.

Lapse Rate and Wind Chill

It may be a comfortable 20°C (68°F) in the valley but as you gain altitude it becomes colder. This is known as the lapse rate. Technically the temperature drops by 0.65°C (1.17°F) for every 100m

(328ft) of ascent. So if it's very hot in the valley you can be assured it will quickly cool off as you go higher. However, the lapse rate can be affected by temperature inversions and also by the humidity in the air – the dryer the air the higher the lapse rate. Temperatures drop noticeably in the shade, at night and during storms.

The wind also dramatically affects the temperature and the combined cooling effect of wind plus air temperature is known as wind chill. For any given air temperature the cooling effect (wind-chill factor) increases rapidly with increasing wind speed. In both summer and winter the wind-chill factor is very important, and good windproof clothing is therefore essential if the effects of wind chill are to be avoided. To give a few examples: with an air temperature of 0°C (32°F) and wind speed of 40kph (25mph) the temperature will feel like –13°C (8.6°F); at –5°C (23°F) with wind speed of 15kph (9mph) it will be –11°C (12.2°F); at –15°C (5°F) with wind speed 20kph (12mph) it will be –26°C (–14.8°F).

WEATHER AVALANCHE – RISK FORECAST NUMBERS

If you are not in the country you're calling you must add the international code + the country code: 33 France, 39 Italy and 41 Switzerland. In the case of French and Swiss numbers drop the first 0 of the number.

French Alps
08 36 68 02 + the number of the department you're in: Haute Savoie 74; Savoie 73; Isère 38.
08 36 68 10 20 is the French Avalanche Risk telephone number.

Swiss Alps
022 162 is the weather forecast number. The introductory language depends on the area of Switzerland that you are in, but you will then be offered a choice of languages – French, Italian or German. There is the same system in place for the avalanche forecast number which is 022 187.

Italian Alps
Aosta valley: 0165 44113; Swiss forecast in Italian: 00 41 91 162. You can speak to someone (in French or Italian) about current conditions in the Italian Alps by calling the Soccorso Alpino Valdostan Protzione Civile: 0165 238222. An avalanche report can be found on 0165 776300.

ONLINE WEATHER AND AVALANCHE INFORMATION

French Alps
www.meteo.fr

Swiss Alps
www.tsr.ch/meteo/meteo.html (Swiss Romande TV forecast).

www.sfdrs.ch/sendungen/meteo (Swiss German TV).

www.wsl.ch/slf/laworg/map.html (Swiss Federal Institute for Snow and Avalanche Research).

Italian Alps
www.regione.piemonte.it/meteo/boll.htm

www.shiny.it/servizi/shinymeteo/index

www.cai-svi.it (Italian Alpine Club site).

www.aineva.it (The Inter-regional Snow and Avalanche Association).

www.regione.rda

General sites
www.csac.org (Cyber Space Avalanche Centre).

www.chamonix.com

www.zermatt.com

www.sac-cas.ch (Swiss Alpine Club).

Lenticular clouds over the Mont Blanc massif; at altitude these high clouds are a sign of strong winds.

BASIC ONE-DAY GEAR LIST

This gear list is given as a basic requirement for a one day summer walk on non-glaciated terrain in the Alps. Things can be left out or added as wished, of course. Additional gear lists are provided for multi-day treks, glacier treks, peak climbing and snow shoeing, but this list applies to all.

Sunglasses

Suncream: lips and face – very high factor, or total protection.

Sunhat

Fleece hat

Gloves

Waterproof jacket: this should be non-insulated, breathable fabric, with hood.

Waterproof trousers: lightweight, breathable.

Boots: comfortable, light, with good ankle support and a secure sole. A rounded heel will not be effective on snowy ground. Trekking shoes can be light and very comfortable, but if you choose boots without ankle support you risk hurting your ankles. Make sure the sole is good. You're almost certain to get wet feet in the rain or snow. Most importantly, you should wear your boots for several walks before embarking on a trek in them.

Spare sweater

Bivvy bag

First-aid kit

Trekking poles

Water bottle

Food

Camera

Rucksack liner or cover

Compass

Map

THE ALPINE FOOTPATH NETWORK

The Alps benefit from a vast network of footpaths, some of which are just local walks while others are long treks that can extend across international borders. These paths are maintained by national bodies, local villages and huts. In France these long distance paths are known as *Grandes Randonnées*, hence the prefix GR for certain long treks. Many footpaths in the Alps are waymarked, the colours usually denoting the type of path. This waymarking is sometimes discreet, sometimes not; on occasion it seems that the people who paint the flashes think that walkers are severely myopic and won't notice a paint flash unless it's a metre square. Also

it's difficult to understand why waymarks are needed frequently along a path where there are no junctions. There is a move in some areas to reduce the size of waymarks, and even to erase some, replacing them with signposts on popular walks.

The GRs in both France and Switzerland are waymarked with red and white paint, whilst in Switzerland local paths have yellow paint flashes. In Italy the system is less defined, although most paths are marked in some way or other. Here many paths have a number, which relates to a number on the map, but these seem to have become a little confused in some areas.

All the treks in this book follow paths and tracks, although they may be sometimes indistinct or obscured by late snow. This is not to say you can't go 'off piste' in the Alps, but the terrain tends to be very rough and staying on the path makes for much steadier progress. In the winter, however, snow shoeing allows you to wander more or less where you like, within the constraints of the terrain.

Despite the waymarks and signs, there is no substitute for map-reading skills. You'll inevitably find path junctions that are not marked, or you'll miss a vital paint mark that was hidden behind a bush or a person. Just because a path has a paint flash doesn't mean it's the way you want to go, and fog, rain or snow can change what is normally an easy-to-follow trail into a very different experience. So don't rely on the waymarks – take a map and compass and be sure you can use them.

The advantage of the alpine path system over non-maintained paths is immediately obvious. People rarely leave well-made paths, and even shortcutting is less desirable when a path is well-graded and easy to walk on; thus further erosion is avoided. It's important to stay on the paths and follow the zigzags, even when descending, otherwise the trails will break down; not only is this unattractive but it also makes walking difficult.

TIMINGS, GRADINGS AND DIRECTIONS
Timings

Timings are included for the treks, snow-shoe walks and peaks. These are **only** a guideline and should not be taken as a challenge, or a yardstick by which your own performance can be measured.

I have worked out the timings on the following basis: that a person walks at a rate of about 3kph (2mph) and climbs at a rate of 300m (984ft) per hour. This is a conservative estimate; many people will go faster than this, and will have to adapt the timings accordingly. I have not added on any time for stops or for descent, which can take a long time if the terrain is difficult or if knees are hurting.

It is important in the mountains to pace the day, and in hot weather to try to make the most of the early, cooler hours, rather than doing the major ascent in the heat of the midday sun, unless this is unavoidable. Timings should be taken into consideration especially when the section is long. Peak timings can vary drastically with conditions.

Gradings

The treks are not graded for difficulty. A trek of several days is so varied that to give a high difficulty grading for just one technical section, which may be avoidable anyway, doesn't seem to be very useful. Read the description carefully – any difficult sections are mentioned, and if they are avoidable this will be indicated.

Directions

In general I refer to compass directions. When right or left are used this is taken to be according to the direction in which the walker is going.

Left and right banks for rivers and glaciers always refer to the true left and right banks, ie as the river or glacier flows down.

GUIDED TRIPS IN THE ALPS

Whilst many people organise their own holidays to the Alps and successfully complete their objectives, others with less time for planning, or insufficient experience for their planned goal, will choose to go with a guided group or to hire a guide privately.

Adverts abound for such services and certain legal requirements apply in Europe. Throughout the Alps, to guide on glaciated terrain, or terrain requiring the use of ropes, the UIAGM (*Union Internationale des Associations de Guides de Montagnes*) guiding certificate is mandatory. To guide on non-glaciated terrain, where a rope would only be used in exceptional situations, a guide must hold the non-glaciated-terrain guiding certificate in France and Italy. These leaders are known as *Accompagnateur en Montagne* in France, *Accompagnatore di Montagna* in Italy and *Berwanderfürher* in Germany. The British qualification 'European Mountain Leader' is also legally equivalent to these certificates. In Switzerland there is no legal requirement at the moment for guides on non-glaciated terrain.

Commercially organised trekking groups have a preordained itinerary, so flexibility is difficult. You will also not have the feeling of adventure that you get from finding your own way, and from never being quite sure what you're going to see next. However, mountain leaders (*accompagnateurs*) are not only qualified in safety techniques and navigation, but are knowledgeable about the area, especially if they are resident in the Alps. They will enhance your enjoyment of your surroundings by pointing out many things that you may otherwise miss.

Privately organised expeditions with a guide clearly offer more flexibility and can be custommade. Whatever you choose to do, if you join a guided group or hire a guide you should check qualifications as this is important for insurance purposes and for the success of your holiday.

MULTI-DAY NON-GLACIATED TREK GEAR LIST

Remember, you want to carry a light rucksack, since the idea is to enjoy the trek, so be sure to keep luxuries to a minimum. Be prepared for the extremes of heat and cold, including rain and snow. This list should be added to the basic one-day gear list (see p30).

Minimal spare clothes – you can always handwash clothes in the evenings.

Clothes for hot and cold weather

Small wash kit

Torch

A very lightweight pair of shoes for wearing in the huts – some huts provide hut shoes so it's worth checking when you reserve as you may not need to take your own.

Sheet sleeping bag – this is recommended in the huts, firstly so that you don't have the blankets next to your skin, and also to keep the blankets cleaner.

Lunch food for the number of days between places with shops. Huts often sell chocolate and picnics.

Ear plugs or some other sleeping aid for the huts.

Diversions – eg a book or pack of cards.

Enough money for the trek – huts often don't accept credit cards, and not all small Alpine towns have banks.

Glacier walking often involves finding your way through spectacular ice and snow scenery.

GLACIER TRAVEL

Hut-to-hut trekking across the glaciers of the Alps is an ideal next step for the walker who, without getting too technical, wants the excitement that the high mountains can give. That is not to say that there is no danger involved in glacier travel – far from it. However, with the right equipment and most importantly the right knowledge, these dangers can be reduced to an acceptable level.

The right equipment is suggested in the glacier-trek gear list (see below). The right knowledge can be gained in part by reading text books, but really there is no substitute for the real thing, either going with experienced friends or by paying for professional instruction from qualified guides.

Glaciers are defined as either dry or wet. A dry glacier has no snow on it. The snow has melted, leaving ice and gravel. You can clearly see any crevasses so you do not need to rope up for this kind of terrain. A rope tends to be as much of a hindrance as a help. Crampons may or may not be necessary, depending on the amount of gravel on the ice and the angle of the slope. By mid-summer the snouts of most glaciers are dry, but conditions vary immensely from season to season, and for this reason it's generally not possible to tell you exactly where you must rope up on the glacier treks.

GLACIER-TREK GEAR LIST

Conditions on glaciers can be very hot in the sun and very cold in the shade, or bad weather. Be prepared for all conditions, but also keep things light, otherwise you'll get very tired. This list should be used in conjunction with the basic one-day and the multi-day non-glaciated trek lists (see pp30 and 31).

Fleece or down jacket or vest

Crampons

Ice axe: 55–60cm for a normal-size person.

Harness

Crevasse-rescue equipment: 2 prussik loops, a long sling, 5 karabiners – 1 screwgate, 1 pear-shaped screwgate (HMS) which can be used for an Italian hitch, 3 snaplinks – and an ice screw. These are minimum requirements, and you may choose other things according to what you're used to.

Extra pair of thin gloves

Thick gloves or mittens

Boots: should be waterproof, take crampons, and have a very good sole, with a non-rounded heel.

Rope: this should be a dynamic rope of at least 8mm, and should be a minimum of about 30m (100ft) long. Clearly if there are lots of people in the group more than one rope should be taken, but bear in mind that weight is also an issue. It was thought until recently that a rope should not be used singly if it isn't designed as a single rope, but on glaciers the force generated by falls is much less than that generated on rock climbs and it is now agreed that 8mm is adequate, provided it is dynamic. However, the down side of a thin rope is that it is harder to grip for rescue manoeuvres, both by hand and with prussiks.

A wet glacier has snow on it, maybe only in small patches at first. This snow hides crevasses, so it's essential to rope up on a wet glacier. Again, crampons may or may not be needed according to the state of the snow and the angle of the slope. If you are on a glacier with just the odd patch of snow, avoid walking on those patches as they are likely to be in depressions, where there are crevasses.

It can be very difficult sometimes to find a way through a crevassed area of glacier, and you may have to retrace your steps frequently to pass circuitously through tortuous terrain. Try to avoid walking along the line of the crevasses, as you could all fall in. Be aware of how the crevasses have formed on the glacier you're on, and ensure that you are not all at risk at the same time. Crevasses most commonly occur on the edge of convexities, on the outside and inside of bends, at the confluence of two glaciers and around jutting features such as rocky buttresses that project into the glacier. Usually you can plan your route on the glacier from looking carefully at the map and trying to avoid these areas, although this doesn't mean you won't find crevasses on flat parts of glaciers. Crossing snow bridges one at a time, with the rope reasonably taut, is another obvious precaution, as is being aware of your surroundings.

Some glaciers are threatened from higher up by seracs (ice pinnacles). If you have to walk under a serac wall, go as quickly as possible – this is not a good place to stop for a picnic. Similarly, if you're following the edge of a glacier, the moraine slopes above may have loose rocks which can come down at any time, especially later in the day.

The glacier treks described in this book are all very popular and in the summer you'll almost certainly find a well-beaten trail across them, unless you arrive immediately after a snowfall. However, the existence of a trail doesn't mean an absence of danger, and snow bridges can collapse at any time.

Glaciers are best travelled in the morning, when the snow is firm underfoot and the snow bridges over the crevasses are at their most solid. An Alpine dawn is one of the joys of the high mountains, whilst another pleasure is arriving at the mountain hut soon after midday and spending the afternoon in the sun on the terrace, knowing that you've had a great day and a safe one. Crossing glaciers on a late afternoon in slushy snow is unpleasant and dangerous. Although timings are given for the glacier treks in this book, conditions can make an enormous difference to the speed at which you can move on glaciers, so these are intended as a guideline only.

SNOW SHOEING

The Alps in winter are magical and beautiful, the mountains and the forests transformed by the blanket of white. Any fine day between December and April will not only see masses of people taking to the ski slopes, but also many setting off on snow shoes. Snow shoeing has become incredibly popular in the last ten years, although its history goes back many centuries.

Given the quantities of snow one can regularly expect above, say, 1000m (3281ft), it is often out of the question to go on foot anywhere that isn't packed down into a hard trail (you can expect at least 2m/7ft of snow at 2000m/6562ft). This would seem to preclude walking in the Alps in winter, unless you equip yourself with the means to avoid sinking up to thigh level, or worse, in the snow. Snow shoeing can be described as winter walking. On snow shoes you can go to places otherwise inaccessible in the snow – walks in the forests, up to the *alpages*, and beyond to some of the Alpine summits.

Snow shoes are basically a large base that you attach to your shoes to make the surface area of your foot bigger, thus enabling you to walk in deep

Snow shoes enable mountain winter walking.

SNOW-SHOEING GEAR LIST

Winter conditions can range from freezing cold in the morning, to baking hot in the midday sun, through to cold, wet blizzards. Gear needs to be taken to cover all these eventualities. Check that your snow shoes can be attached to your rucksack somehow, in the event that you have to carry them for a while. This list should be added to the basic one-day gear list (see p30).

Gaiters: ankle or knee high, it doesn't matter so long as they keep the snow out of your boots.

Boots: should be fairly rigid, waterproof, with a good sole and a heel that isn't rounded at the back (a rounded heel will not provide stability on descents on foot).

Shovel*

Avalanche probe*

Avalanche transceiver*

Warm drink

Spare gloves/mittens

Extra fleece/down jacket/waistcoat

* These items are not necessary if the area you're going to is totally flat and not threatened by any slopes above.

snow without sinking in as much as you would otherwise. People have used such devices to travel in snow since records began, both in Europe and North America.

Nowadays, snow shoes are becoming more and more refined, and the old 'tennis racket' design, often seen in pictures, has been superseded by all sorts of different styles which are each adapted to certain conditions. America and Canada tend to experience a lot of deep powder snow, so snow shoes there are designed accordingly, with a large flexible base area, which works well in soft snow. In Europe conditions vary from powder to crusty to icy snow, so the snow shoes here take this into account and are more rigid, with a crampon underneath, giving good stability and traction.

The popularity of snow shoeing means that manufacturers are continually developing their products, and many variations exist. Initially, the best bet is to hire a few different types, before buying.

Technique

I often hear the comment that 'snow shoeing looks great but it's difficult to imagine how it feels to have snow shoes on your feet'. Five minutes after putting on snow shoes for the first time you'll for-

Well-designed snow shoes with good bindings provide stability when dealing with different snow types.

get they're there. Snow shoeing requires no special techniques, just a love of walking. Unlike skiing, sliding is not the name of the game, and unless you choose to play around, you generally remain upright just as if you were walking. However, this doesn't mean that you won't have fun – running and jumping on snow shoes is part of the experience.

Basic techniques are acquired very quickly, but the more snow shoeing you do the more you will instinctively look at the snow conditions and the slopes around you; and the more you'll become hooked on those sunny days, high up in the mountains, far away from the crowds of skiers and the lifts.

Snow shoes are most comfortable with a relatively rigid pair of boots, since this means your feet won't twist around when you're traversing or descending. There are various types of attachments, from straps to a type of step-in binding which clips on to the heel of your boot. All good snow shoes have a heel raiser at the back of the binding, which can be put up when you're ascending slopes, effectively making the slope less steep, which your calves will appreciate. Under the snow shoes there is usually some sort of crampon. This can vary in size, and some are better than others. These are useful, especially when you want to go up a short steep section, when you'll largely be on your toes. There should also be some sort of traction along the length of the shoe, providing support for traverses and descents.

Poles are essential. Without them you'll look and feel most ungainly, and will be seriously disadvantaged for much of the time.

Where to go

Snow shoes are not designed for certain conditions and very steep terrain is not appropriate. So the type of summits for snow shoes are snowy peaks, often around the 3000m (9843ft) mark or lower, which are extremely beautiful in winter and afford fabulous views of the Alps in their seasonal splendour.

On days when the avalanche risk is high, or when it's actually snowing, the forests are the safest and best place to go – the snow-laden trees are beautiful, the muffled silence wonderful, and the animal tracks are quite fascinating. Great outings can be had in foul conditions – when otherwise you'd be confined indoors – discovering the forest life and the snow.

When the conditions are settled, high plateaux can be reached, where in summer the cattle are

Wide snow shoes are best for deep powder snow.

taken to graze. These are often good objectives in the winter, as they are above the treeline and you'll be able to get spectacular views. Look for small summits on the map, non-glaciated, which would perhaps not be so interesting in summer, but in the snow are really satisfying. Late in the season multi-day treks are possible, though going hut to hut in the winter can be serious, especially if the huts aren't wardened, as you'll need all your food plus cooking things, and it will get cold in the evenings. However, many Alpine huts open for a short season from late March to early May.

Snow shoeing is also a good way to travel on glaciers, but this brings with it all the extra hazards of glacier travel, and the deeper snow and increased cold at high altitude should also be taken into account.

Hazards

Winter in the Alps must be treated with caution. The days are short, and you should always plan to be back well before dark. Although it can be very sunny and warm in the day, as soon as the sun goes down the temperature plummets, and frostbite and hypothermia are very real risks. Fresh snow, or sudden rises in temperature, mean that there will be greater chances of avalanches, so you must be adequately prepared and plan your route very carefully.

It's also important to understand that summer paths will not be found in the winter. Navigation in the snow is often very difficult, and certain terrain that is easy in the summer may not be viable on snow shoes. Some of the most important lessons to learn on snow shoes are outlined below:

What bad weather?

- If the slope is too difficult, turn around.
- If the snow shoes are hindering progress you may need to take them off, but you must be careful if it's icy.
- On snow shoes progress tends to be slightly slower than on foot so plan routes that leave plenty of margin time-wise.
- There are no running streams in winter so take plenty of drink – snow does not quench your thirst unless you have a stove to melt it.
- Learn about avalanches, and find out the local risk rating, but bear in mind that this is only indicative and zero risk does not exist. Err well on the side of caution. You should be equipped with avalanche transceivers and know how to use them, unless the area is very flat, with no slopes above.
- If winter in the Alps and snow shoeing are new to you, consider taking a course run by professionals, to learn the basics of security and to discover the joys of snow shoeing.

TREKKING POLES

In 1990, when I came to live in the Alps I had never walked with poles or even considered it. Many European walkers seemed to use them but I'd never felt a need. However, all that changed when I took the first stage of the assessment course to become an Alpine trekking guide. A long walk/run had to be finished in a fixed time, which seemed totally unrealistic to me. So off we went. Uphill went okay, but on the descents I found myself severely disadvantaged compared to the others, who were almost exclusively using sticks. That decided it for me – I bought a pair of trekking poles and now rarely walk without them, except to do the shopping.

Despite years of publicity, and an increasing use of poles even in the British hills, there is still a lot of prejudice against the idea of using a stick. The idea of old people's walking sticks remains, and some people seem to feel using sticks is the last resort before a walking frame will be required. Far from it! Research has shown that the use of two trekking poles for walking provides incredible benefits: savings of about 30 tons per hour of strain on knees, ankles and hips have been calculated, with each pole prod lifting between 5 and 8kg (11–18lb) from the lower body.

When carrying a heavy load, poles help you to remain upright instead of bending over with the weight. Such an upright stance keeps your chest more open, promoting deeper and steadier breathing. Other advantages include the working of the upper body, which can only be positive; the reduction of swelling in hands which typically occurs in hot, humid weather when your hands are down by your sides all the time; being armed with a deterrent when threatened by dogs or wild pigs or other mountain hazards; and what better than poles for leaning on when taking a breather?

Clearly, if you already suffer from dodgy knees or other leg-articulation problems, using poles is to be advised, but even if you're in fine fettle right now, sticks are a good way to ensure this continues and also to enable more efficient travel, especially downhill. River crossings are easier and safer and you have more chance of negotiating muddy slopes without embarrassing yourself. There is a technique to using sticks though, and you do have to make a conscious effort at first to weight them at each step. Some walkers find them awkward, unnecessarily cumbersome, and some people like to keep their hands free for other things. Certainly it's important to have some means of attaching your poles to your rucksack when the terrain doesn't suit, but in general walkers will decide to get a couple of poles after a multi-day trek in the Alps, if not before or during.

So, is it to be two poles or just one? Personally, I'm an advocate of two, since I think one is unbalanced and after all you don't see many three-legged animals do you? However, this is a question of preference and if you like one then at least it's a start! The telescopic variety is best with the shock-absorbing springs that are now available. All poles have wrist straps which are useful, but they shouldn't be used as a matter of course. On steeper ascents or traverses you may be more comfortable holding the stick further down the shaft to avoid shoulder discomfort or walking with your arms up in the air. All sorts of variations exist – these are just details – but what matters is to try trekking poles over a reasonable distance on rough, arduous terrain, before you decide you'll hang on in there until the trekking wheelchair is invented.

Snow shoeing above Lake Tanay in Switzerland.

Snow-shoe walk grades

Where a good snow-shoe walk covers similar ground to a summer trek featured in this guide, it has been briefly described and the route included on the trek map. The walks will be found on the same maps as the trek, but they do not always follow summer paths. Some knowledge of navigating in winter is necessary to do any of these walks. They are graded 1, 2 or 3 according to difficulty. Grade 1 walks are generally easy, both in terms of navigation, following a valley for example, and in terms of exertion required. Grade 2 will be longer, with some navigation and/or hazards to consider. Grade 3 walks are arduous, often involving navigational skills and winter mountain knowledge.

CLIMBING

In 1741, William Windham and Richard Pococke arrived in Chamonix from Geneva. These two British adventurers had come to explore the glaciers that they had seen glinting in the distance from the Geneva plains. Their journey was widely regarded as reckless and foolish as not only was access to the Chamonix valley very long and difficult, it was generally believed that the glaciers were inhabited by bad spirits and to venture into their midst would invite misfortune. The men and their entourage were not to be daunted however, and their glowing reports of the glaciers, 'like frozen lakes agitated by the wind' encouraged many visitors to the Alps in the next decades.

Modern alpinism really began with the first

ALPINE-PEAK GEAR LIST

Climbing alpine peaks involves a full range of terrain, and the gear you need really depends on the peak to be climbed. Take the list below as a guide, but read the relevant peak description carefully to get an idea of the type of climbing involved.

This list should be used in conjunction with the basic one-day, multi-day trek and glaciated trek lists (see pp30, 31 and 32). Bear in mind that you may be able to leave some gear in the hut whilst you do your peak, picking it up afterwards. Whatever you do, keep your rucksack as light as possible, without sacrificing minimum-safety gear.

Rope: this should be a designated single rope – the lightest are about 9.5mm – and about 30–50m (100–160ft) depending on the route undertaken.

Harness: comfortable enough to withstand long periods of wear.

Helmet: this will not be required on most snow peaks but on any peak that involves climbing a helmet is essential.

Rock or ice gear: requirements vary with the route.

Boots: should be comfortable, waterproof, relatively rigid, and if you'll be climbing rock be sure you're happy doing that in them.

Very light stove, pan and emergency food supplies: these could be life savers if you get caught out at night.

ascent of Mont Blanc in 1786, which itself was a direct result of this interest in the Alps as a place to be explored rather than feared. Following this success most other peaks were climbed in the following decades, many of them by British alpinists with local guides. The Matterhorn was one of the more intimidating summits and was only climbed for the first time in 1865.

Now it may seem that many of the summits are climbed out, that there is little development left to be done. Most summits sport several routes, the 'Normal Route' being either the easiest or the most amenable. However, each season – winter and summer – sees new lines and variations throughout the Alps

The dark forboding north faces of many of the high mountains have become classic mountain challenges and the famous French Alpinist Gaston Rébuffat designated six of these as the 'must do' climbs of the Alps – the Grandes Jorasses, the Eiger, the Matterhorn, the Piz Badile, the Cima Grande and the Dru.

There are sixty-one peaks officially designated as attaining the coveted height of 4000m (13124ft) or above. Climbing all of these provides some people with a lifetime of motivation; others prefer to concentrate on the many peaks with rocky scrambles to the summit or to climb the summits that are accessible on skis; others search for peaks with ice gullies.

Gradings

The peaks are graded following the alpine grading system. In this book there are climbs of F (*facile*), PD (*peu difficile*), and AD (*assez difficile*). F will be snow climbs, with slopes of up to 40°, and maybe some very easy rock scrambling. PD can have slightly steeper snow slopes, and longer, more sustained sections of scrambling, while AD can involve some pitched climbing on rock, snow or ice.

Helicopters are often used for rescue in the Alps.

MOUNTAIN RESCUE IN THE ALPS

Accidents happen in the mountains, it's a fact. You cannot eliminate all risk; if you try to you won't step out of the door, but the skill is to reduce the dangers to an acceptable level, by following standard safety rules for the activity you're engaged in. If you do have an accident in the European Alps, you can at least be relieved to know that usually help will be fairly close at hand. The Alps are covered by a rescue service that is generally fast, efficient and well-practised. Obviously there are occasional places that are less accessible, where you may have to wait longer for help, but for the treks described in this book, should you be unfortunate enough to have an accident, you can expect to receive treatment quickly.

There are four different trekking terrains described in this book. Firstly, the non-glaciated mountains. It may appear that here the chances of needing rescuing are slight but nevertheless the rescue services are regularly called out to incidents involving walkers in these areas. Typical problems are fatigue, damaged ankles and knees, and head injuries from falls.

Secondly, the glacier treks carry the same risks, with the additional hazard of crevasses and icy ground in general. Roping up for glacier travel is not a guarantee against falling into a gaping void. Using a rope badly is probably as dangerous as not using one at all, and every year the rescue services see lots of accidents on glaciers involving one or more members of a party falling into a crevasse. Injuries can be very severe in these cases, including damaged limbs, torso and head, as well as hypothermia caused by a prolonged period in the ice.

The third terrain in this book is that required for winter walking in the Alps on snow shoes. Whilst not necessarily on glaciers, snow shoeing takes place in winter when the days are short and often cold, and there is the added hazard of avalanches. Typical winter accidents (apart from skiing injuries) are cold injuries (particularly hypothermia), slips on icy slopes, and avalanche injuries, either the result of burial or falls caused by the snowpack sliding.

On the fourth kind of terrain, that of Alpine summits, you must also factor in the effects of steeper ground and consequently more technical scrambling and ropework. This regularly results in falls and rockfall injuries. The Alpine peaks are, in general, big and long and require fast and efficient movement. Those who go too slowly can get caught out by nightfall or dangerous afternoon conditions, such as soft snow on the glaciers or afternoon storms. As nightfall comes so the

EMERGENCY NUMBERS

Although 112 is becoming a universally accepted emergency number, it's worth programming into your mobile phone the number of the local rescue service if you can get it. In the Chamonix area the number for the PGHM is 04 50 53 16 89. In Switzerland the rescue number is 117, or 1414 for the REGA rescue helicopter; in Italy 118 is the currently accepted number.

temperatures fall, and frostbite is certainly not unknown in the Alps.

In a remote area any of the above accidents could well be fatal, as help is not near at hand and these types of injuries quickly deteriorate and expose the victim to associated problems of cold and shock. This is not usually the case in the Alps.

Alpine rescue services started out as voluntary affairs, but over the years these services have become more and more complex and significant developments have come about in response to major accidents. In France the most notable event was the deaths of two Alpinists, Vincendon and Henry, who died of exposure on the slopes of Mont Blanc in 1956, following a badly managed rescue attempt. This led to the creation of the *Peloton de Gendarmerie de Haute Montagne* (PGHM) in 1958. The PGHM is a professional organisation and is responsible for the co-ordination of rescues in the Haute Savoie Alps, as well as in some other Alpine regions of France. Elsewhere in the French Alps rescue is organised by the fire service and the police. The same evolution has taken place in Italy, where the rescues are carried out by mountain guides, employed on a rota basis, whilst the Swiss are served by private companies in different regions, using guides and other trained personnel as necessary.

So, what to do if the unthinkable happens and you need help in the mountains? Hopefully, you might be able to get down to the valley with the help of your friends, but if this isn't the case you need to call for rescue. The rapid development of mobile phones over the last few years has made this a much more viable option, even if the rescue service finds itself called out for a considerable number of trivial incidents. If you do have to call the rescue service, you must know where you are and be coherent about your position and your condition. You must also know your own phone number, as the rescue co-ordinator will want to call you back. If the weather is good, a helicopter will generally be sent to locate you as soon as possible. In bad weather, or if your location is very difficult to reach,

Arriving on the summit of Castor (4228m/13827ft) during a winter ascent in the Pennine Alps.

you could be in for a wait, this is when your first aid and survival knowledge and supplies may prove to be essential.

If you don't have a phone you may be able to find a passing walker who does have one. If not, the nearest mountain hut or ski-lift station, or village will be able to help, but be sure to pinpoint the victim's position on the map first and to make sure he/she is well-protected from the cold or further injury. You should always insulate the casualty well – if you have ten pieces of clothing available you should put nine underneath the victim and one on top.

When your ears pick up the welcome sound of the approaching helicopter, there are certain procedures to follow, otherwise you'll either see your salvation heading off into the distance or, worse, more accidents will be caused by you doing something dangerous. You should have already prepared yourself for the helicopter's arrival by making your position obvious (using colourful clothing or getting out an orange bivvy bag, for example). The helicopter will generate a lot of wind, so gear and people should be firmly attached to the ground.

There are accepted signals for indicating to the helicopter pilot that you need help. Put both arms in the air in a 'V' to signal 'Yes, I need help', put one arm up and one down to say 'No, I don't need help'. After this, let the rescue personnel organise everything. Many rescuers in the Alps speak English, so communication shouldn't be a problem. You'll soon be winging your way to the nearest hospital, where they'll doubtless have dealt with hundreds of injuries like yours. In most sectors of the Alps the time-scale from calling out the rescue to arriving at the hospital will be less than an hour, although on very busy days, if you have a minor injury, you may have to wait longer.

Clearly all this changes dramatically if you have an accident whilst alone, or in an obscure area, or if you don't have the means to call for help. In bad weather it may be possible to send up a rescue team on foot, but heavy snow can hinder these efforts, so going out when the forecast is bad significantly increases your risks in an emergency.

So, this is all very well, but what about paying for it? Helicopters cost a lot of money, and the last thing you want to be thinking about when you've hurt yourself is whether your credit card can take it, and that your family's beach holiday will have to go out the window. In France, unlike in Switzerland and Italy, rescue is free, but any medical costs that ensue are not, nor is the cost of repatriation. Moreover, you will often be walking near and over international boundaries.

Insurance is widely available, and should be taken out to cover rescue on the terrain where you plan to walk, and also to cover medical costs incurred and repatriation, should this be necessary. Think about a worst-case scenario: you have an accident and need helicoptering to hospital. They treat you for several days, then you need to return to your own country for further treatment. A doctor and a nurse are sent to accompany you back on the plane, where your stretcher takes up the equivalent of three seats. The doctor and nurse also have to return. Costly!

Statistically very few of the thousands of people who come each year to walk and climb in the Alps ever need to be rescued. The chances are that your only view of a helicopter will be when one is supplying the mountain huts with food, but knowing what to do in an emergency is just one of the facets of trekking in the Alps.

TAKE ONLY MEMORIES, LEAVE ONLY FOOTPRINTS

Everyone has the right to experience the Alpine environment as a place of relaxation and contact with nature; equally, everyone has the responsibilty to protect it. Often the threats to the countryside come from unrestricted developments, to satisfy a demand that has not been correctly evaluated in view of the irretrievable damage done. Other threats are the result of a lack of knowledge or understanding, often caused by those participating in mountain activities – walkers, climbers, mountaineers, paragliders, cyclists and so on.

Wildlife is one of the main attractions of the Alps and the mountains are the last refuge for a large number of species. Co-habitation between animals and people can be difficult, and demands a respect on our part for the animals we come across, a willingness to give them space and to avoid invading their territory.

Numerous plants are also in danger of extinction, and these are strictly protected. The list depends on the region, but in the nature reserves all flora is protected. Even when picking flowers is legal, they should never be uprooted. Two types of terrain deserve particular attention – the forests and the cultivated meadows. Agriculture has dramatically declined in the Alps over the last decades, owing to the growth in tourism, construction and ski development. The last remaining agricultural enterprises should be

respected and walkers must stay on marked paths in forests and meadows.

Litter is a problem worldwide, not least in the mountains. Each person is responsible for his own litter, and even at a refuge don't leave rubbish in the bins if you can carry it down to the valley yourself – most huts use helicopters for supplies, which are expensive and noisy. As for the concept that certain products are biodegradeable – it takes years for orange and banana skins to degrade, so take them with you.

Taking toilet stops outside is a skill in itself. Certain over-busy areas seem to sport more toilet paper than vegetation these days. Don't go next to paths or dwelling places, and if you must use toilet paper make sure it's minimal and buried properly or, better, taken home. Try using leaves or rocks instead of paper.

Finally, bear in mind that people live in the mountain villages where many walks and climbs begin. Respect their homes and surroundings and, if necessary, leave your vehicle lower down the valley and walk or take public transport to the start of the trek.

Take only memories and leave only footprints.

4

THE SOUTHERN ALPS

This area is huge and deserves a book to itself, therefore only a taster is given here of the many different regions to be discovered as you head south from the high major massifs of Mont Blanc and the Pennine Alps. These areas benefit from the earlier arrival of spring, an extensive and varied plantlife, and many unknown and secret valleys and highlands where you can walk alone with only the silence of the mountains as company.

The Graian Alps include the Gran Paradiso and Vanoise National Parks, home to alpine wildlife, as well as extensive flora, tremendous walks, and some very satisfying peaks. Apart from the Gran Paradiso the other summits here don't reach the lofty heights of 4000m (13124ft), but are no less fine for this, providing climbs of all difficulties in truly spectacular situations. Various treks go through these mountains, and the mountain glaciers here don't extend so far as to prevent walkers' passage in their midst.

Further south is the Ecrins massif, part of the Dauphiné Alps, where, by contrast, walkers cannot penetrate the main glaciated massif without glacier travel. But seen from the surrounding foothills, the summits of the Meije, the Barre des Ecrins and all the associated glistening snowy peaks provide a stunning backdrop to the interesting treks in this region.

To the south again are the lesser Maritime Alps, not included in this book. There the glaciers have largely now disappeared, though it remains a fine Alpine region, with the Mercantour National Park as its jewel, forming the last massif before the hills drop down into the Mediterranean.

The Gran Paradiso (4061m/13324ft), as seen on the Gran Paradiso trek.

The Dauphiné Alps stretch from the southern edge of the Vanoise and the eastern edge of the Vercors, and are bounded to the east by the Italian frontier. The three highest mountains in France outside of the Mont Blanc massif are to be found in the Dauphiné – the Barre des Ecrins 4102m (13459ft), the Meije 3983m (13068ft) and Mont Pelvoux at 3932m (12901ft). Before France annexed the region of the Savoie in the 19th century, and gained Mont Blanc in the process, the Barre des Ecrins was the highest French mountain. However, any walk in this region will provide stunning glaciated vistas of the Ecrins National

On the Gran Paradiso trek, the route to the Rifugio Frederico Chabod involves a *via ferrata* (an equipped passage).

Park, where most of the high summits are situated and these summits are thus protected.

The name Dauphin, which literally means 'dolphin' was, for some unrecorded reason, used by a Lord of this region in the Middle Ages and the land he owned became know as the Dauphiné. The land was eventually sold to the King of France by a debt-ridden descendant.

The Graian Alps include the National Parks of the Gran Paradiso and the Vanoise. Nowadays these are Italian and French respectively but until the 19th century the region of Savoie was ruled by the kingdom of Piedmont Sardinia. Only in 1860 was the western part of this region annexed to France, with Italy absorbing the eastern part in 1861, thus politically dividing the Graian Alps, even though they remain geologically inseparable.

Although not home to so many high glaciated summits, they nevertheless have their share of impressive peaks, such as Mont Pourri 3782m (12409ft), a very distinctive peak, the well-known Grande Casse 3852m (12638ft) and of course the Grand Paradiso 4061m (13324ft) – the only summit here to flirt with the 4000-m (13124-ft) mark. However, the Gran Paradiso National park alone apparently contains more than fifty-seven glaciers and the entire area has many peaks of 3000m (9843ft) or more.

The Graians form Europe's largest nature reserve and the area is known particularly for its abundant wildlife, largely a result of the National Parks, which have successfully preserved several species that were threatened in the 19th century. The ibex is especially common in the Gran Paradiso National Park. In the Middle Ages the ibex was present throughout the Alps in large numbers. However, from the 16th century it began to disappear, hunted for its meat, horns, blood and organs – said to cure all manner of ailments. By the 19th century the ibex was becoming a rarity in most alpine regions. In Italy the hunters began to worry there would be no animals left to hunt and in 1856 King Victor Emmanuel II, a passionate hunter, declared the Gran Paradiso region of Italy a royal hunting reserve. The motive of Victor Emmanuel was to preserve the ibex for his own rifle, rather than to save the species, but, paradoxically this was the result he achieved. The ibex survived in this area of Italy, albeit in very small numbers and, finally, in 1922 with the creation of the Gran Paradiso National Park, its future was assured and this became the base for the regeneration of the ibex throughout the Alps, where it had become extinct.

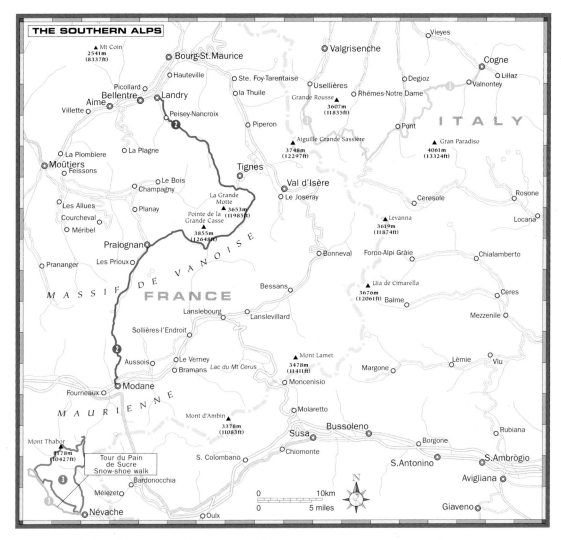

THE SOUTHERN ALPS

▲ Mt Coin
2541m
(8337ft)

○ Bourg-St.Maurice

○ Hauteville

Picollard ○
Bellentre ○
Aime ○   ○ Landry

Villette ○

○ Ste. Foy-Tarentaise

○ la Thuile

○ Peisey-Nancroix

○ Piperon

○ Valgrisenche

○ Usellières

Grande Rousse ▲
3607m
(11835ft)

○ Rhémes-Notre Dame

○ Degioz

○ Pont

○ Vieyes

○ Cogne
○ Lillaz
○ Valnontey

ITALY

▲ Aiguille Grande Sassière
3748m
(12297ft)

▲ Gran Paradiso
4061m
(13324ft)

○ La Plombiere
Moûtiers ○
○ Feissons

○ La Plagne

○ Le Bois
○ Champagny

○ Tignes

○ Val d'Isère
○ Le Joseray

○ Ceresole

○ Rosone

○ Les Allues
Courcheval ○
○ Méribel

○ Planay

La Grande Motte ▲ 3653m
(11985ft)
Pointe de la ▲
Grande Casse
3855m
(12648ft)

▲ Levanna
3619m
(11874ft)

○ Locana

Pralognan ○

○ Prananger   Les Prioux ○

M A S S I F   D E   V A N O I S E

○ Bonneval   Forno-Alpi Gràie ○

○ Chialamberto

FRANCE

Bessans ○

▲ Uia de Cimarella
3676m
(12061ft)   Balme ○

○ Ceres

○ Mezzenile

○ Lanslebourg   ○ Lanslevillard

○ Sollières-l'Endroit

○ Aussois   ○ Le Verney
○ Bramans   Lac du Mt Cerus

▲ Mont Lamet
3478m
(11411ft)

Margone ○

○ Lèmie   ○ Viu

Fourneaux ○   ○ Modane

○ Moncenisio

M A U R I E N N E

Mont d'Ambin ▲
3378m
(11083ft)

○ Molaretto

Susa ○   Bussoleno ○

○ Borgone

○ Rubiana

Mont Thabor ▲
3178m
(10427ft)

Tour du Pain
de Sucre
Snow-shoe walk

○ Chiomonte

S.Antonino ○   ○ S.Ambrògio

○ S. Colombano

○ Bardonocchia

○ Mélezeto

○ Névache

○ Oulx

Avigliana ○

Giaveno ○

0   10km
0   5 miles

N

Enjoying mountain reflections in the Nivolet lakes on the Gran Paradiso trek.

TREK 1: GRAN PARADISO

'Gran Paradiso' is a name that conjures up dreams of paradise in the mountains, and this image is not far from the truth. Situated in northern Italy, just south of Aosta in the Graian Alps, the Gran Paradiso summit at 4061m (13324ft) is the highest in the area. It dominates the national park of the same name (Parco Nazionale del Gran Paradiso) which was created in 1922. The Alta Via 4 is the higher and more spectacular of two routes that cross the park. It crosses high passes, and descends through pastures where chamois and ibex are sure to be grazing. This walk is further enhanced by the superb food and hospitality found in the convivial mountain huts (*rifugios*).

TREK ESSENTIALS

LENGTH 5 or 6 days.
ACCESS Start in Cogne and finish in Valgrisenche, both served by bus from Aosta.
HIGHEST POINT Col Lauson (3296m/10814ft).
MAPS 1:50 000: Kompass Carta Turistica 86 Gran Paradiso Valle d'Aosta; FMB Carte Turistica e dei sentieri Gran Paradiso.
1:25 000: Instituto Geografico Centrale (IGC) 101 Gran Paradiso La Grivola Cogne; 102 Valsavarenche Val di Rhêmes Valgrisenche.
TREK STYLE Mountain refuges available each night, wardened June to September, with two possible hotels.
LANGUAGES Italian and French are spoken in this region.
FURTHER OPTIONS Start in Champorcher and finish in Courmayeur. Or stop in the Rifugio Vittorio Emanuele II and ascend the Gran Paradiso or Ciarforon (3642m/11949ft).

Heading towards the Col Rosset.

The park is unusual in that, although busy during the holiday periods, the visitors are mainly Italian, and, if you don't speak a smattering of Italian or French, you're likely to find yourself doing a lot of gesticulating.

The Alta Via 4 actually starts in Champorcher, but I have chosen to describe it from Cogne, just south of Aosta and to finish in Valgrisenche, rather than going on to La Thuile and Courmayeur. This gives a walk of about five days, with easy access from the Aosta valley. The Alta Via 4 is an east-to-west traverse of the region. The area is split by a series of valleys running north to south and the route climbs over high passes, then descends into these valleys, each very traditional and rural, with old mountain-farming settlements. Each valley has a bus service from Aosta so the trek could be split into smaller sections. This trek reaches very high altitudes for a European non-glaciated trek, so it's worth checking that the passes are relatively snow-free or taking appropriate equipment.

Cogne to Rifugio Vittorio Sella

The bustling village of Cogne is at the junction of the Cogne and Valnontey valleys and is very popular with all kinds of tourists. The flat valley walk along the river from Cogne to Valnontey is likely to be heaving with people on any fine summer's day, and justifiably so since the views of the Gran Paradiso massif far away at the end of the valley are superb. From Valnontey the real climb begins, but still there will be crowds on the big switchback track up to the Rifugio Vittorio Sella (2584m/8478ft). It's possible to reach the hut by crossing the river at a bridge about forty minutes up the path and taking tiny paths up the grassy slopes past the Gran Lauson farm. The Sella hut is a popular place for lunch, and the Italians do take lunch seriously. However, don't panic, many of the day-visitors will descend in the afternoon and you'll be left to enjoy the dusk in relative peace. Take a stroll around the surrounding slopes before dinner and you'll almost certainly find chamois and ibex grazing. There are also some extremely well-fed marmots inhabiting prime locations next to the river.

Rifugio Vittorio Sella to Rifugio Federico Chabod

Looking west from the hut your eyes are drawn to an obvious and apparently very far-off col. This is the Col Lauson (3296m/10814ft) and it is the first objective of the second day. This is a very long day and to go all the way to the Rifugio Chabod requires an early start. If conditions aren't good, or if you don't want to tackle the exposed *via ferrata* (a section of route that goes up rocks, known as *klettersteig* in German) to the Chabod hut you should descend from the Col Lauson to Eaux Rousses and join up with the Alta Via at Pont the next day.

The path to the col is good, but the final part is equipped with chains, and snow could cause problems. You should arrive just as the sun hits the rocky summits next to the pass, casting a magical golden glow. Views to the east are spectacular, but you're unlikely to linger long as it's usually quite chilly, and the steep descent down the western side will be occupying your thoughts. This can be icy, but soon you'll reach the sun as the terrain becomes less barren, and the enticing meadows below are reached in good time for a second breakfast. The Gran Paradiso summit makes a sneaky appearance, but quickly disappears, only to be seen again later. There are herds of ibex and chamois here, and are likely to be feeding in the morning. Flowers are also abundant: high up alpines such as toadflax and purple saxifrage growing in the most inhospitable scree, while lower down are houseleeks, pansies and hawksbeards.

At the very obvious meadow, strewn with boulders, at about 2500m (8202ft) follow the path as it swings round to the south leaving the main trail down to the valley as it continues to the west. The way to the Rifugio Federico Chabod takes a rising traverse through wonderful meadows, and into glacial moraine. Looking back to the northwest, the Mont Blanc massif can be seen far away, snowy summits glistening in the sun. The Gran Serra (3552m/11654ft) and Herbetet (3778m/12396ft) are impressive, towering above as you traverse the foot of the Neyron glacier which issues from Herbetet. The path is indistinct and you need to keep a keen eye on the yellow paint dots marking the way through the boulder fields; whilst looking ahead you'll be wondering how on earth you're going to get through the apparently impregnable rocky ridge of the Punta Money.

On some 1:50 000 maps the way through to the Chabod hut is not marked; on the 1:25 000 maps it's shown as an easy path. In fact, a serious, equipped rocky scramble leads improbably to just below spot height 3254m (10676ft). This could be the high point of the trek if you like scrambling and if conditions are good, but a fall from this climb would have very serious consequences. Arriving at the rocky pass, the Gran Paradiso is seen properly at last, along with its neighbour the Piccolo Paradiso (3923m/12871ft).

The main difficulties are finished for the day, but the descent to Chabod is long and quite tortuous at first. It eases after a long traverse under the Punta Money, and the final stretch to the hut is pleasant, and usually takes you near to grazing chamois. The Rifugio Chabod (2750m/9023ft) enjoys a fabulous position under the northwestern slopes of the Gran Paradiso.

Rifugio Federico Chabod to Colle del Nivolet

The traverse around under the Gran Paradiso is a pleasant rest after the rigours of the previous day, and allows plenty of time to enjoy the views down to the Valsavaranche valley. The main trail to the

Early morning just below the Rifugio Vittorio Emanuele II.

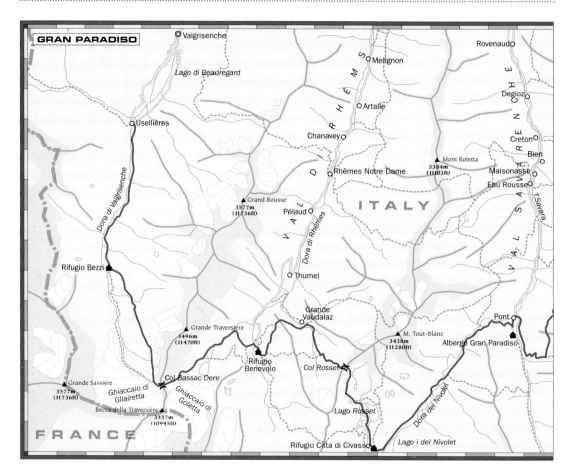

Rifugio Vittorio Emanuele II is joined for the descent to the valley, so you'll be going against the flow in the morning and will meet people heading up to the hut, either for the day or to tackle the summit. Expect to say 'Buon Giorno' many times!

Pont provides a good place for lunch before setting off through larch forest up into the Nivolet valley. The views of the Gran Paradiso are spectacular as you emerge from the trees and, if you're early enough and have binoculars, you'll be able to spot tiny figures descending from the summit.

The flat Nivolet valley is a delight, with a bubbling brook, in places deep enough for a swim, and marmots playing everywhere. Siesta time!

A short stroll takes you to the roadhead (2532m/8307ft) just north of the Col del Nivolet, and there's a small hotel (Albergo Savoia). Alternatively just up on the hillside is the Rifugio Citta di Civasso.

Col del Nivolet to Rifugio Benevolo
Above the col are the fabulous Nivolet lakes, which

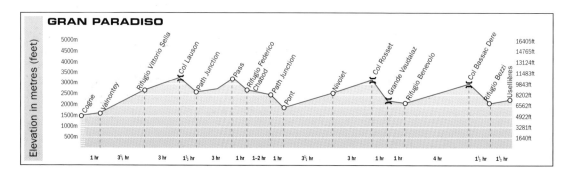

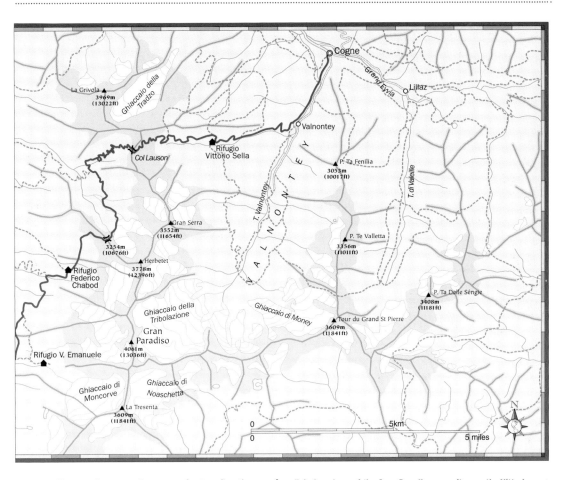

on a still morning can have perfect reflections of the distant mountains. The Alta Via passes the lakes then takes a short climb to the Col Rosset (3023m/9918ft). (It's also possible to cross either the Col di Leynir at 3084m/10112ft or the Col de la Nivolettaz at 3152m/10335ft, both of which have small but dry glaciers on the far side. These provide slightly longer options.) Again views are spectacular and, from the Col Rosset, can be savoured since this is a short day. However, the descent is steep and can be time-consuming. The meadows of the Grande Vaudalaz valley are usually carpeted with flowers and inhabited by marmots, with chamois grazing the more distant slopes, or cooling themselves on patches of *neve* (see glossary, p173) and if you look carefully you should spot the odd ibex high up on the rocks.

Instead of continuing down to the main valley, cross the river at the farm buildings of the Alpe le Grande Vaudalaz and take a rising traverse to reach the Rifugio Benevolo (2285m/7497ft), in a lovely position with glaciated peaks in the distance

Enjoying views of the Gran Paradiso summit, near the Vittorio Sella hut.

and the imposing rock face of the Granta Parei (3387m/11113ft) just above. This is another lunch spot, being easily accessible from the valley road.

Rifugio Benevolo to Valgrisenche

The route ascends into the wild and barren Comba di Goletta, where the Goletta glacier tumbles impressively down from the Punta de la Golettaz (3245m/10647ft) and the Granta Parei. At the base of the glacier is a deep, dark ice cavern from which melt water flows into a huge green lake.

The Col Bassac Dere (3082m/10112ft) gives access to the Valgrisenche valley, which is reached by a high path traversing above the Gliarettaz glacier, with its spectacular crevasses, plunging deeper and deeper as the glacier flows down the valley. You'll see the Rifugio Mario Bezzi far below long before you reach it. The way is quite long, but the terrain constantly interesting, crossing shale slabs, fast-flowing rivers, flower-strewn meadows and boulder-filled canyons. If you're lucky you'll spot the Mont Blanc massif again in the distance.

Don't miss out on refreshments at the rather fine Bezzi hut, where you could spend a very pleasant night enjoying the views up the valley to the glacier and surrounding peaks. Although the descent from the hut is marked on some maps as a road, it's a footpath at first, then becomes a jeep track to the hamlet of Uselères (also known as Usellières). If you can arrange transport from here then do so, otherwise follow the old road along the eastern shore of the Lago di Beauregard to the village of Valgrisenche from where buses run down the valley to Aosta.

THE IBEX

In the Middle Ages the ibex was present throughout the Alps in large numbers. However, from the sixteenth century it began to disappear, hunted for its meat, horns, blood and organs - said to cure all manner of ailments. By the 19th century the ibex was becoming a rarity in most Alpine regions. In Italy the hunters began to worry there would be no quarry left and in 1856 King Victor Emanuel II, a passionate hunter, declared the Gran Paradiso region of Italy a royal hunting reserve. Ironically, therefore, the ibex survived in this area of Italy, albeit in very small numbers and, finally, in 1922 with the creation of the Gran Paradiso National Park, its future was assured. The park became the base for the regeneration of the ibex throughout the Alps, where it had otherwise become extinct.

Now that the bear and the wolf have more or less disappeared, the ibex has very few enemies except the golden eagle which will take young ibex. The ibex is a stockier beast than the chamois, with wider and - in the case of the males - much longer horns. The typical adult ibex measures 70-90cm (2½-3ft) high at the shoulders, the males weighing up to 100kg (224lb). The females are slighter. The huge ridged horns of an adult male can reach a weight of 5kg (11lb), and a length of 90cm (3ft). The female's horns are much shorter, not exceeding 25cm (10in). The ibex belongs to the goat family, as shown by its distinctive eyes, with the characteristic oval, horizontal pupil.

Ibex tend to live in groups - the males together and the females with the young males. They are animals of the rocks, preferring to live at altitude on cliffs, ledges or under overhangs, between 2000-3000m (6562-9483ft). The ibex hoof is made up of two separate toes which can draw apart considerably to give it a good footing, and it moves with ease on rocky slabs and buttresses. In winter they descend, previously to the valleys, but nowadays rarely that low, searching for sunny places out of the wind, yet they do not like the forest, and are not keen on snow either. When forced to descend in winter they stay at the edge of the treeline, in sparse larch forest. Their diet consists of all types of vegetation, including bushes and trees. In winter, lichens constitute much of their frugal diet.

The unhunted ibex has a calm and tranquil demeanour and can be approached to within a few metres. It's rare to see an ibex move quickly, but they can jump impressive distances when necessary - for example, to cross a stream. When the ibex is frightened it makes a sound like a whistle, produced by the sudden expulsion of air from its nostrils. Their life span does not exceed 20-25 years.

In the spring young male ibex can be seen play-fighting, but the real battles take place in the late autumn/early winter, at the start of the mating season, when the hierarchy among the adult males is decided by spectacular fights. The males fight with their horns, which make a loud 'clack' as they bash against each other.

The female gives birth usually to one baby every two years, whereas the chamois can give birth every year. However, despite this relatively limited rate of reproduction, it seems that for the moment, with the regulation of hunting, the ibex population is no longer threatened in the Alps.

PEAK: GRAN PARADISO

CLIMB ESSENTIALS

SUMMIT Gran Paradiso (4061m/13324ft).
PRINCIPAL HUT Rifugio Vittorio Emanuele II (2732m/89641ft).
GRADE PD
HEIGHT GAIN 1329m (4360ft).
APPROXIMATE TIME 4-5 hours.
MAP 1:25 000 IGC 101 Gran Paradiso.

Not only does the Gran Paradiso provide an accessible and interesting ascent, with a glacier approach and a rocky finish, it also affords one of the most wide-ranging views in the Alps. Extending 300km (186 miles) to the south over the plains of the Po to the Mediterranean, and including the Matterhorn, Monte Rosa and other Pennine peaks to the northeast, and the Mont Blanc range just to the northwest, this panorama more than rewards the effort of the ascent.

First climbed in 1860 by a British team led by Chamonix guides, this summit has become justifiably popular, located as it is in one of the oldest Alpine national parks. Any fine summer's day will see many teams on this peak, and the final

rocks can call for some intimacy but this is bearable and even fun, and nothing can detract from those views. On weekdays, outside of the main holiday season, the number of people will be considerably less.

On the pleasant walk up from Pont to the Rifugio Vittorio Emanuele II, (named after the founder of the hunting reserve, later to become the national park) you'll probably encounter ibex and chamois, and at the hut you'll enjoy excellent Italian hospitality.

The normal route to the summit takes the easy-angled west face, by the often icy and gravelly Gran Paradiso glacier. From the hut, head northwards over boulders to the moraines below the Gran Paradiso glacier. The moraine is followed to a small valley that leads to the snout of the glacier. Ascend the glacier keeping to the right and, towards the top, a steeper slope leads to the col at 4026m (13209ft).

Here take to the rocky ridge leading to the summit. An exposed traverse causes a few heart flutters as you are briefly poised above Valnontey far below, then a final rocky scramble brings you to a Madonna on the summit. Return by the same route.

The Gran Paradiso, seen from the traverse from the Chabod hut to Rifugio Vittorio Emanuele II.

TREK 2: TRAVERSE OF THE VANOISE

The Parc de la Vanoise is to be found south of the Mont Blanc massif, bordering the Italian Parco Nazionale del Gran Paradiso, and forms the western lobe of the Graian Alps. This was the first of the French national parks, established in 1963, and is a high plateau punctuated by mountains, which forms excellent terrain for walking. Unlike many other areas where glaciers are a barrier to trekkers, you can hike all the way across the Vanoise. The Traverse of the Vanoise does just that and is superb for its variety of terrain, the proximity of the high mountains, and the flora and fauna that are abundant in this uncrowded region. The Vanoise National Park is twinned with that of the Gran Paradiso, and together they form the largest nature reserve in Western Europe.

TREK ESSENTIALS

LENGTH 5–7 days.
ACCESS Start at Landry in the Isère valley, finish at Modane in the Arc valley.
HIGHEST POINT Col de Chavière (2796m/9174ft).
MAPS 1:50 000 Didier Richard 11 Parc de la Vanoise.
1:25 000 IGN Top 25 3532 ET Les Arcs La Plagne, 3633 ET Haute Maurienne, 3534 OT Les Trois Valleés.
TREK STYLE Mountain refuges available each night, wardened June to September, and run by the national park.
LANGUAGE French.
FURTHER OPTIONS Follow the GR5 instead of the GR55 from Tignes, along the lower route. Ascents of the glaciated peaks in the area, such as La Grande Casse and Mont Pourri.

There are major glaciated peaks in the area, such as La Grande Casse (3855m/12648ft), La Grande Motte (3653m/11985ft) and Mont Pourri (3779m/12393ft), but essentially the Vanoise is an excellent place for non-glaciated walking. The traverse as described here follows, initially, part of the super-long GR5 route, which goes from Holland to the Mediterranean, and then takes the high variant of this route, the GR55 from Tignes to Modane. The trek stays high most of the time and few villages are encountered. You do have to skirt round the Tignes ski resort, which has to be one of the uglier French resorts, at least in the summer,

but it's quickly done and then you're back into the wilds, with not a lift to be seen. There are plenty of mountain huts in the park, all overseen centrally by the national park service, so providing a consistent service. Nevertheless each hut does have its own character.

Snow in August in the Vanoise.

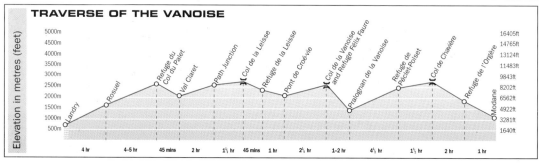

TRAVERSE OF THE VANOISE

Elevation in metres (feet)

5000m — 16405ft
4500m — 14765ft
4000m — 13124ft
3500m — 11483ft
3000m — 9843ft
2500m — 8202ft
2000m — 6562ft
1500m — 4922ft
1000m — 3281ft
500m — 1640ft

Landry · Rosuel · Refuge du Col du Palet · Val Claret · Path Junction · Col de la Leisse · Refuge de la Leisse · Pont de Croé-vie · Col de la Vanoise and Refuge Félix Faure · Pralognan de la Vanoise · Refuge de Péclet-Polset · Col de Chavière · Refuge de l'Orgère · Modane

4 hr   4–5 hr   45 mins   2 hr   1½ hr   45 mins   1 hr   2¼ hr   1–2 hr   4½ hr   1½ hr   2 hr   1 hr

Landry to Porte du Parc de Rosuel

Landry is a small town just south of Bourg-Saint-Maurice, in the Isère valley, which forms the northern boundary of the Vanoise. The first day's walk is not typical of the rest of the trek, being largely in forest, passing small villages and finally emerging into the open at Les Lanches, just before the Refuge de Rosuel. I enjoy this walk for its varied trees – ash, hazel, oak, aspen, walnut and sycamore among others – and the birdlife, as well as the lower-altitude forest flowers, such as foxgloves, campanula, and helleborine. However, if you want to get into the high mountains as quickly as possible this day could be skipped with a taxi ride.

The Refuge de Rosuel, at the entrance (*porte*) of the park, has a special wave-shaped roof with a lawn on it, designed to allow avalanches to flow over the top without it being destroyed.

Rosuel to Refuge du Col du Palet

As you head into the Plagne valley along by the river, among rowan and alder trees, the slopes of Mont Pourri tower steeply on the left, whilst to the right is the Sommet de Bellecôte (3417m/11211ft). The views open up as you climb until you're in the flat valley above the Lac de Plagne. This is an absolutely beautiful area, studded with intensely coloured alpine flowers, and it's tempting to descend to the hut down by the lake, Refuge Entre le Lac, it looks so enticing!

However, your path climbs up steadily towards the Col du Palet where the Refuge du Col du Palet is to be found just below the col at 2500m (8202ft). It's not very far to carry on over to Tignes, where there are hotels, but the refuge has wonderful views of this

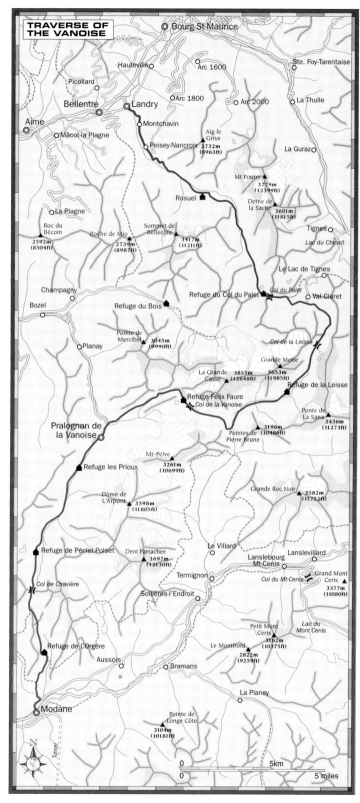

Heading into the Plagne valley.

fabulous valley that you can savour in the evening. On this side of the pass you wouldn't know that there was a major ski resort twenty minutes away, since fortunately no lifts have been constructed on these slopes.

Refuge du Col du Palet to Refuge de la Leisse

Fifteen minutes takes you to the Col du Palet (2652m/8701ft). If you don't need to buy extra supplies, then Tignes can be pretty much avoided by descending to Val Claret and picking up the GR55 path which leads southeast towards the Col de Fresse (the GR5 at Val Claret makes a long loop to the east before coming back west at Modane). Just before the col there is a path junction at 2531m (8304ft) where you head off south-south-westwards among rocks and a wild landscape between the Grande Motte and the summit of the Grande Pré. This takes you up to the Col de la Leisse (2761m/9059ft). Cairns mark the way and in good weather it all seems quite straightforward, but in snow or fog, or both as I experienced on one memorable occasion, this barren moonscape can become quite disorientating.

The Col de la Leisse leads into the Leisse valley and the way soon becomes more defined after the cold and uninviting Lac des Nettes. The Refuge de la Leisse is in fact two buildings, built in the typical style of the park, one for the warden and one for everybody else. The hut is very well organised and woe betide you in high season if you haven't booked!

Refuge de la Leisse to Pralognan de la Vanoise

You will almost certainly be accompanied by the shrieks of marmots as you stroll from the Leisse hut down the valley to the Pont de Croé-vie (2099m/6887ft). Keep your eyes open for chamois grazing the slopes nearby in the early morning. If you go straight on you finally reach the Arc valley at Termignon, but instead the GR55 heads west with a steep but short climb into a flat-bottomed valley under the south slopes of the Grande Casse. The Col de la Vanoise is at 2517m (8258ft), as is the Refuge Félix Faure (also known as the Refuge Col de la Vanoise). This would be a fine place to stay, or you can continue to the village of Pralognan de la Vanoise.

The route follows an old mule track by Lac Long, to enter the ancient glacial valley of La Grande Casse. However, a variant can be taken under the south face of the Aiguille de la Vanoise to descend under the very steep cliffs of le Moriand and through the Cirque de l'Arcelin. The rock faces of the Grande and Petite Arcelin are really impressive and this gorge makes an interesting route to the small resort of Pralognan de la Vanoise.

Pralognan de la Vanoise to Modane

Gentle tracks lead out of the village and the easy walking continues as you pass farm buildings and head up the Doron valley following the river. The Refuge de Péclet-Polset is new, the old one having burnt down in 1996, and is perched on a bluff just below 2500m (8202ft). The path now climbs steadily and you'll be aware of the terrain becoming more and more barren, with just the most hardy flowers here, notably the white and deep-pink glacier crowsfoot. Your objective is the Col de Chavière, which at 2796m (9174ft) has the honour of being the highest pass crossed on any French *Grande Randonnée*.

Many people do the Col de Chavière as a day walk and then return to Pralognan so you may lose some fellow walkers at the pass. The descent to the Refuge de l'Orgère is very pleasant and relatively easy. This big and well-equipped refuge is at the road-head, and a taxi could perhaps be organised to the valley. Otherwise, take the GR5 footpath down through the woods into the rather industrial town of Modane and don't linger!

THE MARMOT

The first time you hear the high-pitched shriek of the marmot you'll most likely look upwards searching for a bird. However, scan the near-by rocks and the chances are that you'll spot a small furry creature sitting up on his hind legs, and that's the culprit. This likeable animal is common throughout the Alps, quite easy to spot, and is a daytime creature. However, much of his time is spent underground in his burrow, and he'll frustratingly nip out of sight as soon as you get close trying to take a photo.

The marmot is about the size of a domestic cat, and it belongs to the rodent family. It has thick fur of variable colour – generally grey on the head with a lighter muzzle, brown-grey shoulders and back, and the underside of the body a paler beige. It has whiskers to enable it to move around its burrow in the dark. The marmot has some impressive front teeth, top and bottom, which are orange.

The strident cry of the marmot is very characteristic, and is not a whistle, but a true cry coming from the larynx. It denotes alarm or fear – if the animal is merely issuing a warning he'll make a series of shrieks, but if he is really scared one shriek will suffice and he'll immediately make for the nearest entrance to his burrow. Marmots are gregarious creatures, living in family groups, and not only do they protect each other by warning of dangers, but also play together, and clean each other's fur. Their main enemies are the fox and the golden eagle. Previously hunted for their fat, marmots are not generally sought-after these days since the meat is no good and they do not have anything worth hanging on the wall as a trophy.

Their extensive burrows have separate sleeping quarters and many entrances. Marmots like the sun, although they avoid the extreme heat, and in the summer will be up early to feed, retreating to their burrows in the midday heat, then emerging for a siesta, lying flat out on a sunny rock, before feeding again before nightfall. On rainy days they don't tend to come out so much.

Their diet consists essentially of vegetation, but they also eat insects, larvae and birds' eggs. They live for about fifteen years and give birth to between two and seven young in May/June, having bred in April. The young are at great risk, and 30 per cent die before their first winter whilst 10 per cent don't survive hibernation.

They hibernate when the days get shorter and the temperature falls, usually early October, not reappearing until April. During the hibernation period they can lose up to 50 per cent of their body weight, their body being almost in a state of suspended animation. Their temperature falls to around 10°C (50°F), so they are deeply hypothermic, and their respiration is reduced to one or two breaths a minute, their heartbeat dropping from two hundred beats a minute to about thirty. If the temperature of the burrow rises or falls noticeably the animal awakes, but otherwise he just gets up once a month to empty his bladder.

TREK 3: MONT THABOR

Mont Thabor stands alone to the northeast of the major peaks of the Dauphiné Alps, most of which are glaciated. At 3178m (10427ft) Mont Thabor is a relatively high non-glaciated peak and, being set just a little apart from the massif, offers superlative views of the snowy summits of the Meije (3982m/13045ft), the Barre des Ecrins (4102m/13459ft) and Mont Pelvoux (3946m/12947ft), as well as views north towards the Vanoise and the Mont Blanc massif.

TREK ESSENTIALS

LENGTH 3 days.
ACCESS Start and finish in Névache.
HIGHEST POINT Mont Thabor (3178m/10427ft).
MAPS 1:50 000: Didier Richard 6 Ecrins Haut Dauphiné.
1:25 000: IGN Top25 3535 OT Névache Mont Thabor.
TREK STYLE Multi-day trek with mountain refuges.
LANGUAGE French.
FURTHER OPTIONS There are many possibilities for other treks in this area, too numerous to mention here.

The ascent of Mont Thabor can be done as a circuit, following part of the GR57 trek, which is a lengthier tour of the mountain. The trek described here begins in the attractive small town of Névache, and features really all that is best about alpine trekking, from meadows and valleys, carpeted with alpine flowers, to higher rocky ground where wildlife abounds, and summit terrain complete with an exciting ridge section.

Névache is in the Vallée de la Clarée, which extends to Briançon and is famous for its sundials, often to be found painted in a very distinctive style on the sunny faces of buildings. The name

From the summit of Mont Thabor, the southwesterly view to the Ecrins is an awesome panorama.

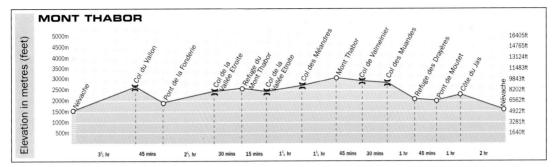

'Névache' has nothing to do with the cattle that graze here in summer (*vache* means 'cow' in French), but comes from the word *nevé*, Névache being a patois variation on this, meaning a very snowy place. Certainly in the winter this area gets heavy snowfall, and this village is the highest one in the Clarée valley to be inhabited year-round.

Névache to the Refuge du Mont Thabor

The path begins just on the outskirts of the village near the St Benoît chapel and follows the Torrent du Vallon up the long valley going north. After a steep start the going becomes easier and you'll pass the St Michel chapel after an hour or so. Streams come down the hillside on either side from small mountain lakes above. The eastern face of the valley is bounded by cliffs and the Rocher Blanc and the Tour du Vallon form the Col du Vallon at 2645m (8678ft). Mont Thabor can be seen from here, to the northeast, whilst to the south views of the Ecrins massif begin to open up.

An initially steep descent soon eases as you traverse under the northern tip of the rocky buttress of the Pointe de l'Enfourant. The path contours around, to descend through rocks to the Pont de la Fonderie (1897m/6224ft). If time or energy is short this point can be reached much more quickly by driving up to the parking at the Vallée Etroite and walking up the valley from there.

The Vallon de Tavernette is followed northwards by relatively gentle terrain to the Col de la Vallée Etroite (2434m/7986ft). Not far above is the Refuge du Mont Thabor at 2508m (8229ft), and this is quickly reached from the col. The hut is beautifully situated in the Combe de la Grande Montagne, above the twin Lacs de Ste Marguerite, descriptively called the Lac Rond and the Lac Long. Mont Thabor is to the west, whilst to the northeast the views stretch down to the hazy depths of the Arc valley, and beyond into the Vanoise. To the southeast is the rocky summit of Cime de la Planette (3104m/10184ft).

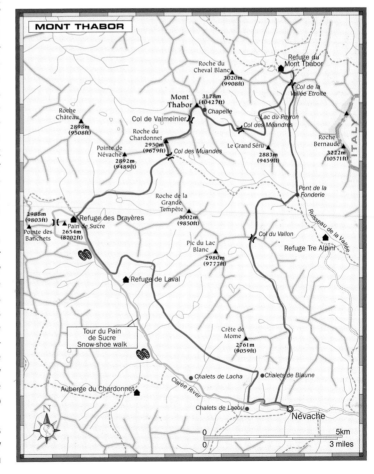

Refuge du Mont Thabor to the Refuge des Drayères

Retrace your steps to the Col de la Vallée Etroite and then take the path that heads first south then southwest into the Vallon de Peyron. The chilly-looking Lac du Peyron is passed, before skirting around the rocks of Les Chances du Peyron and going up to the Col des Méandres (2727m/8947ft). To the south are the impressive pillars of Le Grand Seru. Now the real climbing starts, as the remaining 450m (1476ft) are steep. The path winds up through scree and rocks, quite barren but not without flora and fauna – just keep your eyes

open. Just before the summit you pass the Chapelle du Mont Thabor and then the top is reached. This summit classically proves that you get the best views of the high summits by being outside of the massif. The 360° panorama is stunning and you'll want to spend plenty of time here.

To continue with the route, descend from the summit to pick up a path, just after the chapel, going rightwards under the summit, to avoid the Pointe des Angelières (3093m/10148ft), and then heading back up onto the ridge at point 2943m (9656ft). The route avoids the next obstacle, the

SNOW-SHOE WALK: TOUR DU PAIN DE SUCRE

SNOW-SHOE WALK ESSENTIALS

ACCESS Start and finish at Névache.
DISTANCE 13km (8 miles) to the refuge the first day; 15km (9¼ miles) the second day.
HEIGHT GAIN 580m (1902ft) the first day; 400m (1312ft) the second day.
APPROXIMATE TIME 5 hours the first day; 5–6 hours the second day.
DIFFICULTY 3.
TYPE OF WALK 2-day tour.
INTERESTING FEATURES The rocky peaks and the good views.
MAP 1:25 000: IGN Top 25 3535 OT Névache.

A 13-km (8-mile) walk from Névache is required to reach the Refuge des Drayères in winter. This is largely along a track, albeit a snowy one, and may at first seem to hold no interest when you're keen to get up into the mountains. However, the Clarée valley is extremely beautiful, and this walk to the hut provides pleasant exercise and a good warm-up for the next day's outing.

The Pain de Sucre is an interesting peak, easily recognisable for the vertical strata of its rocky faces. At 2654m (8708ft) it is smaller than its neighbours and is not accessible on foot in the winter, but the tour allows you to get into the midst of the Cerce summits, reminiscent of the Dolomites.

From the hut, head northwest up the main valley, then west. At about 2350m (7710ft) turn to the southwest and follow the subsidiary valley

towards the cirque formed by the Pointe des Blanchets and the Riou Blanc. At 2470m (8104ft) locate the col to the southeast between the Pain de Sucre and the Riou Blanc and climb up to this (2583m/8475ft). As you reach the col you'll be rewarded with fine views far away to the southeast of the summits of the Pic de Rochebrune and Monte Viso.

Initially the descent from the col is steep and should be treated with caution. It soon eases and you follow the delightful Riou Blanc valley back to the Clarée valley. If snow conditions allow, cross the river to reach the main trail back to Névache, but if in doubt stay on the right bank until you reach the Moutet bridge further down.

Animals are often easier to spot in the winter, but keep your distance or they will use up precious energy running away.

PEAK: ROCHE FAURIO

CLIMB ESSENTIALS

SUMMIT Roche Faurio (3730m/12231ft).
PRINCIPAL HUT Refuge des Ecrins 3170m (10401ft).
GRADE F
HEIGHT GAIN 560m (1837ft).
APPROXIMATE TIME 2-3½ hours.
MAP 1:25 000: IGN Top 25 3436 ET Meije Pelvoux.

The ascent of the southeast face of the Roche Faurio, situated above the Glacier Blanc and opposite the north face of the Barre des Ecrins and the Dôme de Neige des Ecrins, guarantees fabulous views. The Glacier Blanc is the busiest place in the Ecrins massif, so during good weather and the holiday season crowds are also guaranteed. Most people come here to climb the Barre des Ecrins, at 4102m (13459ft) the highest summit in the massif, or its shoulder, the Dôme de Neige des Ecrins (4015m/13173ft), easier and equally popular. So the Roche Faurio tends to be quieter. Yet it is a great climb: less difficult, less arduous and less prestigious than its neighbours maybe, but very satisfying.

The Refuge des Ecrins (3170m/10401ft) should be booked at any time except low season. The refuge is reached from Ailefroide, via the Pré de Madame Carle and the Refuge du Glacier Blanc, finally following the left bank of the Glacier Blanc. From the refuge rejoin the Glacier Blanc by the couloir to the east of the hut, then follow the left bank towards the Col des Ecrins. There will inevitably be a track as this is also the route for the two big summits here.

At about 3350m (10991ft), before reaching the col, but having traversed under the rocky spur coming down from the Pointe Xavier Blanc, head right and climb the summit snow slopes to a flattening on the south ridge at 3550m (11648ft). Follow this snow arête, enjoying fine views in all directions, finishing with easy rocks to the summit. The Barre and Dôme de Neige des Ecrins are magnificent when seen from here. Descend by the same route.

Roche Faurio, as seen from the route to the Barre des Ecrins and the Dôme de Neige des Ecrins.

THE GOLDEN EAGLE

When you see a huge bird flying high overhead in the Alps, rarely if ever flapping its wings, you can make a fair bet that it is a golden eagle. This bird has fascinated people for centuries the world over. In mythology it was the sacred bird of Jupiter, whilst for the American Indians it symbolised virility and warrior qualities. In numerous countries the eagle has been chosen as the emblem of glory, because it evokes power, pride and courage.

The golden eagle represents the wildlife of the Alps, living proof of the beauty and grace of mountain fauna. At a distance the eagle can be confused with the buzzard, but closer up it is unmistakable. The golden eagle has a body that is 50 per cent bigger and a wingspan that is 75 per cent wider, from 204–220cm (80–87in). The female is the larger of the species, weighing between 3.8kg and 6.6kg (8.5–14.8lb); it is about 90–95cm (3ft) long, whilst the male is 30 per cent smaller. The bird is brown, in a range of shades, with a darker tail and golden highlights on the neck, head and wings, hence the name. The young have distinctive white marks on the wings, both on the top and the underside, and on the tail, which remain for about four years.

Hooded eyes give the bird a ferocious and cruel look and, armed with a sturdy hooked beak of impressive size, the golden eagle is a fierce and efficient hunter. Its feet are extremely power-ful, equipped with long, black, curved talons which can carry prey of a considerable size. This super-predator enjoys a varied diet depending on what's available. Having a preference for meals that provide considerably more energy than that expended during the hunt, the eagle lives off marmots (in the summer) and other mammals, especially the young of bigger creatures such as ibex, chamois and foxes. Ptarmigan, black grouse, squirrels, martens, ermines, mice and lizards also feature on the menu.

The eagle is active by day and spends the night perched on cliffs or promontories. Golden eagles mate for life, and generally build nests in the cliffs. They produce on average two eggs, but usually only the first baby to hatch survives, the younger one being attacked by the elder. The young birds that survive the first four years of their life can live for up to twenty-five years. The eagle's preferred mode of flight is gliding, and its long graceful spirals are rarely interrupted by the batting of a wing. Huge majestic swoops take it down to catch prey which it generally carries away to consume.

In stormy and windy weather pairs of golden eagles can often be seen high over the mountains, performing spectacular aerial acrobatics, especially in the winter when this also forms part of the mating parade.

The golden eagle suffered a significant reduction in popula-tion in the first part of the 20th century, due to hunting, but it is now a protected species throughout the Alps. It is essential for the Alpine fauna, as it ensures the survival of the fittest animals, tending to kill those that are weak, old, injured or imprudent. It also dispenses with carcasses and diseased animals.

The trail up the Vallée Etroite on the way to the Mont Thabor hut.

Roc de Valmeinier, on the west side, by an exposed section to regain the ridge at the Col de Valmeinier, about 2900m (9515ft). Views throughout are extremely satisfying and the next part of the walk is wonderful as you follow the ridge over the Roche du Chardonnet (2950m/9679ft) to the Col des Muandes (2828m/9279ft). This is exposed and care must be taken – it would be very unwise to be here in bad conditions, and if the weather deterio-rated during your ascent of Mont Thabor you should head back towards the Vallée Etroite rather than continuing on by this route.

Linger as long as you like at the col, before dis-covering the delightful Muandes valley, with its lakes and bubbling stream. The Refuge des Drayères is at the junction of this valley and the main Clarée valley, at the Pont de Pierre (2167m/7110ft). Those with a masochistic ten-dency could plod on down to Névache, but why miss an evening in this charming spot, surrounded by peaks?

Refuge des Drayères to Névache

A lovely stroll can be enjoyed to the roadhead at Pont de Moutet (2023m/6637ft); then either go down the road or, much better, take the steep climb up to Côte du Jas (2396m/7861ft), and contour high above the valley along the Chemin de Ronde, to finally descend to Névache via the Chalets de Biaune. This gives a very pleasant finish to the trek.

THE SOUTHERN ALPS REGIONAL DIRECTORY

GETTING THERE BY AIR

The choice of airport for the Southern Alps region depends on which part you're planning to visit. Geneva airport is quite convenient for the Vanoise area and access is not dificult from here to the Gran Paradiso. The airports of Turin or Milan are convenient for the Gran Paradiso and Ecrins regions. Having landed, there are various options for onward travel to the Alpine regions.

Car hire: several car hire companies operate out of the airports and, as usual, it's normally cheaper to book in advance. From Geneva, French toll motorways via Grenoble lead to the Isère valley and the Vanoise National Park. Good roads lead from Milan, via Turin over the Col de Montgenève to Briançon. Although this pass is at 1850m (6067ft) it is generally open in the winter. The Italian motorways are toll roads and it's wise to have some cash (Italian or French) as occasionally they do not accept credit cards.

Train: from Geneva airport you can link up with the French SNCF railways to reach Landry on the route to Bourg-Saint-Maurice. Modane is also on the main railway line from Paris to Rome. From Milan and Turin the railway comes to Aosta, from where the Gran Paradiso region is served by buses in each of its valleys. Briançon can be reached by train on the Paris–Milan line, stopping at Oulx station in Italy, from where a bus service runs twice daily to Briançon. The Paris–Briançon line goes via Grenoble and Gap so is less direct. From Briançon a bus service (Autocars Résalp) connects with Névache. From Argentière la Bessée, which is on the Briançon–Gap railway line, a bus (Autocars Engelberge) goes to Vallouise and Ailefroide.

Bus: there are bus services from Grenoble to Briançon (VFD) and from Turin to Briançon (SAPAV).

GETTING THERE BY ROAD

The French motorways from the north of France lead to the A41 Autoroute Blanche to Geneva and Annecy from where access is straightfroward to the Isère valley for the Vanoise or to the Gran Paradiso via the Mont Blanc Tunnel or the Grand Saint Bernard Pass. The A43 goes to Modane whereas the A32 arrives here from Italy via the Fréjus tunnel. To reach Briançon from northern France you must come over the Col du Lauteret and from Italy it's necessary to cross the Col de Montgenèvre. Both of these high passes are generally kept open year long, but can be closed in snow. Road information can be had from local tourist offices or from the number in the directory below.

ACCOMMODATION

In the main towns there are hotels or *gîtes*, as well as campsites in the summer. However, some of the smaller towns do not have many hotels and in high season booking in advance is essential. The best sources of information are the local tourist offices, where English is spoken.

Mountain Huts:

There are a lot of huts to choose from in this region, many of which are noted in the trek texts. Since phone numbers change, individual numbers are not listed here. The best way to find out how to reserve a hut is to contact the local tourist office and they may even make the reservation for you. For well-known treks such as the Alta Via 4, the local tourist office can give you a list of hut numbers. If you want to make your reservation before the hut opens you'll need to contact the guardian at his private number, which the tourist offices should also provide. Huts owned by Alpine Clubs or by the National Parks can also be booked direct via the governing body.

DIRECTORY

For all telephone numbers the local numbers are noted – to telephone from abroad add the international code and drop the first 0, except for Italy where the entire number is dialled.

Geneva Airport: tel. 022 717 7111; www.gva.ch
Turin Airport: tel. 011 567 6361; www.turin-airport.com
Milan Airport: tel. 027 485 2200; www.sea-aeroportimilano.it
Swissair: www.swissair.com
Alitalia: www.alitalia.it
British Airways: www.britishairways.com
Air France: www.airfrance.com
Ryanair: www.ryanair.com
Rail Europe: www.raileurope.com
Italian Rail: www.itwg.com
French Railways: tel. UK 08705 848 848; tel. France 08 36 67 68 69; www.sncf.fr
VFD bus: tel. 04 76 47 77 77
SAPAV bus: tel. 0121 322 032
Autocars Engelberge (Briançon–Ailefroide): tel. 04 92 23 33 54; fax 04 92 23 46 52
Autocars Résalp (Briançon–Névache): tel. 04 92 20 47 50
Road info for Col du Lauteret and Col du Montgenève: tel. 04 92 24 44 44

Italian Tourist Offices for the Southern Alps

Gran Paradiso Tourist Office: tel. 0165 95055; fax 0165 95975; email: granparadiso@netvallee.it; www.granparadiso.org
Aosta Tourist Office: tel. 0165 33352

French Tourist Offices for the Southern Alps

For general information and French tourist offices: www.maison-de-la-france.com
Vanoise National Park information: www.vanoise.com
Bourg-Saint-Maurice Tourist Office: tel. 04 79 07 04 92; fax 04 79 07 24 90; email: wlesarcs@lesarcs.com; www.bourgstmaurice.com
Tignes Tourist Office: tel. 04 79 40 04 40; fax 04 79 40 03 15; email: information@tignes.net; www.tignes.net
Pralognan de la Vanoise Tourist Office: tel. 04 79 08 79 08; fax 04 79 08 76 74; email: info@pralognan.com; www.pralognan.com
Modane Tourist Office: tel. 04 79 05 33 83; fax 04 79 05 13 67; www.valfrejus.com
Briançon Tourist Office: tel. & fax 04 92 20 56 45; email: office-tourisme-briancon@wanadoo.fr
Névache Tourist Office: tel. 04 92 21 38 19; fax 04 92 20 51 72; www.hautes-alpes.com/laclaree
Vallouise Tourist Office: tel. 04 92 23 36 12; fax 04 92 23 41 44; www.lavallouise.com

5

THE WESTERN OUTLIERS

The Chablais, Faucigny, Aravis and Beaufortain districts flank the Mont Blanc massif on its western side, yet they are distinct, both geographically and in style and ambience. This is classic trekking country, with vast expanses of meadows and forested valleys, passes and non-glaciated summits.

Traditional farms still exist, producing cheese and breeding cattle. The growth of winter sports has increased the wealth of some of these areas, with the consequent development of ski lifts and pistes, but much of the countryside remains barely, if at all, affected and here you can walk for days enjoying the beauty and tranquillity of these Alpine hills.

Unlike those of the higher granite ranges, the peaks here tend to be limestone, with the associated flora and scenery, namely lakes, cliffs and gorges. Animals and birds abound, different species according to the altitude. The huge Lac Léman (Lake Geneva) is to be seen, if distantly, from many of the climbs, while to the east the glaciated peaks are a constant reminder that this is the Alps.

The treks here are classic in the sense that they contain all that is expected of an Alpine walk, but the names are less well known. Consequently, you're less likely to encounter other walkers doing the same itinerary as you.

Nearing the Brévent on the final section of the GR5 from Lac Léman to Chamonix.

MARTAGON LILY
(LILIUM MARTAGON)

The martagon lily is to be found in light soil, often in mixed forest near to streams and gorges. It is a particularly exotic and intricate flower, its deep-pink petals turned back on themselves like a sort of turban, leaving the long stamens exposed. This flower is pollinated by a moth (the sphinx) which the lily encourages by ensuring that other insects can't land on the smooth, steeply inclined petals. The flower also emits an odour at the end of the afternoon. Anyone who has the audacity to pick this protected species will soon find that it doesn't enhance their house quite as they expected, as its evening scent seems to be attractive only to the sphinx moth.

It is very exciting to find martagon lilies in flower, and if you are lucky enough to do this it will be between June and early August at altitudes up to 2800m (9187ft). The plant can attain a height of 1.5m (5ft) or more.

Much of this region (excluding the Beaufortain) is a huge area of limestone ridges and summits, interspersed with valleys and villages, providing a unique contrast to the granite terrain of the nearby Alps massif. These are the outposts of the main Alpine range and, as such, they benefit from their lower altitudes, enjoying more clement weather and acting as a belvédère for the spectacular views around them. The Mont Blanc massif forms a backdrop to any trek in this region, but the region's own limestone escarpments such as the Rochers des Fiz and the Dents du Midi are equally impressive. Villages perched high on south-facing hillsides enjoy sunshine year-round, offering an almost Mediterranean ambience – you will find the elderly inhabitants sitting outside on benches watching the world go by, even in the depths of winter.

Contrary to the harsh reality of living in the shady valleys created by the high mountains of the main Alpine chain, here there is a more gentle lifestyle, which encourages the existence of agriculture. You'll still find working farms, which produce exceptional cheeses such as Beaufortain and Gruyère. These Alpine cheeses owe their nutty, full-bodied flavour to the richness of the flora in the uncultivated meadows of these valleys, where the cows graze. Although in the summer some cheese is still made up in the *alpages*, most milk is collected morning and evening from the high farms and brought down to the valleys to a local cheese factory where more modern methods are used to make the cheese.

Various breeds of Alpine cattle can be found in these pastures, and most cows that you come across will be wearing bells of varying sizes. The bell acts as identity card for the farmer responsible for the herd and he'll recognise each animal from the sound of the bell. There are two basic types of bells in the Alps: the round iron tend to be small with a dull sound, while the larger bronze variety, which hang from a wide collar and are often very old, are handed down from generation to generation. Many of these bells are decorated, not only with the maker's name but also with religious symbols to provide protection.

Impressive waterfalls abound in the limestone regions, this one can be seen en route to Collet d'Anterne.

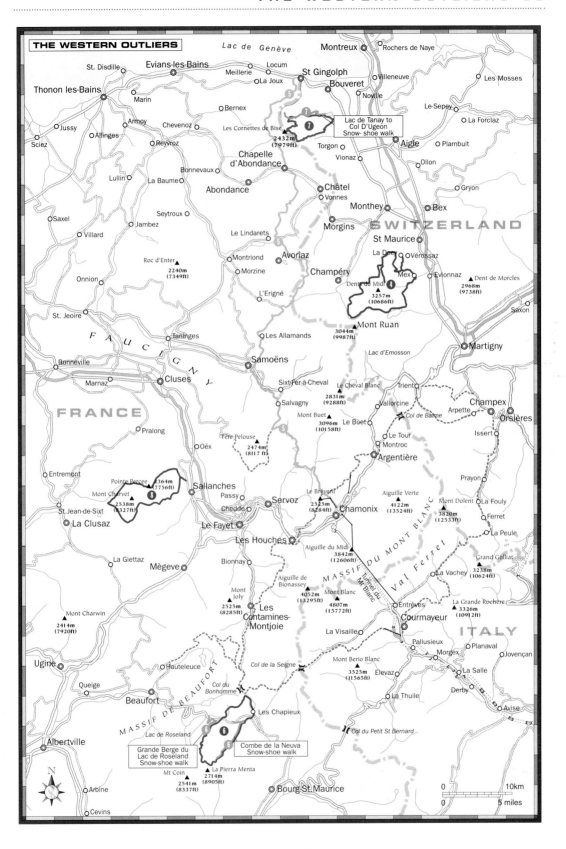

TREK 4: TOUR DES DENTS DU MIDI

The spectacular range of the Dents du Midi towers over the Rhône valley, its spiky summits looking unattainable from here. It is a group of seven summits forming the most westerly mountain group in Switzerland, with only a few of the Jura peaks lying further west than this impressive limestone massif. 'Cathédrale, Forteresse, Eperon' – the very names of the summits evoke better than any description the splendour of this massif.

TREK ESSENTIALS

LENGTH 4 days.
ACCESS Any village along the tour, the most accessible being La Doey.
HIGHEST POINT The Haute Cime (3257m/10686ft).
MAPS 1:50 000: Carte Nationale de la Suisse 272S St Maurice. 1:25 000: Carte Nationale de la Suisse 1304 Val d'Illiez Dents du Midi, 1324 Barberine.
TREK STYLE Mountain huts.
LANGUAGE French.
FURTHER OPTIONS In this trek if you do everything suggested in the description you've just about ticked it!

The Tour des Dents du Midi provides a marvellous trek through the classic alpine meadows and passes of the Swiss Chablais region, with the possible ascent of the highest of the Dents du Midi, the Haute Cime (3257m/10686ft), as well as a couple of other non-glaciated peaks. Generally, views are spectacular, and the terrain encountered is varied, without ever being overly technical or arduous.

The tour can of course be started anywhere along its length, and I suggest you start at La Doey, just above Vérossaz, since this hamlet is easily accessible by postbus from St Maurice in the Rhône valley.

La Doey to Tête de Chalin

From La Doey the Tour des Dents du Midi (TDM) is waymarked along a track to La Sachia and then over the Mauvoisin torrent, to the Fahy *alpage* with its backdrop of impressive waterfalls coming down from Les Trois Merles. Already you are in wild alpine country, a far cry from the ever-busy Rhône valley.

Heading up through the forest, the path then swings around the hillside to reach the viewpoint of Les Jeurs (1560m/5118ft). From here the Dent de Morcles (2968m/9738ft) to the east looks particularly spectacular, whilst to the north you can see down the valley to Lac Léman.

The path continues to traverse, past Chindonne to Valerette. Here, if the weather is good, a superb addition to the TDM can be made by going up the Dent de Valère (2267m/7438ft) and the Tête de Chalin (2595m/8514ft). There is an unwardened

The Great Masterwort (*Astrantia Major*) is found in meadows and hillsides up to 2000m (6562ft).

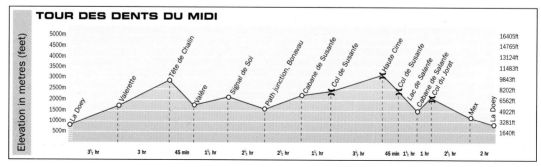

TOUR DES DENTS DU MIDI

Elevation in metres (feet)

5000m / 16405ft
4500m / 14765ft
4000m / 13124ft
3500m / 11483ft
3000m / 9843ft
2500m / 8202ft
2000m / 6562ft
1500m / 4922ft
1000m / 3281ft
500m / 1640ft

La Doey — Valerette — Tête de Chalin — Valère — Signal de Soi — Path Junction, Bonavau — Cabane de Susanfe — Col de Susanfe — Haute Cime — Col de Susanfe — Lac de Salante — Cabane de Salante — Col du Jorat — Mex — La Doey

3½ hr · 3 hr · 45 min · 1½ hr · 2½ hr · 2½ hr · 1¼ hr · 3½ hr · 45 min · 1½ hr · 1 hr · 2½ hr · 2 hr

refuge on the summit, but there are only eight places, so if there's a group ahead maybe think twice about planning to stay there. The path takes you firstly to the Valère chalet, then heads south and east to hit the ridge at point 2019m (6624ft). It avoids the Dent de Valère (2267m/7433ft), although this can be climbed easily, then takes the fine Crêtes de Dardeu to reach the summit of the Tête de Chalin. This is a fabulous spot, right under the steep walls of the northernmost summit of the Dents du Midi, the Cime de l'Est (3177m/10424ft). Views are extensive over the Valaisan Alps, and the Grand Combin is particularly impressive. If, for some reason, you can't stay at the refuge, the nearest lodging is a dormitory in the Centre Sportif at Les Jeurs.

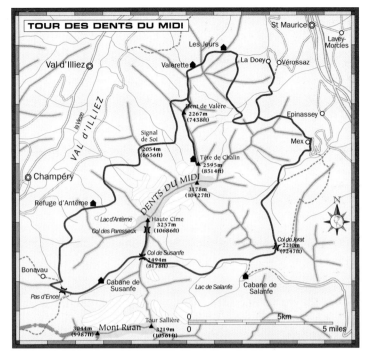

TOUR DES DENTS DU MIDI

St Maurice
Lavey-Morcles
Les Jeurs
Val d'Illiez
Valerette
La Doey
Vérossaz
Dent de Valère
2267m
(7438ft)
Epinassey
Signal de Soi
2054m
(6656ft)
Mex
Tête de Chalin
2595m
(8514ft)
Champéry
3178m
(10427ft)
Refuge d'Antème
Lac d'Antème
Haute Cime
3257m
(10686ft)
Col des Paresseux
Col du Jorat
2210m
(7247ft)
Col de Susanfe
2494m
(8178ft)
Bonavau
Cabane de Susanfe
Lac de Salanfe
Cabane de Salanfe
Pas d'Encel
VAL D'ILLIEZ
la Vièze
DENTS DU MIDI
Tour Sallière
3044m
(9987ft)
Mont Ruan
3219m
(10561ft)
0   5km
0   5 miles

The magnificent northwest face of the Dents du Midi. The highest point, the Haute Cime, is climbed during the trek.

ORCHIDS

Alpine flowers are all beautiful, and orchids are no exception. Orchids particularly like wet and shady ground, and are common along the banks of streams and in marshy areas. These attractive flowers share a common shape, whereby the flowers are generally in dense spikes with the lowermost petal developed into a lip that hangs down.

One of the more unusual members of the orchid family is the vanilla orchid. This dark red plant, which is striking despite its small size, is exceptional amongst orchids for its tiny, tightly packed flowers, forming what appears to be a single flower but which is in fact about forty. The theory here is safety in numbers, to afford protection from the wind and tough climate. Thus as a group they become much more robust and hardy. The flowers themselves are unlike other orchids, being upright. Various legends are attached to the bulbs of the vanilla orchid – it was thought that one of its bulbs was an aphrodisiac whilst the other would induce impotence (risky if you got the wrong one); it was also believed that if the bulbs were uprooted between 11pm and midnight it would provoke an amorous encounter; whilst bulbs slipped into a wallet or handbag would guard against the loss of money.

These delightful flowers will be found in meadows and grassy places up to 2800m (9187ft), flowering from late May to July.

Tête de Chalin to Cabane de Susanfe

Retrace your steps to the TDM trail at Valère and continue around the hillside into the glaciated cirque of Chalin, dominated by the north face of the Dents du Midi, and the hanging Chalin glacier. Continuing west, the path climbs steadily to just below the Signal de Soi (2054m/6739ft), which can easily be climbed to make the most of the fine views from here – the Val d'Illiez just below, with the French frontier visible to the west, whilst away in the distance are the Jura and the pre-alps (alpine foothills) of Fribourg. The route traverses under the Glacier de Soi, crossing several impressive glacial torrents, to come around the Arête de Sélaire, past the Lac d'Antème to the Refuge d'Antème (2030m/6660ft). This is a wonderful and impressive cirque, under the Haute Cime, and the refuge would be a fine place to stay if you have the time.

The TDM continues west, descending past Métécoui, and through the Rossetan *alpage* to just above Bonavau, where it meets the Tour des Dents Blanches. The two treks continue on together into the deep gorge of the Pas d'Encel, where a hand-line protects the only exposed section. The trail crosses the Sauffla torrent and leaves the gorge to climb up to the Cabane de Susanfe (2102m/6897ft), situated in a fine wilderness under the northern slopes of the Tour Sallière (3219m/10561ft) and Mont Ruan (3044m/9987ft).

Cabane de Susanfe to Cabane de Salanfe via the Haute Cime

In good conditions it is highly recommended to include the ascent of the Haute Cime (3257m/10561ft) in this trek. The Col de Susanfe (2494m/8183ft) is reached easily from the hut,

and is splendidly encased by the Tour Sallière and the Haute Cime. The way to the summit is obvious, directly north from the col, passing by the interestingly named Col des Paresseux (3056m/10027ft) – 'the pass of the lazy people'.

In the summer you are unlikely to be alone here, but this doesn't change the fantastic panorama of almost all the major summits of the northern Alps that greets your arrival at the top: to the south the Mont Blanc massif, to the east the Combin, the Dent Blanche, the Weisshorn, the Matterhorn, and further north the Bernese Oberland. This is a sight to enjoy at length, and since you're just going to the Salanfe hut you have plenty of time to sit and stare if it's warm enough.

Descent is by the same route to the Col de Susanfe, then down to Lanvoisset. From here the dammed Salanfe lake is not visible, and the path to it is sometimes hard to find, but after you cross a rocky barrier it suddenly appears. Head along the northern shore of the lake to the Cabane de Salanfe, where you can spend the rest of the day enjoying this wild and unusual cirque, bounded by all seven of the Dents du Midi summits, with the sparking Lac de Salanfe like a jewel at its centre.

Cabane de Salanfe to La Doey

A short steady ascent and you're at the Col du Jorat (2210m/7251ft); then it's downhill all the way. However, the descent is quite long and steep, taking you from the splendours of the summits back into the gentler meadows and forests. Mex is the first civilisation you come to, from where a traverse through the woods takes you to La Sachia and then you're on known ground back to La Doey.

TREK 5: LAKE GENEVA TO CHAMONIX

This trek begins on the shores of Lac Léman (Lake Geneva) – the biggest lake in Western Europe – and heads through increasingly impressive mountain scenery to finally arrive right opposite the magnificent Mont Blanc massif. The GR5 is one of the French Grande Randonnées, although it actually starts in Holland. The Alpine GR5 is usually begun on the edge of the Alpine chain at Lac Léman, finishing at the Mediterranean, near Nice, and can be comfortably completed in four weeks. Lake Geneva to Chamonix is the first stage of this Alpine GR5.

For most of its length the trek swings back and forth over the Chablais Franco–Swiss frontier, before reaching the Mont Blanc region. The terrain is varied, ranging from meadows and villages – where you can sample both French and Swiss hospitality – to the impressive high plateau of Anterne.

St Gingolph to Refuge de Bise

The French side of the border town of St Gingolph provides the starting point for the trek. Do be sure to venture down to the shore of the lake before heading off into the hills. After probably taking a couple of wrong turns in the town, you'll start climbing up towards the village of Novel on a track above the Morge river, which itself forms the border with Switzerland. The altitude is relatively low here and it's usually quite humid in the trees, but don't worry as this doesn't last very long. Enjoy a cold drink at Novel before continuing to La Planche.

Here the real climbing starts, and steep, flower-bordered paths take you up into the meadows of Neuteu. Now the views open up and you'll be delighted to see how far your efforts have brought you from the lake. Only a little more ascent and the Col de Bise is reached at 1915m (6283ft). Quite a difference from the 370m (1214ft) you started at. You can see the day's objective just below, although in reality it takes a little longer to reach the refuge than you might imagine. However, you should have time to contemplate the wonderful

TREK ESSENTIALS

LENGTH 7 days.
ACCESS Start at St Gingolph on Franco-Swiss border at Lake Geneva (Lac Léman), finish Chamonix.
HIGHEST POINT Col du Brévent (2368m/7765ft).
MAPS 1:50 000 Didier Richard 3 Chablais Faucigny Genevois; 8 Mont Blanc.
1:25 000 IGN Top 25 3528 ET Morzine, 3530 ET Samoëns.
TREK STYLE Mountain refuges, *gîtes* and small hotels.
LANGUAGE French.
FURTHER OPTIONS Continue the GR5 southwards, following the Tour du Mont Blanc (Trek 9, p89) to Col de la Croix de Bonhomme, and the first part of the Pierra Menta circuit to Col de Bresson (Trek 6, p73). Then south to the Isère valley, from where the Traverse of the Vanoise (Trek 2, p52) continues the route to Modane. Ascents of Aiguilles de Crochues, Mont Blanc (see associated peaks, p103 and p98).

panorama from here, with the limestone slopes of the Cornettes de Bise (2432m/7975ft) dominating the views to the southeast (see Trek 7, p77, for the ascent of this). To the north beyond the lake is the Oche chain.

A quick jaunt and you're down at the Refuge de Bise, a traditional working farm – washing in the trough will probably be an unforgettable experience. Ibex roam the slopes of the Cornettes de Bise, so be sure to take a stroll around in the evening armed with binoculars and camera.

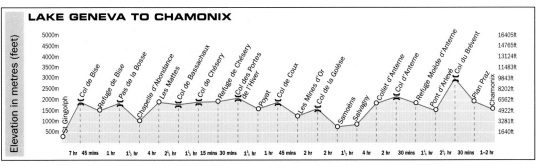

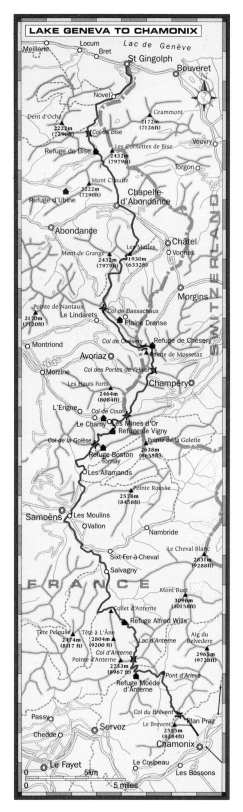

LAKE GENEVA TO CHAMONIX

Refuge de Bise to Chapelle-d'Abondance

This is a short section and could be combined with an ascent of the Cornettes de Bise in good conditions, or just enjoyed as a restful day with plenty of time to contemplate the delights of the pastoral scenery, and then to fully experience the patisseries in Chapelle-d'Abondance.

The Pas de la Bosse (1816m/5958ft) is reached quickly and steeply from the hut, and on a clear day the views of the Dents du Midi and the Grand Combin are superb. It is from here that you can ascend the summit of the Cornettes de Bise, but beware of bad weather, late *nevé* or a nervous disposition, since the route is exposed.

The descent from the col is equally steep and horribly muddy in the rain, and you'll be quite happy to reach relatively flat ground at the Chalets de Chevenne. This section can be lengthened by taking the track southwest from the refuge, skirting round the rocky ridge of the Dent du Chat, to the Refuge d'Ubine, which is privately owned, and often occupied. You may be lucky enough to be invited in for a drink. A pleasant path leads over the Col d'Ubine (1694m/5558ft), then down to the Chalets de Chevenne, rejoining the GR5 just before Chapelle d'Abondance. It's best to stay here as there is little accommodation for several hours afterwards, short of leaving the route and descending to Châtel. The Abondance valley is famous for its cows (which have circles of white round their eyes like spectacles) and fine cheese. The village of Chapelle is worth exploring, with its charming architecture and, of course, its chapel.

Chapelle-d'Abondance to Refuge de Chésery

Take your life in your hands and walk very quickly out of town along the main road for 2km (1.2 miles), then turn off and breathe a sigh of relief. The 900-m (2953-ft) ascent to Les Mattes (1930m/6332t) is gained quite steeply, but not unrelentingly, and the views from the top provide ample reward. After a short descent you pick up a traversing trail that contours high above the Châtel valley around the hillside, under the southern slopes of Mont de Grange, which at 2432m (7979ft) is the highest peak in the Savoyard Chablais.

The walking becomes easier, with just a slight climb to the Col de Bassachaux (1778m/5834ft), and its restaurant, where the bilberry tarts should not be missed. There is a *gîte* down the road at Plaine Dranse, or you can continue on to the Col de Chésery (1992m/6536ft). This is not too far from the Col de Bassachaux, but the views are spectacular and it would be a shame to do this section in a hurry as dusk falls.

At the Col de Chésery you step into Switzerland, and the deserted customs buildings testify to the border crossing. The very basic Refuge de Chésery (also called Refuge Lac Vert), which must be reserved beforehand, is to be found on the shores of the often frozen Lac Vert.

The Refuge de Bise.

Refuge de Chésery to Les Mines d'Or

Hope for a clear sunny morning, and hurry to the Col des Portes de l'Hiver (2157m/7037ft). The breathtaking views will stop you in your stride. The great thing is you'll enjoy this vista for the best part of the day, so be sure to have plenty of film for the camera. To the west the Pointe de Mossetaz (2284m/7494ft) is visible, then the Dents du Midi 3257m/10686ft), the glaciated dome of Mont Ruan (3040m/9974ft), the Dents Blanches (2711m/8895ft) and the Tête de Bossetan (2406m/7894ft). The next few hours are passed in Switzerland, with its tidy pastures and neat chalets – distinctly different from the French Alps.

The way is straightforward, although you should keep your eye on the waymarks for the GR5 as this area abounds in local paths, each perfectly signed in true Swiss style. The yellow marks denote a local walk, whilst the GR5 has the usual red-and-white flashes. Chaux Palin provides a refreshment stop, time to sample some Swiss fare, then onwards and finally upwards to the Col de Coux (1920m/ 6299ft), and back to France.

Les Mines d'Or is a slight detour from the GR5, but is worth it for the quality of the accommodation. Previously a site for gold mining, this is now a hotel and restaurant, providing food of a standard not commonly associated with trekking. There is dormitory accommodation, or you could splash out and get a room. Either way, you get to eat in the smart restaurant, so be sure to have a clean shirt at the ready.

Les Mines d'Or to Samoëns/Salvagny

Head up the road then past the Refuge de Vigny, alternative accommodation to Les Mines d'Or, then on again through tranquil meadows to the Col de la Golèse (1660m/5447ft), which is an important migratory-bird route. The Refuge Bostan-Tornay is just a few minutes from here and does a good morning coffee. The way down to Samoëns is quite long and knee-crunching, but console yourself by imagining all the goodies you're going to sample in town.

Samoëns is a very pleasant resort, tucked far enough away from the main areas to have retained its charm and individuality. Its Place de Gros-Tilleul, dating from 1438, is surrounded by ancient monuments, which are fine examples of the style of the Samoëns builders. In the 17th century, these builders were known far and wide for their skills, and left their mark in such distant places as Poland and Louisiana. The botanical gardens, founded by a local lady, are also famous and well worth a visit.

After looking around, settle down under a sunshade at one of the cafés on the main square, order whatever you've been dreaming of for the last five days, and indulge in a bit of self-congratulation.

There are plenty of hotels to choose from in town, but to be ideally placed for the long day ahead it is better to continue on to Salvagny. For

Climbing up to the Col d'Anterne, nearing the end of the Brévent on the GR5 trek.

the trail takes an improbable passage above the imposing Faucilles de Chatet to reach the Collet d'Anterne (1796m/5893ft).

Suddenly you feel that the trek is changing, the surrounding peaks are getting higher, and in the distance to the south there it is – the Mont Blanc massif, its summit just peeping out. Mont Buet (known locally as the Ladies' Mont Blanc) is much closer, to the east, and in the foreground is a wonderful expanse of limestone boulders and intensely coloured flowers. Definitely a place to savour.

The Plateau d'Anterne is one of the gems of this trek, and you'll understand why as you wander among the rocks and burbling streams, with cattle grazing peacefully and the gigantic Rochers des Fiz towering overhead. A late lunch stop at the Refuge Alfred Wills is a must before continuing on south towards the Col d'Anterne (2257m/7405ft). The Lac d'Anterne offers yet another tempting stop, but don't linger too long since the col is your objective and beyond is a visual feast.

As you climb the last few metres to the pass you will forget your weariness as you're held spellbound by the spectacle opening up before your eyes. The Mont Blanc massif is magnificent. Not far below is the Refuge Moëde d'Anterne, from where you can watch the last dying rays of the sun on the glistening rose-tinted summits.

Refuge Moëde d'Anterne to Chamonix

An unusual day in that it begins with a descent. Meadows lead to the Pont d'Arlevé, which is the only passage over the Diosaz Gorge, scene of many epics when people unwittingly try to descend to the valley by this route. Only one more climb left now, and it's a very pleasant one, taking you through alpenrose and alder bushes, past ruined shepherds' buildings, to the Col du Brévent (2368m/ 7769ft). If you still haven't had enough of Mont Blanc it re-emerges here to reveal the whole massif, from Mont Blanc at the southern end, its neighbours Mont Maudit and Mont Blanc du Tacul, the characteristic spire of the Aiguille du Midi, with its two-stage cable car, and the Chamonix Aiguilles, flanking the Mer de Glace glacier, with the Drus and the Aiguille Verte to the north.

As you descend towards Plan Praz and the Brévent resort you may feel a tinge of regret to be returning to the bustle of civilisation, but the restaurant is a fine place to end the trek, watching the paragliders take off from the slopes below. Those with masochistic tendencies or anaesthetised knees may choose to walk down to Chamonix; others will take the lift!

those with time to spare, a day could be spent exploring Sixt and the spectacular Fer à Cheval.

Salvagny is reached by strolling along the Giffre river and then via the Gorges des Tines, where the water-eroded rocks bear testament to the power of the torrential water. Salvagny has an excellent *gîte* with superb facilites, owned by a local guide, on the road through the village.

Salvagny to Refuge Moëde d'Anterne

This stage heads back up into the mountains today, headed towards the Mont Blanc massif. Enjoy the early morning warm-up along the small roads, past the sometimes impressive Cascade de Rouget, to the big car park near le Lignon. This is a popular place to begin day walks so don't be too alarmed by the numbers of people. Most of them will not be doing the GR5. Pleasant forest gradually thins out as you climb high up past several vertical waterfalls. Huge impressive yellow cliffs flank the valley to the east, whilst

TREK 6: BEAUFORTAIN PIERRA MENTA CIRCUIT

At 2714m (8905ft) the Pierra Menta can hardly be described as a major peak in the Alps, and it in fact only rises a couple of hundred metres above the neighbouring cols, but this unusual conglomerate monolith is surprisingly well known. Standing as it does above the tranquil pasture land of the Beaufortain, the Pierra Menta provides a rugged contrast to the green meadows below.

Legend has it that the mythical hero Gargantua, whilst crossing the Alps towards what is now Italy, was stopped in his tracks by the snowy mass of the Mont Blanc massif. He searched for a way through to the right and tripped over the Aravis range. In anger he kicked the mountains, and sent a piece of rock flying through the air to land in the heart of the Beaufortain, leaving a *brêche* (or notch) on the Aravis ridge which is now known as the Porte des Aravis. So was born the Pierra Menta. It was first climbed in 1922 by Zwinglestein and Loustalot, and now has several climbing routes to its summit.

This short trek provides an opportunity to discover all the joys and variety of these mountains. The late and well known alpinist Roger Frison-Roche, in his book *Le Versant du Soleil*, described the Beaufortain as 'a privileged massif, still preserved today, enclosed between the Isère and Arly valleys, with Mont Blanc behind'. Its privilege comes from the fact that it has all the attributes of a mountain area, but none of the hardships. Its people have never been poor as they benefit from extremely good grazing land and are able to live off their land, their main wealth being cattle. The Beaufortain receives a lot of rain, and this coupled with the schists of the area, makes for very favourable terrain. The Beaufortain cows produce exceptional milk, which is used for the famous regional cheese, similar to Gruyère.

TREK ESSENTIALS

LENGTH 2 days.
ACCESS Start and finish in Les Chapieux, accessible from Beaufort or Bourg-Saint-Maurice.
HIGHEST POINT Col du Grand Fond (2671m/8763ft).
MAPS 1:50 000 Didier Richard 8 Mont Blanc.
1:25 000 IGN Top 25 3531 OT Megève, 3532 OT Massif du Beaufortain.
TREK STYLE Mountain refuge.
LANGUAGE French.
FURTHER OPTIONS Continue from the Col de Bresson on the GR5 to the Isère valley and beyond to the Vanoise.

The Beaufortain is on the extreme western edge of the Alps and is classic Alpine-pasture country, nestled under ridges and peaks, none more than 3000m (9843ft) high. Lying at a slight remove from the glaciated peaks this region is quieter and very traditional. There are usually fewer people walking the paths here and time seems to move a little more slowly.

Les Chapieux to Refuge du Plan de la Lai

The trek starts in the small hamlet of Les Chapieux. This is on the Tour du Mont Blanc (TMB) and has for centuries provided hospitality for travellers crossing between Italy and France. Our first day starts by following the TMB trail up to the

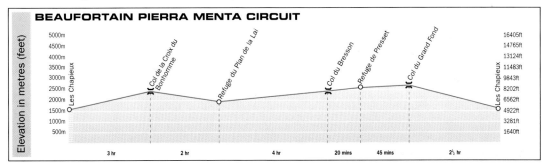

BEAUFORTAIN PIERRA MENTA CIRCUIT

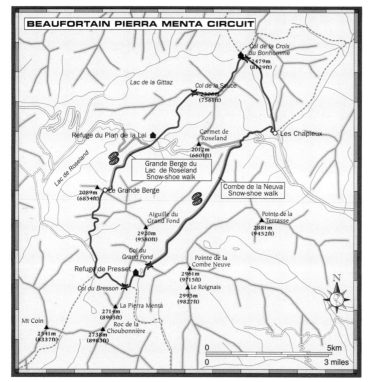

BEAUFORTAIN PIERRA MENTA CIRCUIT

Refuge du Plan de la Lai to Les Chapieux

The next day you're headed into the Beaufortain massif. One August I awoke at Plan de la Lai to find a metre of fresh snow had fallen overnight. On that occasion it proved to be quite a feat to find the path around the hillside past the Petite and Grande Berge farm buildings, and even more so up to the Col du Bresson (2469m/8101ft). However, in normal summer conditions the path is fairly clear, although it can be a bit confusing after the Grande Berge, through the farmland before the climb up to the col.

Emerging from the pastures and bushes into the barren scree leading to the pass, you'll walk through several levels of vegetation, each with its own flowers and wildlife. Below, the Lac de Roseland stretches out, and ahead is the unmissable spire of the Pierra Menta. Popular for rock climbing in the summer, this area also provides the site each winter for one of the most famous ski-touring competitions in the Alps.

The pass is a wonderful place to linger if it's warm enough, enjoying the monolithic Pierra Menta, reminiscent of the Dolomites. Immediately to the east is the Aiguille de la Nova (2893m/9492ft) and the Pointe de Gargan (2767m/9078ft), whilst views southeast to the Vanoise are dominated by the glaciated Mont Pourri (3779m/12399ft). Situated just above at 2514m (8248ft) is the Refuge de Presset, next to the hidden Lac de Presset, where refreshments will be available in high season. This gives an even better opportunity to study the vertical walls of the Pierra Menta, and from the other side of the lake on a fine calm day you'll find it perfectly reflected in these clear still waters. The GR5 heads off south from the col, alongside the Orente Torrent to the Isère valley.

When you're finally ready to leave this fabulous wild spot, you continue northwards from the refuge to the Col du Grand Fond (2671m/8763ft). Here the views are again stunning, especially of Mont Blanc in the far distance. The path is at first indistinct for the descent, but you'll easily spot the

Col de la Croix du Bonhomme (2479m/8133ft). From here the views away south towards the Vanoise are wonderful and even on a hazy day the misty far-off hills lead you to believe the mountains stretch away forever.

At the col you leave the TMB and head south along the Crête des Gittes. This ridge is very attractive and often threatens to tempt TMB candidates away from their objective. The path snakes back and forth across the crest, and is an absolute joy to walk. Views into the Beaufortain open up and you can see the blue-green waters of the huge Lac de Roseland glinting far away. This is also the GR5 walk, which heads through the Beaufortain, then south into the Vanoise, with the ultimate objective being the Mediterranean.

At the end of the ridge you arrive at the Col de la Sauce (2306m/7566ft). Gentle strolling down through meadows, where you may well find local farmers milking the cows with mobile milking machines, takes you to a boulder-strewn area just before the road where you'll find the Refuge du Plan de la Lai (1818m/5965ft). Being accessible by car, this French Alpine Club hut attracts some passing day-time trade, but is rarely very busy overnight. The boulders behind are a fine place for spotting marmots as well as harbouring many varieties of alpine flora.

small lakes under the characteristic Brêche de Parozan, which is worth ascending if you have the time, for a final look at those views. This notch is supposedly again the work of a giant; this time the fellow was said to have lifted a piece of rock from the ridge and found it to be rather heavier than he expected. Afterwards he couldn't put it back so he left it nearby, leaving the *brêche* in its place.

From here the trail descends, mainly gently, down the Pointe de la Combe Neuve, taking you under the steep slopes of the Aiguille du Grand Fond (2920m/9580ft). On the eastern side of the valley the Pointes de la Combe Neuve (2961m/9715ft), Motte (2718m/8918ft) and de Pralognan (2663m/8737ft) provide an impressive line of cliffs. This valley was frequented in times past by crystal hunters searching for quartz and precious metals. Note that at certain times the area is used as a firing range, so ask at the hut to be sure you won't inadvertently become a target.

You are now on part of the Tour du Beaufortain, and this good path leads all the way to the road from Plan de la Lai to Les Chapieux, coming out at la Fauge, a couple of kilometres (about a mile) from Les Chapieux.

Very snowy conditions on the Col du Bresson, with the Pierra Menta behind.

SNOW-SHOE WALK: GRANDE BERGE DU LAC DE ROSELAND

SNOW-SHOE WALK ESSENTIALS

ACCESS Start and finish at Col des Sauces (1645m/5397ft).
DISTANCE 10km (6¼ miles).
HEIGHT GAIN 460m (1509ft).
APPROXIMATE TIME 4–4½ hours.
DIFFICULTY 1
TYPE OF WALK 1-day round trip by same route.
INTERESTING FEATURES The Roseland Lake and the surrounding mountains.
MAP 1:25 000: IGN Top 25 3532 OT Beaufortain.

The southeast bank of the Roseland Lake provides beautiful walking terrain, especially in winter, and the Grande Berge (2089m/6854ft) is a good objective for a day's snow shoeing, with superb views of the lake to the east, and the surrounding mountains to the north and south.

Access to this area is difficult in winter and you need to check that the Col de Méraillet has been cleared of snow – this usually happens in early spring. Park at the Col des Sauces (1645m/5397ft). Follow the road up past the Roc de Biolley to reach the Refuge du Plan de la Lai (1818m/5965ft). Here leave the road to head southwest, already enjoying extensive views, to the chalets of La Petite Berge. A short climb takes you to the Petite Berge summit at 2071m (6795ft). A gentle, undulating traverse continues in the same direction to attain the Grande Berge summit (2089m/6854ft), with a chalet close by. It is possible to continue on beyond this, even as far as Etrus on the far side of the lake if you wish. Return by the same route.

SNOW-SHOE WALK: COMBE DE LA NEUVA

SNOW-SHOE WALK ESSENTIALS

ACCESS Start and finish at the Cormet de Roseland.
DISTANCE 13km (8 miles).
HEIGHT GAIN 704m (2310ft).
APPROXIMATE TIME 6 hours.
DIFFICULTY 2
TYPE OF WALK 1 day round trip by same route.
INTERESTING FEATURES The beautiful and wild valley.
MAP 1:25 000: IGN Top 25 3532 OT Beaufortain.

This superb long valley gives a magnificent walk, penetrating right into the heart of the mountains. As with all walks in this area, though, it can only be envisaged in the spring when the road has been cleared of snow.

From the Cormet de Roseland take the track which goes around the hillside under the slopes of the Dent d'Arpire and into the Combe de la Neuva. There are steep slopes above so do not go here after fresh snowfall.

The way is easy to see as you're basically following the valley. At the head of the valley you'll enter a cirque, defined by the Aiguille du Grand Fond, the Pointe de Presset, the Aiguille de la Nova and the Col de la Nova.

To reach the vantage point of the Col du Grand Fond (2671m/8763ft) climb up the slopes on your right, under the Brêche de Parozan, to about 2550m (8366ft) then traverse under the Pointe Presset and up to the col. Directly ahead to the south is the impressive spire of the Pierra Menta and, beyond, the Isère valley and the Vanoise National Park. Just below can be seen the Refuge de Presset, but if you want to go down to this, better to take the neighbouring Col de Petit Fond (2622m/8603ft), not named on the map, which provides an easier way through. Return by the same valley, varying the way a little as you wish.

THE ALPINE CHOUGH

Sit down at any regularly visited Alpine col for your picnic and you'll soon find yourself joined by at least a couple of feathered fellow-picnickers, keen to share your sandwiches. The alpine chough is as black as a crow, of similar size (about 38cm/15in long), with a bright-yellow beak and red legs and feet. In Europe it lives exclusively in the Alps, and seems to like the company of people, especially those armed with food.

This bird is a great acrobat and you'll often see choughs performing incredible aerial ballets, clearly having great fun as they soar on the currents and gusts. Whole groups will descend en masse only to shoot up again with seemingly effortless ease. In winter the choughs will not hesitate to visit villages for food, whilst good summer conditions will see them up at 4000m (13124ft) and higher. In the Himalaya they have apparently been seen at over 8000m (26248ft).

Choughs are gregarious birds and often gather in large flocks of more than twenty. Cliffs and rocks are their preferred roosting sites, and they never choose to live in the forests. In winter they descend to the valleys by day but return to their rocky niches at night. Choughs eat anything they can find, from berries to insects to carcasses to whatever you happen to have in your picnic box.

They nest on cliffs, on ledges and in cavities and produce between three to five young each year. The young chough has a black beak that doesn't become yellow until adulthood.

TREK 7: CORNETTES DE BISE

This is one of my favourite walking summits. It's got everything you need for a great mountain outing – pleasant and varied terrain, wildlife, flowers and fabulous views. It is a very popular peak, justifiably so, and on any fine day in the high season you share the vast panorama over Lake Geneva, but, so what?

Of course it's wonderful to find solitude some times during a walk, but on the Cornettes de Bise I've met all sorts of people from little kids tasting the thrill of their first mountain, to octogenarians sipping red wine on the top. Don't be misled – this is not an easy day; but it has something for everyone, and the social spirit is an essential part of the experience.

From Lac de Tanay

There are several routes up the mountain, and my favourite is to begin and end at the Lac de Tanay. Parts of Tanay are crowded in high season, but you can always find a place on the lake shore that's deserted, and there's nothing better than a dip in the cold and refreshing water after a long sweaty walk.

Since this is a circular route you can go either way round. The way described tends to be less frequented. From the charming hamlet of Tanay you head west past the last houses into the Echercies valley. The path meanders up alongside the flower-bordered stream to join the small road leading up to the Montagne de l'Au *alpage*. Views north to the twin summits of the Jumelles (2215m/7267ft) and the Grammont (2171m/7123ft) are spectacular, and the latter also provides a good day walk from Tanay.

Just as you reach the farm buildings a sign takes you on a footpath to the left. The general direction is still west and there are occasional paint flashes, but it all gets a bit confused with cattle tracks around here. However, continue heading towards the Col d'Ugeon until this path seems to head off to the right at around 1900m

> **TREK ESSENTIALS**
>
> **LENGTH** 1 day.
> **ACCESS** Start and finish at Lac de Tanay, above Vouvry in the Swiss Rhône valley.
> **HIGHEST POINT** Cornettes de Bise (2432m/7975ft).
> **MAPS:** 1:50 000 Carte Nationale de la Suisse 271 Chablais. 1:25 000 Carte Nationale de la Suisse 1284 Monthey.
> **TREK STYLE** 1 day.
> **LANGUAGE** French.
> **FURTHER OPTIONS** The Grammont (2171m/7119ft).

(6234ft). You should then be able to pick up the trail heading off south around the hillside towards the northern slopes of the Cornettes de Bise. This soon becomes clearer and there are no more real difficulties, though for a brief while you may be wandering on almost trackless terrain, and the farmer's fences can further confuse the issue.

Once on the proper trail again the way traverses steadily east and upwards. There are a couple of exposed parts, but nothing too technical. The path leads around a rocky spur to the delightful Chaux de Milieu, a wonderful area of limestone boulders where flowers abound. From this point onwards you should keep your eyes open for ibex, since a large herd lives under the Cornettes de Bise and if you're lucky you'll find both the male group and the females accompanied by the younger animals.

Wander through the boulders and you'll reach a long narrow traverse, which it would be unwise to step off. This brings you to a small col on the Rochers de Chaudin, the junction with the path

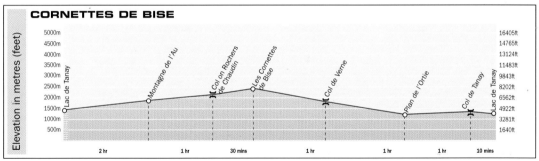

CORNETTES DE BISE

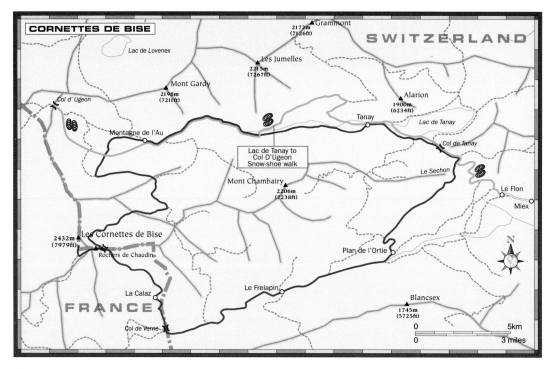

from the Vallée de Verne, your descent route, and you will almost definitely meet other hikers here.

It's about thirty minutes to the summit, but the ground is rocky and quite slippery, worn from the passage of thousands of feet and ibex hooves. Red flashes mark the way and there are several variants, so you can make it more or less exposed as you wish. Winding your way up, you'll join people coming up from France from the Refuge de Bise and finally there's the cross marking the top. Be sure to not wander beyond the cross or you'll make a quick descent to the Abondance valley.

The presence of a cross makes this feel like a proper summit and the views are as good as any to be had from the high mountains. Away to the north is the vast Lac Léman (Lake Geneva), the biggest lake in the Alps. To the east is the Diablerets massif, south the Dents du Midi, and, beyond, the high mountains of the Alps. Even on a hazy or slightly cloudy day this summit is worthwhile, for if nothing else you're more or less assured sightings of ibex and, as with many peaks in the foothills, there is a real feeling of being on top of the world.

When you tear yourself away you need to retrace

Looking north from the summit of the Cornettes de Bise.

SNOW-SHOE WALK: LAC DE TANAY TO THE COL D'UGEON
(2019M/6620FT)

SNOW-SHOE WALK ESSENTIALS

ACCESS Start and finish at Le Flon.

DISTANCE 13-km (8-mile) round trip.

HEIGHT GAIN 987m (3237ft).

APPROXIMATE TIME 8–9 hours.

DIFFICULTY 3

TYPE OF WALK Round trip, returning by the same route.

INTERESTING FEATURES Tanay lake, surrounded by the steep rocky summits of Les Jumelles, Alamon and le Sechon, the fantastic wild scenery, the Cornettes de Bise and the view from the col down to the Refuge de Bise.

ADDITIONAL INFORMATION Even when the track up to Tanay is clear of snow, it is only authorised for four-wheel-drive vehicles.

MAP 1:25 000: Carte Nationale de la Suisse 1284 Monthey.

This is a pleasant outing on snow shoes, which although not difficult is quite long and should not be attempted after fresh snow as the surrounding slopes are very steep and avalanche-prone. The summer path up the valley above Tanay is not recommended in winter as it is threatened by avalanches and also goes very close to the river which will be snow-covered and consequently difficult to avoid. There is a jeep track up to the Montagne de l'Au farm which can be followed on the north side of the valley. Even here expect to encounter avalanche debris which can be awkward to cross.

If you find yourselves weary by the time you reach the farm buildings, turn back as the col is a lot further than it appears. To continue on from the farm, head northwest over undulating terrain towards the col, which is the lowest point directly ahead. This walk is delightful wherever you get to, as it takes you into a wild and unfrequented area, beautiful in the snow, with the impressive steep walls of the Cornettes de Bise (2432m/ 7979ft), the highest summit in the region, to the south. Keep your eyes open for chamois and ibex. If you go just beyond the flat Col d'Ugeon you have reached the Franco-Swiss border.

your steps to the col. From here your objective is the Col de Verne (1814m/5952ft) which lies on the frontier with France. This is reached by a pleasant trail past the deserted *alpage* of Calaz, then down steep switchbacks to the welcome flat of the pass. Here you can stand with one foot in Switzerland, one in France.

A steep path takes you into the Vallée de Verne which is followed easily down to the Plan de l'Ortie (1281m/4203ft). This beautiful pastoral valley, flanked by steep limestone cliffs to the north, is very peaceful, with just a couple of farms providing some activity. At the Plan de l'Ortie a path leads you up into the mixed forest under the impressive cliffs of le Sechon where there are three exposed sections – two of which are equipped with cables – to traverse under the cliffs. The ground below is very steep and in wet or snowy conditions extreme care is needed. As the way gets easier you arrive at the Tanay jeep road a short distance below the Col de Tanay (1440m/4725ft), just beyond which is the lake, and your swim.

ALPINE PASQUE FLOWER (PULSATILLA ALPINA)

Known in France as the *Anemone des Alpes*, this beautiful flower belongs to the buttercup family. There are many varieties of pulsatilla, but this is the best known in the Alps. The alpine anemones or Pasque flowers can be either yellow or white, both being equally common. They are poisonous, like all pulsatillas, and after flowering they form a hairy seedhead which in French is known as *l'homme gris*, 'the grey man'. This seedhead is almost as attractive as the flower itself, especially when jewelled with droplets of early-morning dew. It is finally carried away by the wind to scatter its seeds. The word 'anemone' comes from the Greek *amenos* meaning wind.

The Pasque flower was formerly used to treat bites and blood problems in cattle, but it is now protected. It grows as high up as 2700m (8853ft) and flowers from May to July.

TREK 8: THE ARAVIS CIRCUIT

The highest point in the Aravis range is the Pointe Percée (2750m/9023ft), which stands proudly above its neighbouring peaks. This summit is very beautiful, especially in the morning and evening light, when its limestone faces are tinged pink and orange. The ascent of the Pointe Percée is, however, quite a serious undertaking, and there are more amenable summits such as the Quatres Têtes (2364m/7756ft), which afford equally fabulous views.

The beauty of this area is that it is ideally placed to give the best vista of the Mont Blanc massif, and the trek provides a visual extravaganza, crossing some surprisingly varied terrain, ranging from gentle Alpine meadows to comparatively demanding barren passes, allowing a circular tour through this rocky massif.

Burzier to Refuge de Doran
A four-wheel-drive track leads up to the Doran pasture and is quite popular with those who have such a vehicle. This means you'll have to move over on the track from time to time, but don't let this put you off. The walk is still pleasant through shady forest, and as you gain height the views stretching out to the Arve valley below become increasingly spectacular, with the splendid Arpenaz waterfall on the other side of the valley.

High cliffs line the way at times and the bends look like they'd be a bit hairy in a car. As you near the refuge you'll begin to get glimpses of steep limestone rock faces, dazzling in the sun, and just as the trail flattens out you'll see the Doran chapel

TREK ESSENTIALS

LENGTH 4 days.
ACCESS Burzier, above Sallanches in the Arve valley.
HIGHEST POINT Les Quatres Têtes (2364m/7756ft).
MAPS 1:50 000: Didier Richard 8 Mont Blanc.
1:25 000: IGN Top 25 3430 ET La Clusaz Grand Bornand.
TREK STYLE Mountain refuges.
LANGUAGE French.
FURTHER OPTIONS Ascent of the Pointe Percée, either from Doran or Gramusset.

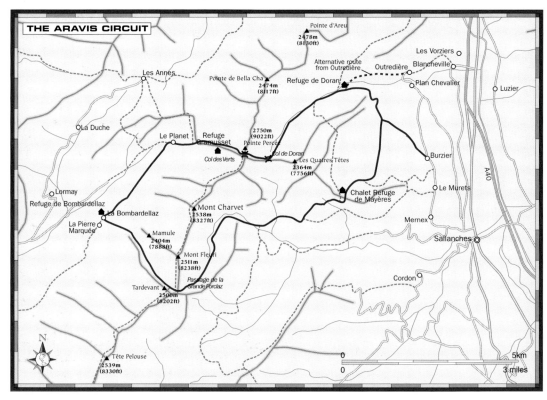

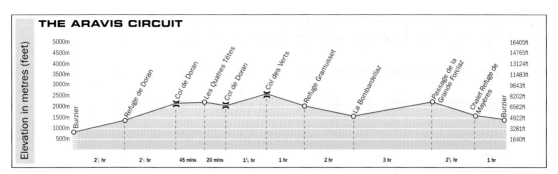

THE ARAVIS CIRCUIT

and behind it the impressive east face of the Pointe Percée. Alternatively, there is a recently created footpath that starts at Outredière, along the road from Plan Chevalier and to the north of Burzier, where there is a car park. (This path is signposted to Refuge de Doran and avoids the jeep track, but is not marked on all maps.)

The Doran farm and refuge is a traditional summer *alpage*, and the refuge provides true Alpine fare, with the background melody of cowbells. As the evening arrives, so the majority of the tourists will descend and you'll be left to enjoy the superb ambience of this magical spot. To the north are the six distinct buttresses of the Tours d'Areu, home to many fine rock climbs. This sector is separated from the rest of the cirque by the Col de la Forclaz. From here eastwards, limestone cliffs form an impressive cirque, which appears to have no possible exit, dominated by the Pointe Percée and in front of it the stocky bulk of Les Quatres Têtes.

Refuge de Doran to the Refuge Gramusset

The sun will be kissing the summits as you head off in the early morning up towards the Col des Arêtes Noires – also named Col de Doran – at 2178m 7146ft). Keep your eyes open for the paint flashes as the path crosses the river in places. The route up the Quatres Têtes takes a left turn before you reach the col, and joins the slabby ridge heading directly east to the summit. You can make this ridge as easy or difficult as you wish, since it's possible to climb some easy slabs at the top to add a bit of exposure if you like.

The summit feels like a promontory with nothing beneath. The view of the Mont Blanc massif is nothing short of grandiose, and the proximity of the forbidding rocky ramparts heightens the impressiveness of the surroundings. Retrace your steps down the ridge then continue the short way to the pass. The Pointe Percée slopes are extremely steep, and the next 400m (1312ft) to the Col des Verts (2595m/8514ft) are exposed. The traverse

of this slope would not be a good idea in bad weather as it can be very slippy. At the Col des Verts you're right under the summit of the Pointe Percée and you may well be tempted to ascend. However, this ascent is rocky scrambling and the way is not easy to find. Unless you have lots of time and are sure to be able to ascend and descend safely, this should not be attempted. If you do decide to go up the Pointe Percée from the Cols de Verts the line of ascent is basically by a series of exposed chimneys, starting from a commemorative plaque – green paint flashes mark the way, and along the route from time to time there are metal rings in the rock. Some scrambling is involved.

A steep path leads down into the west-facing Combe des Verts, which can hold snow until very late in the season. This might mean you can enjoy a quick *glissade* (see glossary, p173), or it may mean you have to take a long time being careful not to fall over hidden boulders. Look out for climbers on the buttresses of the Pointe Percée as you descend to the rather ugly Refuge Gramusset (2164m/7100ft).

From the hut you could spend a pleasant day climbing the Pointe Percée by the west face route, which provides the easiest way up. In the direction of the face you stay left rather than taking the Col des Verts path, your objective being the obvious scree couloir that splits the centre of the face.

The steep, southwest face of the Mamule dominates the Forclaz valley and sports some fine rock climbs.

THE GENTIAN
(GENTIANA)

The gentian family includes several flowers, each very different from the other, and some not recognisable as being in the same family. The classic alpine flowers are the trumpet gentian (*Gentiana acaulis*) and the spring gentian (*Gentiana verna*). Both these are the wonderful deep blue that most people associate with the gentian flower.

The trumpet gentian has large trumpet-shaped flowers and blooms from May until August. It tends to be in flower early in the lower meadows and is a sure sign of spring. The spring gentian has a star-shaped flower composed of five petals and is found up to 3000m (9837ft), again until August or even later. These flowers are sometimes found in autumn and winter and it isn't known if this is a second flowering or just a mistake of the calendar.

There are several other blue gentians which are to be seen in various soils throughout the Alps, most commonly the short-leaved gentian (*Gentiana brachyphylla*) which flowers in clumps on stony ground in July and August and has been found up to 4200m (13772ft). Also commonly found in the Alps is the great yellow gentian (*Gentiana lutea*), which can grow to be very tall, reaching 1.5m (5ft). This flower has been sought after since pre-Roman times for its curative properties, as well as for the production of alcoholic drinks.

There is also the spotted gentian (*Gentiana punctata*) with its pale greenish-yellow, spotted, upright bells, and the rather unusual purple gentian (*Gentiana purpurea*) which has flowers that are sometimes almost brown. These are also used to aid digestion, since they regularise intestinal activity and have a positive effect on the vascular system. Unfortunately, the gentian's beneficial properties are to be found in its roots, so nowadays this practice is not to be encouraged. The spotted gentian can apparently live for a hundred years or more, and doesn't start to flower until it's at least ten years old.

Beware of loose stones and *neve* – if there is late snow here an axe would be needed and the ascent could be difficult. From halfway up this gully, red paint-marks take you on to the Crête Faitière ridge, which joins the chimney route near the summit.

Refuge Gramusset to Chalet Refuge de Mayères
This is a long day, so be sure to get an early start. From Gramusset you have to make a steep descent to Le Planet and then head down the valley, past the hamlet of La Bombardellaz, with its oratory, to the Refuge de Bombardellaz. This would be an alternative place to spend the night after Stage Two, making that stage longer but this stage shorter. From the refuge a path meanders east through woods and unfortunately all that altitude you so quickly lost has now to be regained – that's the mountains for you! Your objective is the Combe de la Grande Forclaz (marked as 'Forcle' on signs), at the head of which is the only possible way back over the chain of summits to regain the Arve valley. The Forclaz valley is enclosed by steep cliffs, including the imposing double summits of the Mamule. Look out for climbers ascending its steep limestone face.

The way up to the pass is fairly obvious, and the glacier marked on the map is no longer there, although *neve* can remain in shady spots for the season. The small hummock marked as point 2001 can be avoided by taking the path which skirts it on the left.

The Passage de la Grande Forclaz (2311m/7582ft) is flanked by the Ambrevetta (2463m/8081ft), which it is possible to ascend on foot, and by Mont Fleuri (2511m/8238ft). A steep descent takes you into the more spacious Combe des Fours where chamois and ibex live, testifying to the tranquillity of this area.

The sense of being far off the beaten track continues as you pass under the precipitous slopes of Mont Charvet. The Torrent des Fours gushes out of the corrie as the spectacular Cascade des Fours, which you almost follow. The path takes an unexpected line down the cliffs, giving you a great view of the waterfall. Soon after descending the cliff be sure to take the lefthand path to traverse interesting terrain above and through cliffs to the Chalet Refuge de Mayères. If you're lucky you'll arrive in time to see light aircraft landing and taking off at the small steep airstrip here.

Les Mayères is another *alpage* ('*mayer*' in fact being another word for this) and is in a stunning position with expansive views of the valley and the Mont Blanc massif. By this stage you may have had enough of the views, but if not you're in for another unforgettable visual delight.

Chalet Refuge de Mayères to Burzier
Again a four-wheel-drive track leads down through meadows and forest to Burzier. This last stage could be done at the end of the third day, but that would make a very long day and you'd have to have a very good reason to pass up on a night at Mayères.

THE WESTERN OUTLIERS
REGIONAL DIRECTORY

GETTING THERE BY AIR
Geneva airport is the most convenient airport for the Western Outliers region. The airport is served by many different airlines including Swissair, British Airways and Easyjet. Having landed, there are various options for reaching the trekking areas in this region.

Car hire: cars can be rented from the airport, and all the start points for the treks here are accessible in an hour or two from the airport. It's normally cheaper to book the car before you arrive.

Taxi transfer: Airport Transfer Services operate from Geneva to Sallanches.

Train: a good train service runs from Geneva airport to St Gingolph, St Maurice and Monthey. From the train stations the local Swiss Postbus service (PTT) will take you to the trek start points (see bus details below). To reach the Aravis area there is a rather slow and tortuous train service from Geneva to Sallanches. For the Beaufortain area, a train service runs from Geneva to Annecy from where a regular service continues to Albertville.

Bus: the Swiss Postbus service (PTT) is efficient and reliable. From Geneva buses run along the lake to St Gingolph then on to Monthey and St Maurice. There is a postbus to le Flon, to Vérossaz and to Dorénaz. Postbus tickets should be purchased at the Post Office during office hours, otherwise directly from the bus driver. The Postbuses leave from the Post Offices, and usually have pick-up points at train stations.

The French bus services are not quite so extensive. From Sallanches there is no bus serice to le Burzier so a taxi will be needed for this short journey if you have no car. From Albertville a bus service (Autocars Blanc) runs to Beaufort throughout the year, and to the Cormet de Roseland in the summer season.

GETTING THERE BY CAR
By car, a good motorway system (toll roads) leads down through France to the Autoroute Blanche (A41) which leads to Geneva and Annecy and onwards. To drive on the Swiss motorways you must buy a "*vignette*", which can be obtained at the border. The French roads are very busy on Friday evenings and Saturdays during the holidays, Sundays being much quieter. In winter, snow tyres or chains are often necessary on the smaller roads to access the mountain towns and villages. The local tourist offices will be able to advise.

ACCOMMODATION
In the main towns there are many choices of hotels or *gîtes*, as well as campsites in the summer. However, some of the smaller towns do not have many hotels and in high season booking in advance is essential. The best sources of information are the local tourist offices, where English is spoken.

Mountain Huts:
There are a lot of huts to choose from in this region, many of which are noted in the trek texts. Since phone numbers change, individual numbers are not listed here. The best way to find out how to reserve a hut is to contact the local tourist office and they may even make the reservation for you. For well-known treks such as the Tour des Dents du Midi, the local tourist office can give you a list of hut numbers. If you want to make your reservation before the hut opens you'll need to contact the guardian at his private number, which the tourist offices should also provide. Huts owned by Alpine Clubs or by the National Parks can also be booked direct via the governing body.

DIRECTORY
For all telephone numbers the local numbers are noted – to telephone from abroad add the international code and drop the first 0, except for Italy where the entire number is dialled.

Geneva Airport: tel. 022 717 7111; www.gva.ch
Swissair: www.swissair.com
British Airways: www.britishairways.com
Swiss rail: www.sbb.ch
Rail Europe: www.raileurope.com
French Railways: tel. UK 08705 848 848; tel. France 08 36 67 68 69; www.sncf.fr
Air Transport Services: tel. 04 50 53 63 97; email: andy@cham-ats.com; www.cham-ats.com
Autocars Blanc: tel 04 79 38 10 50

Swiss Tourist Offices for the Western Outliers
For contact numbers for all tourist offices in the Valais/Wallis region of Switzerland: tel. 027 327 3570; fax 027 327 3571; email: info@valaistourism.ch; www.matterhornstate.com
For the whole of Switzerland: www.myswitzerland.com
Geneva Tourist Office: tel. 022 909 7000; fax: 022 909 7075; email: info@geneva-tourism.ch; www.geneva-tourism.ch
Champéry Tourist Office: tel. 024 479 2020; fax: 024 479 2021; email: champery-ch@portesdusoleil.com; www.champery.ch
St Maurice Tourist Office: tel. 024 485 4040; fax 024 485 4080; email: tourisme@st-maurice.ch; www.st-maurice.ch
Val d'Illiez Tourist Office: tel. 024 477 2077; fax 024 477 3773; email: ot.illiez@bluewin.ch; www.val-d-illiez.ch
Monthey Tourist Office: tel. 024 475 7963; fax 024 475 7949

French Tourist Offices for the Western Outliers
For general information: www.maison-de-la-france.com
Albertville Tourist Office: tel. 04 79 32 04 22; fax 04 79 32 87 09; email: albertville.tourisme@wanadoo.fr; www.tourisme.fr/albertville
Beaufort Tourist Office: tel. 04 79 38 15 33; fax 04 79 38 16 70; email: otareches-beaufort@wanadoo.fr; www.areches-beaufort.com
Bourg-St-Maurice Tourist Office: tel. 04 79 07 04 92; fax 04 79 07 24 90; email: wlesarcs@lesarcs.com; www.bourgstmaurice.com
Sallanches Tourist Office: tel. 04 50 58 04 25; fax 04 50 58 38 47
Grand Bornand Tourist Office: tel. 04 50 02 78 00; fax 04 50 02 78 01; email: infos@legrandbornand.com; www.legrandbornand.com
La Clusaz Tourist Office: tel. 04 50 32 65 00; fax 04 50 32 65 01
Chapelle d'Abondance Tourist Office: tel. 04 50 73 51 41; fax 04 50 73 56 04
Chatel Tourist Office: tel. 04 50 73 22 44; fax 04 50 73 22 87
Morzine Tourist Office: tel. 04 50 74 02 11; fax 04 50 74 24 29; www.avoriazski.com
Samoëns Tourist Office: tel. 04 50 34 40 28; fax 04 50 34 95 82
Sixt Tourist Office: tel. 04 50 34 49 36; fax 04 50 34 19 57
Servoz Tourist Office: tel. 04 50 47 21 68; fax 04 50 47 27 06
Chamonix Tourist Office: tel. 04 50 53 00 24; fax 04 50 53 58 90; email: info@chamonix.com; www.chamonix.com
Reservations: tel. 04 50 53 23 33; fax 04 50 53 87 42

6

THE MONT BLANC RANGE

Relatively compact given the number of high peaks contained within, the Mont Blanc massif measures less than 40km by 15km (25 miles by 9 miles), with Mont Blanc, the highest summit of Western Europe, reaching 4807m (15767ft). The Franco–Italian frontier snakes along the range, the Italian side of Mont Blanc being impressively steep compared to France's rounded slopes.

This is where alpinism began. When awe-inspired visitors decided that the peaks should be climbed rather than feared and that the glaciers were majestic not monstrous. Many battles against the elements have been played out in this arena, not to mention more violent confrontations during the First World War. However, the best trekking terrain is not within the massif, but around it, in the non-glaciated Aiguilles Rouges massif, the wild slopes above the Emosson lake, and the delightful Ferret valleys of Italy and Switzerland.

From these belvederes the snow-capped summits and tumbling glaciers of this impressive range are seen at their best. Although Mont Blanc is the most famous peak in Europe, and consequently attracts many visitors, it is still easy to escape the crowds of the main valleys and towns. There is such a wealth of footpaths that the choice is almost limitless. A few are extremely popular, and these are the ones most visitors choose. However, near every busy walk there is a more secret one, where you'll find animals, flowers, and peace and quiet to enjoy the splendours of these mountains.

The Aiguille Noire de Peutérey, with the summit of Mont Blanc behind in the first light of dawn.

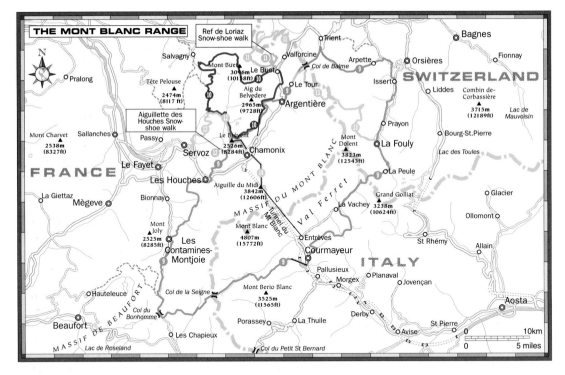

When tourism in the Alps first began in the 18th century, the tourists, many of them British, came with the sole intention of seeing the glaciers, whilst the summits remained shrouded in mystery and suspicion. Only the crystal searchers and the chamois hunters ventured up high and nobody entertained the idea of trying to get to the top of the peaks. In Chamonix, in 1760, Horace Bénédict de Saussure looked across towards the Mont Blanc massif from the vantage point of the Brévent. He asked his guide the names of the snowy summits. 'I don't know', replied the guide. 'Those are bad mountains, where they say there is no grass, no vineyards, not even any stones for building. Nothing but snow, sir. We call them the *montagnes maudites*' (the cursed mountains). De Saussure decided he couldn't rest until he'd been to the summit of Mont Blanc. He offered a reward to the first person who could find a route to the top.

Several local people were vaguely tempted by the idea and the following years saw some half-hearted attempts, and several near successes, notably instigated by de Saussure and the like-minded Marc-Théodore Bourrit, chorister at Geneva Cathedral; but the idea of climbing high, snowy summits was still revolutionary. One of the biggest problems was that accepted opinion held that to spend a night out on the glaciers would be fatal, either because of the cold, or because of the demons that inhabited these deadly seas of ice. It was assumed that anyone caught out by nightfall would not come back alive.

In 1786, an attempt was made that was to point the way to success. Two parties of men met at the Dôme de Goûter, having come up by different routes. Together they discussed the possible routes onward from the Dôme, coming to the conclusion that to go on up the Arête des Bosses was impossible. The weather was deteriorating and they decided to retreat as quickly as possible since night was drawing in.

One of them, Jacques Balmat, a loner and not much liked by the others, strayed briefly from the group to look for crystals. When he returned, he found they had gone on down, leaving him to fend for himself, with no tracks to follow, due to wind and snow. Balmat continued on alone, but in the bad weather he was forced to stop at the Grand Plateau, and to spend the night on the glacier. The next day, with time to spare, Balmat took the opportunity to check out the possible routes from the Plateau to the summit, and spotted what seemed to be the most feasible line. His return to the valley, to the complete disbelief of the locals, dispelled the theory that a night out was not possible. After that it was just a question of time, and Balmat couldn't keep his reconnaisance a secret for long.

Balmat's daughter, Judith, was ill and the Chamonix doctor, Michel-Gabriel Paccard, visiting the little girl, had far more interest in Mont Blanc than in the well-being of the child. He had already tried for the summit, and he proved to be the partner Balmat needed for a successful attempt. Paccard's motivation, unlike Balmat's, was not financial; rather he dreamed of being the first scientist to reach the top. This was ideal for Balmat as he quickly figured that with Paccard he wouldn't be obliged to share the reward, so he told Paccard he knew the route and agreed to be his guide. During 7–9 August 1786, Balmat and Paccard reached the summit of Mont Blanc in a three-day push, bivouacking first at the Gite Balmat (a big boulder) at the top of the Montagne de la Côte and then getting to the summit via the Rochers Rouges at 6.23pm on the 8 August. Dr Paccard took several measurements on the summit, then they set off down. At around midnight the two men regained their bivouac on the Montagne de la Côte.

How well Balmat had really reconnoitred the route has been much debated over the years, but as a team they made it, thanks to their own determination, mountain sense and some degree of luck – after all, they had none of the gear we take nowadays, not even a rope. On their return to Chamonix, Balmat's daughter had succumbed to her illness, but the fame of the two men was assured as they arrived hand-in-hand, with Paccard suffering from snow blindness, having lost his hat near the summit.

Balmat set off for Geneva to claim his reward from de Saussure, but was allegedly mugged on his way back and the money taken. However, he was awarded other benefits and afterwards was always in demand to guide on Mont Blanc. He was to die years later at the age of seventy-two, searching for gold on the slopes of Mont Ruan. For a long time Balmat was solely credited with the ascent and was always known as 'Jacques Balmat dit Mont Blanc', while Paccard was just portrayed as a passenger. That was set right in later years and now the names go together as the pair responsible for opening up this fine mountain to future climbers.

De Saussure finally made it to the summit on 3 August 1787 after a four-day siege, accompanied by eighteen guides, including Jacques Balmat, and vast quantities of scientific equipment. He spent four-and-a-half-hours on the top, conducting

Mont Blanc, as seen from the Chamonix valley.

The magnificent Brenva face of Mont Blanc.

Any fine summer's day sees many people go to the top, but at least there are several normal routes. Needless to say the views are superlative, but don't expect to be alone – if you are something's probably wrong!

One of the key access routes to the Mont Blanc range is the Chamonix valley, whose development was closely linked to the history of Mont Blanc. For many centuries Chamonix was just another unknown village, tucked away under the towering high summits that inspired fear in the locals. Today it is one of the most celebrated towns in the world, a mecca for mountaineering, both in winter and summer. This incredible development didn't begin until the second half of the 18th century.

Buried deep beneath the massif, the Chamonix valley culminates in a cul-de-sac at its northern end. The priory was founded in 1091, and this date marks the official beginnings of Chamonix. The severe climatic conditions of this shady valley meant that for a long time it held little attraction to outsiders. The high summits were thought to be home to dragons, and the long glaciers snaked down to the valley, at certain times threatening the houses themselves. Every winter would see terrible avalanches devastate the hillside, and despite some cultivable land, the harvests were poor.

Little by little this closed world was discovered by adventurers from afar. In 1741, two British travellers, William Windham and Richard Pococke, ventured into the valley with the express intention of seeing the glaciers, visible from the Geneva plains. Their glowing reports attracted other wealthy travellers, and the valley was soon an essential stop-over on any adventurer's itinerary. Some twenty years later Horace Bénédict de Saussure's encouragement led to the first ascents of Mont Blanc, from there on the future of Chamonix as a tourist venue was more or less assured.

Visitors came from far and wide, and in 1860 the visit of Napoleon III and the Empress Eugenie did much to further publicise the importance of the valley and its massif. The 20th century saw the rapid development of skiing with the result that in the winter season Chamonix now receives as many visitors as in the summer. In 1907, the town hosted the first international ski competition and in 1924 the first winter Olympics were staged on its slopes.

Its location on the frontier of both Italy and Switzerland makes this French town a truly international centre, with rail and road links to the neighbouring valleys of Valais and Aosta.

numerous experiments, and concluded that the summit was at 4775m (15667ft). The descent was a bit quicker than the ascent, especially as some of it was done glissading on their feet, or in de Saussure's case on his bottom. De Saussure subsequently had all pictures destroyed that showed him in this unflattering position.

This climb was much publicised in educated circles in Europe, laying down the guidelines for later ascents and ensuring the fashionability of mountaineering over the next few years. Mont Blanc saw success after success, and in 1808 Marie Paradis, a local girl from Saint Gervais, working at the time for an inn in Chamonix, made the best business move of her life by getting herself dragged to the top. Credited with the first female ascent 'La Marie du Mont Blanc' became a celebrity and set up her own café. In terms of women's mountaineering though the second women's ascent, by Henriette d'Angeville in 1838, is perhaps more noteworthy, since she did the ascent under her own steam and was fuelled by her personal motivation.

Mont Blanc never since seems to have lost its popularity. The construction of the Aiguille du Midi cable car in 1955 obviously added immensely to the accessibility of the massif in general. But we can at least be glad that the plans to build a railway from Le Fayet to the Mont Blanc summit faltered in 1914 at the Nid d'Aigle and fortunately this venture was not resumed after the First World War.

TREK 9: TOUR DU MONT BLANC

The very name of this trek is exciting and conjures up images of snowy peaks. This is *the* famous long-distance walk in the Alps, and the Tour du Mont Blanc (TMB) has got it all: fine views, variety of terrain and scenery, different countries, high passes, beautiful Alpine valleys... this is the yardstick by which all others are measured. For the first-time walker in the Alps, this trek will clearly provide a fulfilling experience and probably whet the appetite for more. For the seasoned Alpine visitor, it won't disappoint either. What could be better than walking through three countries, seeing the Mont Blanc massif from all sides, with distant views of other huge peaks, even the Matterhorn if you're really lucky?

The trek was first done in its entirety in the 1760s by pioneers such as Horace Bénédict de Saussure and Marc-Théodore Bourrit. In the early days it was mainly undertaken by mules on old rough tracks, but between 1820 and 1850 a veritable network of lodges was set up on the tour. Many of the paths are centuries old, used as routes between the Alpine valleys for trading and for grazing animals.

Its fame means that the TMB attracts a great many hikers and at the height of the summer season it can be busy on some parts of the tour. However, even then it's possible to escape most of the crowds and to walk in relative isolation for the day, only meeting lots of people on the descents to the valleys or on arrival at a popular refuge.

Being a circular tour, the TMB can be begun anywhere along the route. I have a preference for starting in France in Argentière, since this way the first day is spent traversing the Aiguilles Rouges, looking at the Mont Blanc massif and getting a feel for

TREK ESSENTIALS

LENGTH 8–10 days. More with detours or rest days.
ACCESS Suggested starting points are Argentière, Courmayeur, Champex, or any other town on the tour.
HIGHEST POINT The Col des Fours and the Fenêtre d'Arpette are both 2665m (8744ft).
MAPS 1:50 000: Didier Richard 8 Mont Blanc.
1:25 000: IGN Top 25 3630 OT Chamonix, 3531 ET St Gervais.
TREK STYLE Huts and hotels.
LANGUAGES French and Italian.
FURTHER OPTIONS Numerous detours are possible on a tour like this, by taking more time. For example, you could take a day to visit higher huts such as the Cabane d'Orny or the Refuge Albert Premier, or spend a day up at Lac Blanc. The maps are well marked with paths and to be able to take the time to wander is highly rewarding.

Descending from the Col des Fours towards La Ville des Glaciers.

the general layout of the mountains. Other good starting places are Courmayeur in Italy or Champex in Switzerland.

You can go clockwise or anti-clockwise. Take note if you choose the former – my first TMB was done in this direction and I spent a lot of time saying *Bonjour*, and even on occasion being stopped and told I was going the wrong way! For those with a non-conformist nature this is probably the best option, but for the rest of us, anti-clockwise is a good bet. I'm not sure whether there are real advantages to going in one direction and not the other – there are certainly a couple of slopes that I prefer to do as descents not ascents, but this could be through force of habit. Anyway, after a decade of bi- or tri-annual trips round the tour, all but the infamous first one in the same direction, that's the way I'm going to describe it. So if you decide to go the other way you'll have to read backwards!

The TMB has several high variations and whether or not you choose to do these depends on

TOUR DU MONT BLANC

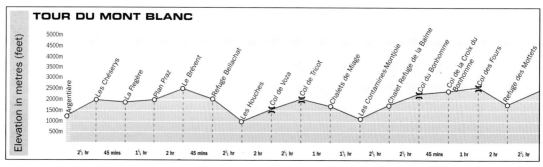

TOUR DU MONT BLANC

several factors: weather, fitness, time and preferences. The trek described here is the TMB in its highest form. The normal lower variations are all well marked on the maps. Unlike the other treks in this guide, the TMB isn't described day by day – there are so many different places to stay that this would be too selective. So it is split into stages that cover two or more days instead, though all major lodging possibilities are mentioned in the text.

FRENCH SECTION
Argentière to Les Houches
Starting in Argentière (1252m/4108ft), your first day is a traverse of the Aiguilles Rouges range – the 'red needles', named after the reddish tints in the rocks. From the centre of Argentière the trail heads gently uphill into the larch and spruce forest. Although you can take the lowest path and go straight to La Flégère in a couple of hours, it's better to head up to Les Chéserys, under the popular crags of this name, with a short section on ladders and cables.

After a couple of hours of climbing you reach the large cairn of Les Chéserys (2000m/6562ft) which makes a great place to rest. Views of the Mont Blanc massif are superb and now's the time to start learning the names of the peaks. Mont Blanc is fairly obvious, although the snowy dome as it is from this side is scarcely recognisable as the same peak when viewed from Italy, where its steep south face is spectacular. From this vantage you can clearly see the Aiguille du Midi (3842m/12606ft), with its two-stage cable car. The Aiguille Verte (4122m/13524ft) is directly opposite, next to the Drus (3754m/12317ft), and the sweeping valley of the Mer de Glace. Far away is the rocky spire of the Dent du Géant (4013m/13167ft), on the Italian frontier, and to the left the brooding dark buttresses of the famous north face of the Grandes Jorasses (4208m/13806ft). Looking back you can

Descending towards the Rifugio Elisabetta, having passed into Italy by the Col de la Seigne.

see the village of Le Tour with its glacier above, and on the northeastern horizon the lowest point is the Col de Balme (2191m/7184ft), an important landmark as, if all goes well, that will be the return point to France at the end of the trek.

The Flégère ski area, your next objective, is clearly visible, just forty-five minutes walk away. However, above is the Lac Blanc (2352m/7717ft), a justifiably popular venue for day walkers, especially those who take the lift to La Flégère. The panorama is fabulous, and this is surely the place to go if you want to get those photos of the massif. From Lac Blanc it's a little less than an hour to La Flégère from where it is said that you can see fourteen glaciers. There is also dormitory accommodation below the lift building. The walk from La Flégère to Plan Praz (2000m/6562ft) – the middle station of the two-stage cable car up to Le Brévent – along the Grand Balcon, is a beautiful stroll, bordered by alpenrose and bilberry bushes. The path is undulating, easy underfoot, allowing you to fully appreciate the fabulous vista. Plan Praz is one of the principal take-off zones in the Chamonix valley for paragliding and on most summer days there will be people laying out their chutes ready to jump.

The next section takes you up to the Col du

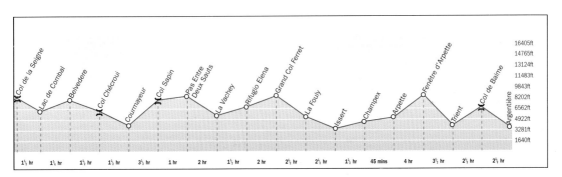

On the summit of the Tête Nord des Fours, 2756m (9042ft).

Brévent (2368m/7769ft), and around to the Brévent summit. The views to the west and north open up, revealing a wild and undeveloped area, bounded by the high cliffs of the Rochers des Fiz. This section can remain snowy late into the summer season, and I have known it to be difficult to find the trail – those little red-and-white flashes tend to get covered. The summit of the Brévent is at 2525m (8284ft) and gives superlative views of Mont Blanc and the surrounding peaks. It was from here in 1760 that Horace Bénédict de Saussure first came up with his audacious plan to climb Mont Blanc.

The path heads down and south above the Lac du Brévent to the Refuge Bellachat (2136m/7008ft). This private hut is in a superb position, perched high above the valley and you will certainly want to spend time studying the summits and the glaciers. The Bossons glacier is particularly eye-catching. It allegedly boasts the biggest elevation drop of any glacier in the world, from its source at 4807m (15772ft) to its base at 1300m (4265ft). Lower down it breaks into spectacular crevasses and seracs, glinting blue and green.

The path down to the valley is, well, down – and down and down. If you (or your knees) don't like descents you can console yourself with dreams of the patisserie in Les Houches which, if you find the right one, is the best ever. It's a long way to go though, even for a great chocolate croissant. The path signs are plentiful, although ignore the signposted timings or you may think you're walking backwards – how does 50 minutes to Les Houches then become 1 hour 10 minutes a quarter of an hour later?

Les Houches (1008m/3305ft) is a lively town, where you can get all supplies. It's on the main railway line to Chamonix from St Gervais, so escape is possible here. It has a post office, bank, supermarkets, hotels, *gîtes* and a market on Mondays.

To find the patisserie, take a look down the steps opposite the church.

Les Houches to Les Contamines-Montjoie
The path out from Les Houches can be a little hot on summer days but as you get higher it will cool off. There's also a choice of two cable cars to go to the same place. From the Col de Voza (1653m/5423ft) you can see back to the Rochers des Fiz and the Brévent. You're heading round the side of Mont Blanc, which you won't see again for a while. However, the Aiguille du Goûter (3863m/12674ft) and the Aiguille de Bionassey (4052m/13295ft) are superb. The normal TMB goes down to the village of Bionnassay, then through a couple of other hamlets to emerge in the Contamines valley. A series of paths and back roads leads in to Les Contamines-Montjoie, the next destination.

The alternative higher route goes over the Col de Tricot (2120m/6956ft). This way is to be recommended in good weather, for its proximity to the glaciers. The path follows the tramway from the Col de Voza to Bellevue. Constructed early in the 20th century, this tramway was originally intended to go from St Gervais to the summit of Mont Blanc. Funds and men ran out in 1914 so it finishes on a slope at the Nid d'Aigle and provides a convenient ride up for Mont Blanc aspirants. Look closely at the Aiguille du Goûter and you'll see the Refuge du Goûter, starting point for ascents of Mont Blanc by the Arête des Bosses. On a fine summer morning, with binoculars, you should see lots of people returning to the hut from the summit, and an equal number heading up from the lifts, rucksacks laden, going to the hut.

To go to the Col de Tricot (2120m/6956ft) the route leads down and around to the snout of the Bionnassay glacier. Then it winds its way through beautiful meadows, covered with flowers in July, and up to the col. The other side of the col may look alarmingly steep at first glance. Take a deep breath and look again – it's not so bad and the path is good. At the base of this slope are the Chalets de Miage – a traditional restaurant and refuge, under the imposing slopes of the Dômes de Miage.

Onwards, you climb up to the Col de Truc (1720m/5643ft), where there's another refuge. Both this and Miage offer a genuine taste of Alpine life, being also summer farms or *alpages*. Bronze Age remains found here suggest that this was the first place to be occupied in the Contamines region, 4000 years ago, possibly by people in search of copper, essential for the composition of bronze.

From Le Truc the descent to Les Contamines-Montjoie is easy, on forest tracks. Les Contamines-Montjoie is a town similar in size to Les Houches, with all the necessary services. The continuation of the TMB takes the road briefly to get out of town, then a flat track to Notre Dame de la Gorge. It is thought there has been a chapel here since the Middle Ages and it is a well frequented site, both by hikers and by pilgrims.

Here you are following a very ancient route which comes from the valleys of the Tarentaise, used since pre-Roman times to reach what is now Switzerland, via the Col de Voza and the Col de Balme. The Romans came through here, hence the 'Roman road' which, as was the Romans' wont, takes a direct line. It's a little steep and, depending on the time of day, you could be going against the flow as it's a popular site for day walks. Heading up this track you pass firstly the Chalet Hotel du Nant Borrant and then an hour later the Chalet Refuge de la Balme. Both provide dormitory accommodation and good food.

Les Contamines-Montjoie to Courmayeur

The TMB heads directly south and an early start on this next section allows the major climb to be completed in cool shade. You are going to the Col du Bonhomme (2329m/7641ft), the 'bonhomme' (gentleman) being the visible rocky lump to the left of the col, and his lady the smaller lump left again. This path is very pleasant since the steep parts are interspersed with flat sections. A huge cairn provides an obvious stopping place. Legend has it that an English lady expired at this spot – whether she was doing the TMB has never been confirmed! – and was subsequently buried here. Her lady-in-waiting of course did the honourable thing and died too. However, it's also thought that this could be an old altar dedicated to Mercury, the god of travellers. It is regarded as good luck to add a stone to the pile.

The way on is all too obvious – up. There is often *nevé* remaining until well into the season, but it doesn't generally present any problems, and from the col in good weather the views south over to the Beaufortain are wonderful.

The next pass is a giveaway – just 45 minutes and 100m (328ft) of ascent, and is gained by a traverse, with those views just getting better and better. On reaching the Col de la Croix du Bonhomme (2479m/8133ft) you may spot Mont Pourri (3779m/12399ft) away to the south in the Vanoise. The Refuge de la Croix du Bonhomme was renovated in the early 1990s and now provides spacious accommodation. The normal TMB continues south from here to the hamlet of Les Chapieux, where the Auberge de Nova is a comfortable place to stay.

The high alternative route goes over the Col des Fours (2665m/8744ft) to the east. If you go this way you will miss Les Chapieux. From the col it is possible to ascend one of the small summits forming the col – the Tête Nord and the Tête Sud des Fours – from where on a very clear day you can see the Matterhorn. From the col the way down is obvious, and steep. This way should be avoided in early season, unless you are experienced on snow slopes. If you like snow, however, this slope provides a good *glissade*. The flowers are fabulous at the right time and as you descend you go through several different zones, from the high alpines, such as the toadflax and the glacier crowsfoot, to the meadow flowers low down. When you hit the track at Les Tufs look out for the short cut – in July this meadow is overflowing with gentians, hawksbeards, orchids and rampions.

After this long descent it's a relief to arrive in the valley. La Ville des Glaciers is really just a farm and a car park. The normal route comes along the road

With the Italian face of Mont Blanc as a backdrop, the ascent to the Col Chécroui is one of the highlights of this trek.

The impressive spire of the Drus.

The climb is really good, through meadows, the only problem being that for the first part the views are behind you — however, this provides a fine excuse to stop from time to time.

Looking back you'll soon see the Lac de Miage formed at the edge of the Miage glacier, although it's hard to see the glacier as the ice is covered in gravel and the lateral moraine has been colonised by larch trees.

The path continues up to finally arrive at a high point, which is one of the finest viewpoints on the tour.

From here the Peutérey ridge to the summit of Mont Blanc is very impressive, starting with the Aiguille Noire de Peutérey (3773m/ 12379ft), which shelters the spiky spires of the 'Dames Anglaises' (English ladies) – apparently so-called because they are cold and inhospitable! The huge snowy summit of the Aiguille Blanche de Peutérey (4108m/13478ft) leads up to the summit of Mont Blanc de Courmayeur. This is without doubt a place to savour.

Gentle walking leads through meadows to the edge of the Courmayeur ski resort and the Col Chécroui. A ski bar in the winter, Maison Vieille provides dormitory accommodation in the summer. Many people who had planned to go as far as Courmayeur fail to resist the temptation of spending a night here. Not only is the welcome good, the situation is fabulous. Watching the sun set behind the Aiguille Noire is a must, and the early morning is equally impressive. The misty pink views away down the Aosta valley to the magical summit of Grivola, are beautiful. And, best of all, at Maison Vieille there are sunloungers! What better way to rest those aching muscles?

Courmayeur is the Italian equivalent of Chamonix. The centre of the town is attractive, with plenty of cafés and shops – quite welcome after several days in the hills. An old Roman city (Curia Major), Courmayeur was close to the Alpis Graia road, leading to the Col du Petit St Bernard, and on the road to Gaul, which went over the Col de la Seigne. The houses here are noticeably different to those seen in France: the slate-covered roofs are typical of the Aosta valley.

To reach Courmayeur from Col Chécroui there are several options: one is to descend through the forest to the north of the Maison Vieille, to the road at Notre Dame de la Guérison, or there is a cable car down to Courmayeur from just below Col

to here and just along the track by the river is the Refuge des Mottets. This *alpage* provides dormitory accommodation, and possibly the biggest dormitories you may ever sleep in. Two old barns have been renovated (slightly) to sleep about a hundred people. The owners of the refuge breed donkeys and their dulcet tones will accompany your dreams. You can hire a donkey to carry your rucksack to the next col, but the donkeys are not that keen to go up, and they certainly don't hurry. It's not rare to arrive at the Col de la Seigne (2516m/8255ft) and find several donkeys up there – understandably they're not keen to head down and do the whole thing again!

ITALIAN SECTION

This is the frontier with Italy, so your greeting should now be *buon giorno*. However, in this area of Italy most people also speak French, some as a first language, since the borders have shifted in recent history.

If possible pick a sunny day for this section. On the final grind up to the pass, Mont Blanc slowly comes into view, making you hurry to get the full picture. The Italian face of the massif is spectacular, and views stretch away as far as the Grand Combin in Switzerland, straight ahead to the east. An easy descent takes you to the flat area of the Alpes Inférieures de la Lée Blanche (2035m/ 6677ft), with the Rifugio Elisabetta just above. This is a popular hut, with impressive views of the glacier just behind.

The TMB descends to the valley and takes the road for a short while. If you're desperate by this stage for a comfortable hotel and a private room, it's best to head straight down to Courmayeur, the next town, preferably by bus. Otherwise the variant by the Col Chécroui is to be recommended.

Chécroui at Plan Chécroui. The main trail descends directly to Courmayeur, passing through the charming village of Dolonne. Courmayeur provides all facilities and there is a daily bus from here back to Chamonix, as well as buses up the Val Ferret towards the Swiss frontier.

Courmayeur to Champex

There are two options to get out of town and up the Val Ferret. The shortest is to walk or bus up the valley itself. However, the true TMB leaves town by the back road just beyond the church, which leads to Villair. The path continues up the Val Sapin to the Col Sapin (2436m/7992ft). The best way, though, is to go steeply left up to the Rifugio Bertone (1991m/6532ft) – Chalets du Pré on some maps. From just above here there are fantastic views, especially of the Grandes Jorasses. Mont Saxe provides a very fine ridge walk, with soaring cliffs and tumbling glaciers on the other side of the valley, and it comes down to rejoin the TMB at the Col Sapin.

Heading round the back of the Tête Entre Deux Sauts summit, you descend through meadows past the new Rifugio Walter Bonatti to La Vachey and some wonderful restaurants – (the polenta is definitely worth stopping for). At this stage you hit the road, joining up with the alternative Val Ferret route, and continue along the road to Arnuva from where the next objective is the Swiss border. An easy track leads to the rather smart Rifugio Elena. Constructed in the early 1990s, this hut is large and impressive and is perched opposite the Aiguille de Leschaux (3759m/12333ft), the Aiguille de Triollet (3870m/12697ft) and the attractive summit of Mont Dolent (3823m/12543ft), meeting point of France, Switzerland and Italy.

The climb up from here to the next pass is much easier than might be expected: relatively steep, but less rocky than the rest of the trek so far and if you stick to the most well-worn zigzags then it goes very well. You soon arrive at an obvious viewpoint from where the Grand Col Ferret is clearly visible. Looking north you'll see the Petit Col Ferret, which is a less frequented and steeper option for this stage. Your path continues, much flatter, to arrive at the Swiss border at 2537m (8324ft). All this will seem quite straightforward on a normal dry and sunny day. However, beware – this section changes drastically in the wet. The consequences of slipping on these paths are more amusing or embarrassing than dangerous, but the Grand Col Ferret is one big mud slide in inclement weather. A nice diversion from the col is a quick ascent of the Tête de Ferret (2714m/8905ft) which gives even better views of the Swiss peaks ahead.

SWISS SECTION

Descending, you are immediately conscious that things feel different. The general ambience is more pastoral, green meadows, no longer the towering peaks, and, if you're lucky, masses of starry blue gentians, edelweiss if you look hard and, lower down, orange hawksbeard, asters and sainfoin. Descend past the *alpage* of La Peule and arrive on a wide jeep track. This leads down to the valley, but you'll get there a lot quicker if you keep your eyes open for the red arrows marking the short cuts. For those who enjoy jogging down this can be a blast, especially when combined with a refreshing dip in the river at the bottom.

Ferret has a couple of hotels, at least one of which also has dormitory accommodation, but many people go on to La Fouly for the night, where there are shops, a post office, *gîtes*, hotels and a campsite. A bus service runs from Ferret down the valley to Orsières, where connections are possible to Martigny and Champex.

From Ferret to La Fouly there is a footpath along the river, or you can stroll down the road. The advantage of this latter option is that you get to see a remarkable contraption, just by the hamlet of Le Clou, which is amazingly simple and clever at the same time – a post adorned with metal tubes,

Checking out the local specialities near Les Contamines.

carefully angled, allows you to easily identify all the peaks within sight – if it's clear.

The TMB now becomes a pleasant stroll across the river and through larch forest and alder bushes, going very close to the Dalle d'Amone, a famous rock climbing site. The path is well marked and has been re-routed to stay high above the river, which floods impressively in heavy rain. You emerge from the woods at a track on the outskirts of the traditional old village of Praz de Fort. Follow the main road through here until you get to the centre of the village, where a right turn will take you past some ancient farm buildings, testimony to hundreds of years of farming in this area.

A lovely tranquil section follows, to be savoured for as long as possible. The back road goes through the village of Les Arlaches, where an intriguing sign informs one that this is the Swiss customs post. The village is charming, and the vegetable gardens impressive. Meadows of wild flowers or hay, depending on the season, border the track, and it's just slightly downhill. That said, don't look too far ahead or you'll spy the buildings of Champex, your next objective, rather depressingly high up on the hill. Make the most of the hamlet of Issert, where the path rejoins the main road, with its waterwheel and café.

Strolling into Praz de Fort.

Cross the road and take a deep breath – the next bit to Champex is up! The problem with the Swiss Val Ferret is that most of it is so gentle that it's easy to get into a nice strolling rhythm, and then this relatively short climb can feel disproportionately hard. It's almost inevitable that you'll arrive here early afternoon, a bit drowsy after lunch, at the hottest time of day, when your body's really hoping that you'll let it lie down in a meadow for a while. The path is good and although it can be a bit hot and sticky in the trees, there are some good places to take a break. If you choose the right one you'll enjoy superb views down the valley to Orsières.

Champex is in a class of its own on the TMB. An upmarket resort, it caters equally well for the well-heeled tourist wanting to stroll along the attractive shore of the immaculate lake and the sweaty, boot-clad hiker looking for a *gîte* and a cold beer. The cafés are all delightful, and by this stage of the trek it's a real treat to sit by the lake, eating an ice-cream extravaganza. All necessary facilities are available, including a couple of *gîtes* offering dormitory accommodation. There are also plush hotels if that's your wont, and a campsite. A bus service runs to Orsières and onwards to Martigny.

Champex to Argentière

When you manage to tear yourself away from this oasis, walk up the road to the track leading off left to the Val d'Arpette. Here a final decision must be made. The track left is for the high-level variant over the Fenêtre d'Arpette. The normal route goes 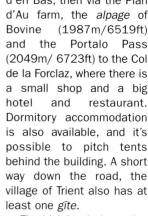 straight on to Champex d'en Bas, then via the Plan d'Au farm, the *alpage* of Bovine (1987m/6519ft) and the Portalo Pass (2049m/ 6723ft) to the Col de la Forclaz, where there is a small shop and a big hotel and restaurant. Dormitory accommodation is also available, and it's possible to pitch tents behind the building. A short way down the road, the village of Trient also has at least one *gîte*.

The high-level alternative path should not be attempted too early in the season, when steep *nevé* can remain on either side of the pass, nor in bad weather. However, in fine dry conditions, when you know the snow has gone, it can be the highlight of the trek.

A tempting chairlift goes up from the start of the Arpette track, but unless you want to visit the Cabane d'Orny, don't take this – it just looks as if it goes your way. Only a few hundred metres up the track, a path leads off to the right under the chairlift. Signposted variously to 'Petit Ruisseau' or 'Arpette', this is the nicest trail to follow. It ambles alongside a man-made irrigation channel (*bisse*). The clear bubbling waters gushing down in the shady forest provide a haven of freshness on a hot day. Then, suddenly, you arrive on the jeep track again and are greeted by a magnificent view. With the route heading back towards the high mountains, directly ahead of you are the spiky summits of the Pointe d'Orny (3269m/10715ft) and the Pointe des Ecandies (2796m/9174ft). There is a cluster of buildings here, the Relais d'Arpette, including restaurant, dormitories, rooms and a campsite. This is the last accommodation before Trient.

The crux of this stage, the Fenêtre d'Arpette (2665m/8744ft), is out of sight from here, but is only slightly lower than the Col des Ecandies, clearly visible as the lowest point on the ridge straight ahead.

The path from Arpette takes you up the valley, becoming progressively narrower, steeper and rockier. If you've chosen to tackle this climb in the early morning, you'll have welcome shade for much of the way, and will certainly be accompanied by the shriek of marmots. Be sure not to miss the right turn, leaving the trail to the Col des Ecandies, to traverse around the mountainside. The pass finally comes into view – it looks dauntingly distant and high from here so take in the sideways' views instead! Teasingly, the col peeks out then disappears for some time until finally the traversing is over and you find yourself in an area strewn with boulders. The red-and-white flashes draw you on and the pass starts to look encouragingly closer. The final obstacle is a deceivingly short-looking zigzag section before you arrive at the small rocky notch of the Fenêtre d'Arpette.

Views are great in all directions. Behind you the sun will have risen fully by now, outlining the distant peaks in a misty glow. The other side of the col reveals a completely different world. The Trient glacier tumbles down in a chaotic mass from the high peaks of the Aiguille du Tour (3544m/ 11628ft), the Aiguille Purtscheller (3478m/ 11411ft) and the Tête Blanche (3422m/11227ft). Far off to the northwest is the distinctive dammed lake of Emosson, where dinosaur tracks are to be found on the wild limestone slopes. Behind this are the peaks of the Tour Sallière (3219m/10561ft) and Mont Ruan (3044m/9987ft). If you arrive here in good time you may be able to spot tiny figures making their way down from the summit of the Aiguille du Tour, probably the most popular high mountain for novices in the area.

The way down is steep and rocky, and requires care, especially in wet or cold conditions. Watch out for hidden icy sections, since this west-facing slope may not have seen any sun at the time you start descending. There are almost always numerous parties toiling up this path, and you'll doubtless be glad your own ascent is over, although sore knees will complain on this relentless slope. You will certainly stop often, the glacier being so very compelling with its twisting, ever-changing crevasses and the myriad colours of the ice.

Soon you lose sight of the high summits as height is quickly lost, heading into the valley below. When you reach the main trail, which will probably take much longer than you expect, turn right and descend for another ten minutes to the Chalet du Glacier, where welcome refreshments are available in the season. It's possible to head out from here in forty-five minutes to the Col de la Forclaz (hotel/gîte) and the main road from Martigny to the French border, where a summer bus service runs infrequently.

From the chalet the nearest accommodation is in Trient, just fifteen minutes away. For those who don't need to go to Trient, the best way from the bridge is to head left and up to the alpage of Les Grands. However, this Swiss Alpine Club refuge is private, so Trient is the only place to stay in these parts. The path from Les Grands takes a wonderful high-level traverse around the hillside to the Col de Balme, but it's long and combined with the Fenêtre d'Arpette makes for a very arduous day.

From Trient the TMB heads south, back out of the village, to disappear almost immediately into the forest. A well-graded zigzag path climbs up and up. Emerging from the forest you finally get to see the long-awaited Col de Balme, at 2191m (7189ft) the gateway back to France, and if you started in Argentière this will be your last pass. The path is easier now and, as you approach, the Refuge de Balme comes into view. When you can see the colour of its shutters you know you're getting close and when you can see your cold beer waiting on the table outside you've cracked it. Before the drink though you'll doubtless be stopped in your tracks by the amazing views. You've returned to the Mont Blanc massif and you'll be able to recognise all those peaks you became so familiar with on the first part of the tour, so many days ago. The refuge is a working alpage, but provides food and drinks.

Either take the easy track down past the ski pistes and the lifts to the village of Le Tour, reputedly the snowiest village in the Alps, or throw ethics to the wind and take the lift. Le Tour has a bar and a church with limited accommodation. Down in the village of Montroc, fifteen minutes away, there is a hotel. There's also a gîte at Tré le Champ, reached by taking the path behind the railway tunnel entrance. To get to Argentière from Montroc village follow the road to the second bridge over the river. To avoid taking the main road stay on the true left side of the river, to follow the quiet back road down to Argentière, coming out at the church. Then celebrate!

The snowy dome of Mont Blanc's French face provides a relatively straightforward climb compared to the steeper slopes of the Italian face. Route 1 is the Goûter Route; Route 2 is the Grands Mulets Descent Route.

PEAK: MONT BLANC

The highest peak in Western Europe is inevitably very popular and the only way you'll usually get the summit to yourself is either to go out of season or in bad weather, or to arrive there very late or extremely early. For many people Mont Blanc is the peak to do, and it's certainly the one your friends at home will have heard of. The views are wonderful; after all you're higher than everything else around, and all the massif peaks are very close – the Aiguille Verte and the Grandes Jorasses are particularly prominent. On a clear day you can see for many miles, to the other high mountain ranges all around, and also over to the French and Italian plains.

Mont Blanc was originally climbed from Chamonix via the Grands Mulets. Nowadays this

CLIMB ESSENTIALS

SUMMIT Mont Blanc (4807m/15772ft).

PRINCIPAL HUTS Refuge du Goûter 3817m (12524ft), Refuge des Cosmiques 3613m (11854ft), Refuge des Grands Mulets 3051m (10010ft).

GRADE All the routes described here are PD, but be aware that conditions can vary.

HEIGHT GAIN 990m (3248ft) for Goûter route; 1372m (4502ft) for the Three Mont Blancs routes.

APPROXIMATE TIME 4–5 hours for the Goûter route; $4^{1}/_{2}$–7 hours for the Three Mont Blancs routes.

MAP 1:25 000 IGN Top 25 3630 Chamonix, 3531 ET St Gervais.

route is frequented in winter on skis, or as a descent, but for the ascent there are safer options. The normal routes from the French side are the most amenable, and two possibilities present themselves, one technically easier though more hazardous than the other.

The Goûter Route

The Tramway de Mont Blanc from Le Fayet takes you up to the Nid d'Aigle at 2372m (7782ft). This railway can be joined by taking the Bellevue cable car from Les Houches. From the Nid d'Aigle follow the path to just before the Tête Rousse refuge, then head up diagonally across the small glacier to reach the Grand Couloir, which must be crossed and regularly raked by stonefall. Be very careful here, go early and quickly and wear a helmet. Easy scrambling up the ridge, with a few cables towards the top, leads you to the Refuge du Goûter (3817m/ 12524ft). This hut gets very crowded in the season and a reservation is essential.

Relatively flat ground begins the next day, steepening towards the Dôme de Goûter, which is passed on the left to reach the Col du Dôme (4237m/13901ft). Next you'll pass the emergency shelter of the Refuge du Vallot (4362m/ 14312ft) and you'll feel you should be almost there. However, you've got the Grande Bosse (4513m/14807ft) and the Petite Bosse (4547m/14919ft), before reaching the narrow summit crest. The ridge can get rather crowded on busy days and great care should be taken as most people you meet will be tired and perhaps not too keen to make way. Descend by the same route, or by the Grands Mulets, described below.

The Three Mont Blancs Route (Mont Blanc du Tacul, Mont Maudit and Mont Blanc)

This route has become increasingly popular since the construction of the Cosmiques refuge some years ago, and also because of the risk of stonefall in the Goûter couloir. But it is a long way and conditions can vary dramatically on Mont Blanc du Tacul and Mont Maudit. The first day is very short, from the top of the Aiguille du Midi cable car to the Refuge des Cosmiques (3613m/11854ft). The next day you follow the well-worn track up the glaciated north face of Mont Blanc du Tacul, missing the summit by traversing round the shoulder to go to the Col

Maudit (4035m/ 13239ft). Sometimes huge crevasses and seracs form on this face and make for a difficult passage, which can cause traffic jams.

From the col you traverse onto the steep north face of Mont Maudit and take the easiest way through the sometimes dangerous seracs, again missing the summit to go to the Col du Mont Maudit (4345m/14254ft). A slightly descending traverse leads to the Col de la Brenva (4303m /14118ft). The Mur de la Côte is a final obstacle before the last interminable slope, which is a grind for tired bodies, and the final pull to the summit can often seem to take an eternity.

Grands Mulets Descent Route

It is sometimes safer to descend by this route, either to avoid the Goûter couloir later in the day, or the Three Mont Blancs traverse if you found there to be a steep section you're not happy to descend.

However, the Grands Mulets descent is long. The Jonction, where the two upper branches of the Bossons Glacier meet, is extremely crevassed and complex, and late in the season the crevasses are likely to be very open. Follow the Goûter route down as far as the Col du Dôme, then turn right to reach the Grand Plateau at around 4000m (13124ft). A steeper section leads to the Petit Plateau. Race across this and the next steep section, as there are menacing seracs overhead.

At around 3250m (10663ft), depending on the state of the glacier, head right towards the Grands Mulets Refuge, continuing straight down, then right through the chaos of the Jonction. Leave the glacier shortly before the Gare des Glaciers, at about 2500m (8202ft), and pick up the path going under the north face of the Aiguille du Midi, across the dry Glacier des Pélerins and then down to the Plan de l'Aiguille cable car.

The Mont Blanc massif seen from the Aiguilles Rouges.

TREK 10: TOUR DES AIGUILLES ROUGES

The Aiguilles Rouges is the name given to the range of mountains on the western side of the Chamonix valley, opposite the Mont Blanc massif. It is a fabulous place to walk for the views alone – Mont Blanc and its associated peaks are seen in all their splendour from here.

The Tour des Aiguilles Rouges can be done as a four- or five-day trek, beginning on the southern side of the range, but then heading into the wilder northern area. It includes the ascent of Mont Buet, known locally as the 'Mont Blanc des Dames' (the Ladies Mont Blanc), being at 3096m (10158ft) considerably smaller than the real thing, but nevertheless a fine challenge, and a wonderful summit – just the thing for a 'lady'!

The Aiguilles Rouges range now has few remaining glaciers, and features largely rocky peaks, attaining a maximum height of around 3000m (9843ft). The area is designated a nature reserve so any development is regulated. It does, however, have two ski resorts on its south-facing slopes and the relative ease of access provided by the ski lifts, coupled with the views, means that the southern side of the Aiguilles Rouges is quite busy. But as soon as the walker drops over to the north-facing slopes, there are far fewer people, and the area is much more of a wilderness.

Vallorcine to Lac Blanc

I suggest this tour is begun in the tiny hamlet of Le Buet, in the Vallorcine valley, since this is where it finishes. A good track leads up from Le Buet, on the far side of the railway line and the river, to the Col des Montets (1461m/4793ft). From here a well made path heads up in switchbacks into the Aiguilles Rouges. It flattens out on the broad rounded ridge of La Remuaz and you pass the tempting Lacs des Chéserys on the way up to Lac Blanc. There are usually lots of people here during the day, drawn by the stunning views, but in the evening

TREK ESSENTIALS

LENGTH 4 or 5 days.
ACCESS Start and finish in Le Buet in the Vallorcine valley, on main railway line Chamonix-Vallorcine-Martigny.
HIGHEST POINT Mont Buet (3096m/10158ft).
MAPS 1:50 000: Didier Richard 8 Mont Blanc.
1:25 000: Top 25 3630 OT Chamonix, 3630 ET Samoëns.
TREK STYLE Mountain refuges available each night, wardened June to September, reservation essential at Pierre à Bérard.
FURTHER OPTIONS Mont Buet by the normal route, which does not involve exposed ground: from the Refuge Moëde d'Anterne go northeast over the Col de Salenton, then follow the often snowy path around the Aiguille de Salenton and up to the summit; descend the same way to the Refuge de la Pierre à Bérard. Ascent of Aiguille Crochues from La Flegère; Ascent of Aiguille du Belvedere from Lac Blanc - this scramble is exposed and requires a rope.

calm returns and this is a great spot from which to watch the dying rays of the sun on the mountains. The dominant feature is the Aiguille Verte (4122m/13524ft), with the Dru (3754m/12317ft) in the foreground. The Refuge du Lac Blanc was rebuilt in 1991, after the old building was destroyed by avalanche, and the new hut is very attractive, set in a much safer position. Keep your eyes open in the evening and you are likely to see ibex roaming the nearby slopes at dusk.

Lac Blanc to Refuge Moëde d'Anterne

The path from Lac Blanc descends easily to La Flégère, where the first ski lifts are encountered.

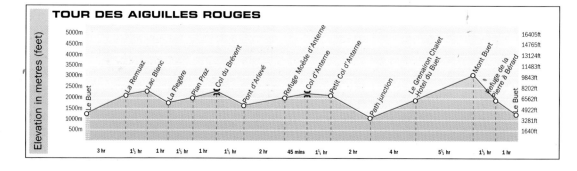

TOUR DES AIGUILLES ROUGES

Elevation in metres (feet)

Escape these quickly by the pleasant traverse which leads around the mountainside to Plan Praz. This path undulates slightly, but is relatively flat and allows a full appreciation of the panorama ahead. The slopes are carpeted in alpenrose, which in July will be blooming with pink flowers, whilst later in the season your progress will be hindered by the masses of bilberries bordering the trail – purple tongues are a real giveaway! Plan Praz is part of the Brévent ski area, and is also a major take-off zone for paragliders. Take the time to watch them as you enjoy refreshments here. This is the last real civilisation you'll see for a while.

A choice presents itself – either walk up to the Col du Brévent (2368m/7769ft), or take the second stage of the cable car to the top of the Brévent (2525m/8284ft), and walk round the back to the col. The view changes immediately you get to the pass, where you leave behind the chaos of Chamonix: the dark depths of the Diosaz gorge lie immediately below, and ahead are the impressive limestone walls of the Rochers des Fiz. South and west is the Arve valley, stretching away hazily towards the Geneva plains, to the southeast the ever-present snowy peaks of the Mont Blanc massif and to the north is the large rounded summit of Mont Buet.

The path descends gently towards the gorge, amongst alpenrose and juniper bushes, passing the ruins of old shepherds' buildings. Your destination is visible on the other side of the valley, where the *alpage* buildings, the Chalets de Moëde, can be seen, and the refuge is not far beyond.

Descend all the way to the Pont d'Arlevé at 1597m (5240ft), and then head up through flowery meadows to the Refuge Moëde d'Anterne, also marked as the Refuge du Col d'Anterne on some maps. It commands a superb view of the massif,

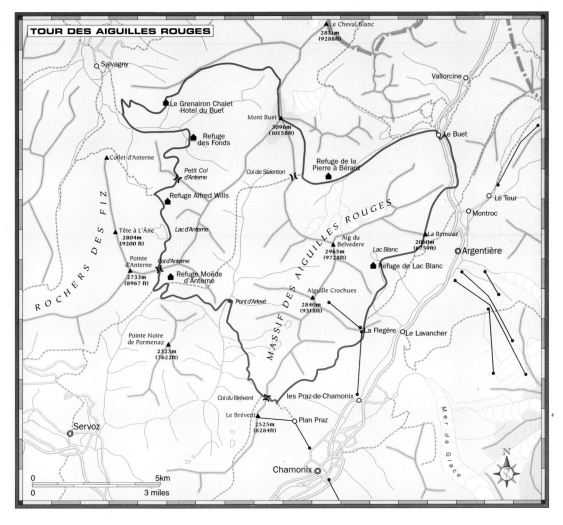

and is large and well equipped, having been enlarged and improved these last years.

Refuge Moëde d'Anterne to Le Grenairon Chalet-Hotel du Buet

From Moëde d'Anterne a choice must be made. There are two different possibilities for the ascent of Mont Buet on this trek, one considerably more demanding technically than the other. If you are not happy on exposed ground, protected by cables, then take the option described in 'Trek Essentials' on p100. The harder variant described here involves steep and committing terrain, and should not be attempted in anything but perfect weather, with no remaining snow on the slopes.

The way goes over the Col d'Anterne (2257m/7405ft) and into the splendid Plateau d'Anterne, where the lake lies sheltered by the huge rocky ramparts of the Rochers des Fiz. The Refuge d'Anterne Alfred Wills (named after a British alpinist, a founder member of the Alpine Club who wrote prolifically about his Alpine exploits and who also came to search for fossils in this area) provides a convenient morning-coffee stop, but don't linger too long before continuing up to the Petit Col d'Anterne (2038m/6687ft).

The scenery changes quite dramatically as you leave the idyllic pastoral meadows of the plateau and head down through steep forested slopes to the Refuge des Fonds. Another refreshment stop presents itself, before pressing on down the valley. Don't dwell too much on the map here since you'll be frustrated at having to descend to go back up to Le Grenairon Chalet-Hotel du Buet. The way up to

Nearing the summit of Mont Buet, having climbed from the Bérard valley.

the refuge is steep and you don't emerge from the trees until just before the refuge at 1974m (6477ft). This is quite a climb, so it's important to pace this day carefully and not spend too much time sunbathing on the plateau!

Le Grenairon Chalet-Hotel du Buet to Refuge de la Pierre à Bérard

The next day is the big one and if the weather is not set fair for the day don't hesitate to head back to Moëde d'Anterne and down to Servoz in the Chamonix valley. This route up Mont Buet – 'La Route des Crêtes' – should not be attempted in anything other than excellent conditions, both of the weather and the walkers. The path is immediately rough and steep as it heads up the Frêtes du Grenier and for the first part is exposed, becoming slightly less so after the summit of La Cathédrale (2531m/8304ft). A traverse leads to another steep climb up to the ridge, arriving just below the summit of the Pointe de Genevrier (2870m/9416ft).

Now comes the Arête du Buet, the north ridge of the peak, equipped in part with cables. The terrain climbed is quite steep in places, but the difficulty is minimal, so long as there is no remaining *nevé*. After the cabled section, the angle eases and a rounded ridge leads to the summit at 3096m (10158ft) and fantastic views. There is a superb panorama in all directions, and Mont Blanc is seen in all its splendour from here, towering over the neighbouring peaks

The descent is by the normal route up the mountain, and the path is good, but in bad weather it would nevertheless be easy to lose your way here. The upper part, as far as the Col de Salenton, is often snowy even in midsummer and there are some steep sections lower down where tired legs will complain – more than 1000m (over 3000ft) must be descended to reach the Refuge de la Pierre à Bérard.

Refuge de la Pierre à Bérard to Vallorcine

Although it's only another hour and a half to the valley from here, the refuge could be welcome after the long summit day. Then the descent of the charming Bérard valley can be savoured slowly, with frequent stops in the sun by the river, rather than hurrying down, tired and ready to finish the day.

Amble down the valley, accompanied by the bubbling brook, to Le Buet. Just before emerging from the valley don't miss the view of the big waterfall: at the small Café de la Cascade follow the way behind the café and through the rocks to a superb viewpoint opposite and below the waterfall. Whilst

PEAK: AIGUILLES CROCHUES

CLIMB ESSENTIALS

SUMMIT Aiguilles Crochues (2840m/9318ft).
GRADE Normal route PD, east face AD.
HEIGHT GAIN FROM INDEX CHAIRLIFT 455m (1493ft)
APPROXIMATE TIME 2½–3 hours
MAP 1:25 000 IGN Top 25 3630 OT Chamonix.

Situated in the Aiguilles Rouges, on the west side of the Chamonix valley, the traverse of the Aiguilles Crochues provides a fine rocky traverse, at a very moderate level, with a short snow slope to descend at the end. It can be done in a day by using the cable car and the Index chairlift at La Flegère.

From the top of the chairlift follow the path around the hillside heading northeast, to then zigzag up to the Col des Crochues (2704m/8872ft). Follow the vague path right from the col to a chimney in the west side of the ridge of the Petites Crochues. From the top of the chimney easy slabs and ridges lead over the Pointe Sud des Crochues to the main summit (2840m/9318ft). It is also possible to gain the Petite Crochue by climbing its attractive east face, which is reached by a ledge system leading out of the gully under the Col des Crochues. The route follows a rightwards traverse, a chimney, then a ramp, followed by a steep wall in four pitches.

Continue along the ridge from the summit to the Col des Dards (2790m/9148ft) and descend

the usually snowy slope to Lac Blanc. In good conditions this slope can be 'glissaded', but be careful as boulders lie below, which can catch you, or the snow could be slippier than expected and you could arrive more quickly than desired at the bottom. If in doubt, wear crampons and descend slowly. From Lac Blanc a good trail takes you back to the cable car.

Heading up to the Col des Crochues in winter.

you're there take a look at Farinet's cave – Farinet lived in the 18th century, and was allegedly famous for forging money which he gave to the poor. He managed to avoid capture with the help of friendly villagers who protected him whilst he was hiding out in caves.

The last section down to Le Buet takes you past some of the oldest dwellings in the Vallorcine valley, which are now being renovated as summer residences, and you arrive at the main road just next to the well placed bar of the Hôtel du Buet.

ALPINE TOADFLAX (LINARIA ALPINA)

This flower sports the wonderful combination of orange and purple, in some of the tiniest and most intensely coloured flowers you'll find in the Alps. It is especially amazing as it grows in the most barren and uninviting ground you can imagine. Gravel, scree, boulders - this is where you'll find alpine toadflax, forming a small cushion, its long slender roots just under the surface sometimes attached to neighbouring plants for greater purchase against the harsh conditions. Alpine toadflax can be found throughout the Alps above 1500m (4922ft), but seems to favour the higher altitudes, the more hostile the location the better, and has been found as high as 4200m (13780ft) on the Rimpfischhorn in Switzerland.

TREK 11: THE DINOSAUR TRACKS OF EMOSSON

The dinosaur tracks above the Vieux Emosson lake were discovered in 1976 by a French geologist. They date from the Triassic period, 200–230 million years ago when dinosaurs were relatively new on the earth. These dinosaurs were still quite small creatures and the footprints are about the size of a large hand. The fact that they remained undiscovered until so recently is a testament to the wildness of this area, and when I first saw the tracks ten years ago it was still necessary to search them out among the rocky slabs above the lake.

TREK ESSENTIALS

LENGTH 2 days, or 1 if starting at Emosson itself.
ACCESS Start and finish at Le Buet, or start at Emosson and finish at Le Buet.
HIGHEST POINT Col des Corbeaux (2603m/8540ft).
MAPS 1:50 000: Didier Richard 8 Mont Blanc.
1:25 000: IGN Top 25 3630 OT Chamonix.
TREK STYLE Dormitory accommodation at Refuge de Vieux Emosson.
LANGUAGE French.
FURTHER OPTIONS From the Refuge de Vieux Emosson it's possible to ascend the Cheval Blanc then continue along the ridge to the summit of Mont Buet (3096m/10158ft). This is very exposed and involves a short equipped section. Note that descent from Mont Buet directly into the Tré les Eaux valley is not possible, so either return to the Cheval Blanc and go over the Col des Corbeaux, or take the normal route down from Mont Buet into the Bérard valley.

The last few years have seen some development in this area and the owners of the Emosson dam have recognised the potential of the site and also the need to protect the footprints. During the summer season you'll have no trouble finding the tracks as the site is fenced off and there are explanatory signs and even an on-site guide to give further details. However, don't let this put you off – the area is still worth a visit, especially if the walk

described here is undertaken, since the Emosson lakes are beautiful, and the descent via the largely unspoilt Tré les Eaux valley is very special.

This walk should only be tackled well into the summer season, when all the snow below 3000m (9843ft) has gone, since earlier you won't see the dinosaur tracks (they don't come out in the snow) and the descent to the Tré les Eaux valley would not be advisable in anything other than perfect summer conditions.

Emosson can be reached by car, or by a combination of funicular and train from Chatelard, just on the Swiss side of the Franco–Swiss border. The funicular is quite exciting, reputedly ascending slopes at 87° (they say this is the steepest funicular in the world). It was built in 1920 to aid the construction of the Barberine dam, and has now been renovated for the transport of visitors.

This walk can be done in a day if you take transport early to Emosson. However, I think it is best done as a two-day tour, by walking from the small hamlet of Le Buet, just near Vallorcine, the last French village before the Swiss frontier.

Le Buet to Vieux Emosson

From the car park at Le Buet, a footpath leads alongside the railway down into the village of Vallorcine. At the railway station cross the main road and walk towards the church, then onwards to Le Mollard. Take the forest footpaths towards

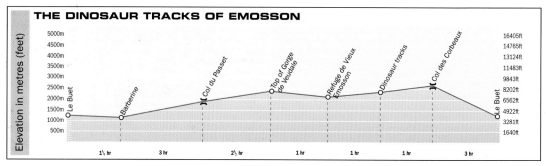

THE DINOSAUR TRACKS OF EMOSSON

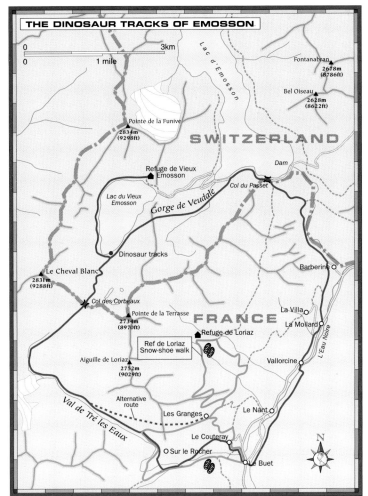

THE DINOSAUR TRACKS OF EMOSSON

Looking across the lake to the north you can see the little-visited summits of Mont Ruan and the Tour Sallière, where Jacques Balmat, one of the first climbers of Mont Blanc in 1786, went looking for gold and never returned. To the west is the Pointe de la Funive and south-west is the striking rocky spire of the Aiguille du Van.

As you walk over the dam look carefully and you'll spot an unlikely line of artificial climbing holds snaking up the most impressive part of the wall. If you're lucky there may even be people climbing this, one of the more audacious man-made climbing structures around.

You need to get to the old Emosson lake and there are two possible routes. One is to follow the tarmac road, closed to cars, that leads through tunnels to the lake. If you've walked from Vallorcine and are tired this is probably the best bet since it brings you out at the Vieux Emosson refuge, where you can spend the night. Far more secluded, however, is the Gorge de Veudale, the path for which breaks off on the left soon after the dam. This valley is a delight — quiet, with abundant flowers and the ever-present shriek of marmots. If you are doing the two-day tour this path can still be taken, but it will be necessary to walk around the old lake to the refuge, then back again the next morning — about forty-five minutes each way.

Barberine, heading off left at the signs for the waterfall (*cascade*) and the Col du Passet. The waterfall is worth a look, before embarking on the steep climb up to the impressive Emosson dam. As you ascend, the views open up behind you, and from the Col du Passet the panorama is rewarding. You don't need to go on to the dam itself, but I recommend that you do. Don't panic when you arrive at the big lake with hoards of other people — the majority won't venture beyond the lake. The place is justifiably popular, with its magnificent views of the Mont Blanc massif, and the splendour of the 150-m (492-ft) dam itself, which is designed to hold back 225 million cubic metres of water.

Constructed in 1975 in a joint Swiss–French operation, this dam replaced the smaller Barberine dam which was built in 1926. A third dam forms the Vieux Emosson lake – the old lake. Even though the area has been radically changed by man, it somehow retains a sense of wilderness.

Leave only footprints!

The Emosson Lake is surrounded by wild, unfrequented mountains.

The Veudale path is not always obvious, but small cairns mark the way. After an hour or so the valley gives way to a barren rocky ridge. The old lake is just below, and ahead are the summits forming this cirque, notably the Cheval Blanc (2831m/9288ft), the Tête de Grenairon (2647m/8685ft) and the Pointe de la Funive (2834m/9298ft).

Nowadays it's not difficult to spot the site of the dinosaur tracks – green posts and chain-link fencing being a bit of a giveaway – but don't forget that this is the most important site of its kind known at present in Europe and the footprints need to be protected from people clambering all over them, otherwise they will soon be destroyed.

Some 230 million years ago the region that was to become the alpine chain was part of a vast zone covered by water of variable depth in which, for tens of thousands of years, sediments had been accumulating. The layer of rock in which the tracks are fossilised was a sandy beach at the edge of a vast expanse of submerged land. There are very clear fossils of wave marks as well as the footprints and it's incredible to think that these were once on the seashore. This beach, cooled by a breeze from the sea and occasionally submerged at high tides, was highly appreciated and frequently visited by essentially herbivorous dinosaurs. The tracks were made in sand and sediment and some of their footprints hardened and became fossilised, preserved forever.

Around 80 million years ago compressional movements led to the disappearance of the ocean and to the collision of the African and European continental plates, shunting everything upside down and creating the Alps. Rocks formed below sea level were thrown out and landed at considerable altitudes, as seen here.

Vieux Emosson to Le Buet, via Tré les Eaux

From here it's obviously possible to return to the Emosson Lake by the path around the old lake and the road, but the continuation is superb and in good weather it provides a fine outing. The Col des Corbeaux (2603m/8540ft) is straight up ahead, to the south-south-west. Be careful not to confuse it

THE MOUNTAIN OR BLUE HARE

The mountain hare or blue hare, like the ptarmigan with whom it shares its territory, is an expert at camouflage. The colour of its coat changes according to the season, allowing it to merge into its terrain throughout the year. The mountain hare is in fact a survivor from the last Ice Age when most mountain hares followed the retreat of the glaciers, returning to the far north of Europe, whilst a few of them stayed in the Alps where they found a suitable climate.

The mountain hare moults twice a year, once in spring when its coat becomes grey brown, and once in October when it gradually becomes white all over (except for the tips of its long ears which remain black all year). The animal can adapt to either forest or open country, preferring sparsely forested clearings, and it is found anywhere beween about 1400 and 3000m (4593-9843ft). It is a nocturnal creature and in the day will stay hidden near a rock or a tree if possible. In winter its characteristic tracks testify to its wanderings in search of food. The print is shaped like a 'Y': the hare almost always runs or bounds, pushing vigorously off its back feet, which are side by side, and landing on its front feet, one in front of the other. It can achieve speeds of more than 50kph (over 30mph) and jumps of 2m (6$^{1}/_{2}$ft).

The blue hare tends to be solitary, probably because there are not enormous numbers of them in the Alps. Although very shy, they are not, however, troubled by bad weather, being well adapted to a rigorous climate. Their diet consists of vegetation: plants, leaves and flowers in the summer, or dry grass, lichens, moss and seeds in the winter. The hare also feeds on branches, cutting them very neatly with its sharp incisors.

Its main predator is the fox, but also martens and stoats can kill young hares, whilst the golden eagle and the owl are the birds it most fears. A hare can live for up to ten years, but this is exceptional in the wild, where it is in great danger.

The female mountain hare gives birth to between two and five young twice a year, once in May/June and again in August/September. It is this relatively high reproduction rate that enables the species to survive in a dangerous world.

with the Col du Vieux just to the right. A vague path leads up steep scree to the col. To descend into the valley on the far side it's best to try to follow the paint flashes. If you lose them, look carefully at the map and note that the path turns left (south-east) before the base of the valley. This is an exciting and wild place in good weather, but could be a bit of a nightmare in fog. The eastern slopes of Mont Buet on the other side of the valley are impressively steep, and rather sinister.

The path becomes much clearer as it descends into the base of the Tré les Eaux valley. This valley is close to the popular Bérard valley, but is far quieter. Look out for wild columbines and martagon lilies in early summer, and chamois on the slopes on the far side.

The flat valley starts to descend steeply and the path stays on the true left bank. It maintains height as the valley descends and becomes increasingly rocky. A relatively easy *via ferrata* section equipped with cables and chains is passed and more rocks, which can be treacherous in wet conditions, take

you to a short ascent and an obvious resting place. Alpenrose cover the slopes here, providing a carpet of pink flowers in July.

It's decision time: if you're not at home on rocky slabs equipped with cables in a downward mode, take the left-hand path. This is no second-best option, and gives a lovely descent to Le Buet via the hamlet of Les Granges. If you choose the right-hand route be prepared to come back up if you feel wobbly. It involves the descent of a rocky slab, which is well protected with metal cables, chains and pitons to step on, but which it would be unwise to fall off. There is an exposed short traverse to reach the slab, which looks deceptively easy. Children should only be taken this way when roped-up by adults who know what they are doing; dogs might be a problem; and in wet conditions this descent could be very dangerous.

The path continues much more easily alongside the fast-flowing torrent to emerge at the tiny hamlet of Sur le Rocher, and then down through forest to Le Couteray. Le Buet is just up the main road.

SNOW-SHOE WALK: REFUGE DE LORIAZ

<table>
<tr><td>

SNOW-SHOE WALK ESSENTIALS

ACCESS Start and finish at Le Couteray, or Le Buet if going via Sur le Rocher.

DISTANCE 4.75km (3 miles) from le Couteray to Loriaz by the forest track; 3.5km (2¼ miles) from le Couteray via the footpath. The section from Le Buet to Les Granges adds about 3.5km (2¼ miles).

HEIGHT GAIN From le Couteray to Loriaz is 668m (2192ft), from Le Buet it's 690m (2264ft).

APPROXIMATE TIME From Le Couteray via the forest track is 5½ hours return, via the footpath takes about 5 hours and for the Le Buet extension add on another hour.

DIFFICULTY 2.

TYPE OF WALK 1-day round trip, possibly a circuit if conditions are suitable.

INTERESTING FEATURES The Bérard valley, which is magical, especially in deepest winter; the pleasant forest section, and the views of the massif and the Trient peaks.

ADDITIONAL INFORMATION A good short circuit can be made from Le Buet, Vallon de Bérard, Sur le Rocher, Les Granges, Le Couteray, Le Buet.

MAP 1:25 000: Top 25 3630 Chamonix.

</td></tr>
</table>

The Loriaz refuge is a good objective on snow shoes and can be reached in various ways. Either of the summer paths starting in Le Coutéray is possible in the winter, but after heavy snowfall the footpath is threatened by avalanches, especially at the Pont du Nant de Loriaz, and you should stick to the forest track all the way.

A delightful extension of the walk can be had by starting at Le Buet and taking the Vallon de Bérard as far as the bridge over the river at La Vordette. Then double back on the other side of the river to go through the woods to Sur le Rocher. From here head into the Tré les Eaux valley, breaking out of the trees at Les Granges, and then picking up the trail to Loriaz.

From Loriaz the views of the north faces of the Aiguille Verte, the Droites and the Courtes are particularly superb, as are views of the Aiguille du Chardonnet and the Aiguille du Tour. To the south-west is the Vallon de Bérard with the obvious Col de Bérard and Brèche de Bérard at its head. If you have the time you could continue on up to the summit of Le Charmoz (2366m/7763ft) directly north of Loriaz, or take in the Tête de Chevrette (2039m/6690ft) just before you head into the forest on the descent via the forest track.

TREK 12: POINTE NOIRE DE PORMENAZ

The Pointe Noire de Pormenaz (2323m/7617ft) is situated to the north of the Mont Blanc massif on the far side of the Chamonix valley. It can be reached via the Brévent, from where Henri Bénédict de Saussure in 1760 first nurtured what was to become his obsession with Mont Blanc and came to believe that the peak could be climbed. Seen from the Pointe Noire the 'three Mont Blancs' as they are known locally – Mont Blanc du Tacul, Mont Maudit and Mont Blanc itself – are quite simply magnificent. Indeed the views throughout this walk are superb and this trek is included largely for this reason.

Chamonix to Servoz

The walk can easily be done in a day from the top of the Brévent lift system. In this case follow the path around the northern slopes of the Brévent to reach the Col du Brévent (2368m/7769ft). Looking north you'll see the fine rounded summit of Mont Buet (3096m/10158ft), the ascent of which is described in Trek 10 (see Trek Essentials on p100). To the northeast are the rocky ramparts of the Rochers des Fiz and, away below, the Arve valley.

From here the path leads down into the deep, dark depths of the Diosaz gorge. This is a lovely descent, through alder bushs and alpenrose, past the ancient ruins of shepherds' dwellings, and down to the pont d'Arlevé (1597m/5240ft).

In the Alps what goes down first thing in the morning generally has to go back up again, and this walk is no exception. Having lost all that height, you must regain it. The path rises gently through the

Moëde meadows. Above can be seen the impressive Rochers des Fiz, but before reaching these you'll arrive at the Refuge Moëde d'Anterne after a couple of hours of ascent. If you wanted to take two days over this trek then the night would be spent here, allowing the evening light to be enjoyed on the Mont Blanc massif. If this is the plan then it would seem a good idea to walk directly to the Col du Brévent from Plan Praz, the middle station of the Brévent cable car.

Whatever the decision, stop and enjoy refreshments at the hut, which has been renovated in recent years and is run by friendly local people. It is a popular venue – I've even stayed here at the same time as a wedding party. Needless to say it poured with rain and hail.

Onwards from the hut towards your destination, the spectacular Rochers des Fiz contrast beautifully with the rounded green of the Pormenaz site. It's not far to the Pointe Noire from the hut – a couple of kilometres and 300m

Almost at the summit of the Pointe Noire de Pormenaz, with the Lac de Pormenaz below.

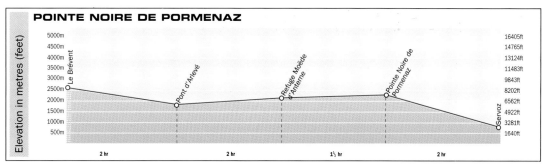

POINTE NOIRE DE PORMENAZ

(about a mile and 1000ft) of ascent. The path is pretty obvious in good weather, but this changes totally in bad conditions. It would be very easy to lose the trail in poor visibility, and it isn't a good idea to head off down into the Diosaz gorge, since it is not possible to descend this without ropes. Every so often, people have epic adventures, both in winter and summer, when they lose their bearings in this area.

The lake is a delightful place to stop, with its border of white cottongrass, and the summit even more so. I don't know why it's the Pointe 'Noire' – I've seen it green in summer, white in early, late and occasionally mid-summer, but never particularly black. The views from here will make you want to stand and stare. The Aiguille Verte and the Aiguilles des Dru are particularly prominent from here, as well as Mont Blanc. The path from the lake to the summit isn't marked on the current IGN Top 25 map, but it's there alright.

When leaving the summit head for the Chalets de Pormenaz to pick up the main trail leading down through the forests to Servoz. This path does get better, but at first it is indistinct in places and this is not a good place to be in thick fog.

The village of Servoz is at 814m (2671ft) altitude, so it isn't difficult to figure out that there is some serious 'down' to be done. This is where the wisdom of a two-day trek becomes apparent: you'll be on the summit well before lunchtime, so will be able to make a leisurely pace for the

rest of the day. As a one-day trip it is perfectly feasible but you need to be sure that both you and your knees realise that by the time you're jogging down the forest trail you'll have covered a lot of ground and the last part could seem like hard work.

Servoz is an attractive village with all amenities, and the railway station at the far end is signposted from the centre. Trains run up the valley to Chamonix fairly regularly until early evening.

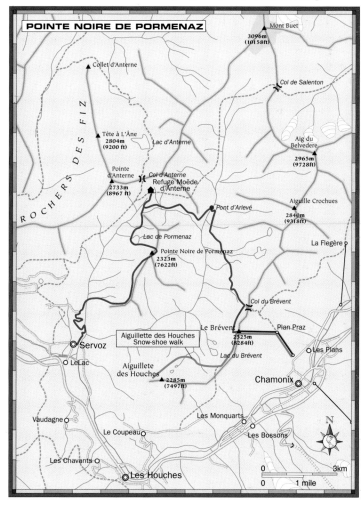

SNOW-SHOE WALK: AIGUILLETTE DES HOUCHES

This has to be the best vantage point in the valley for the massif, and the Aiguillette des Houches (2285m/7493ft) not only benefits from this view but also provides a fantastic snow-shoe summit. Although the Aiguillette can be ascended directly from Le Coupeau without the use of lifts, I recommend taking the Brévent cable cars since they make life much easier and you are soon away from the ski pistes.

Follow the ski piste from the cable car for one zigzag, then duck under the rope marking the edge of the piste. Already you'll be confronted with breathtaking views, not just of the Mont Blanc massif but also of the Rochers des Fiz and the Diosaz gorge. Take the easiest line heading south and staying above the Lac du Brévent. You're aiming to more or less follow the summer path as far as the Tête du Bellachat then to descend to the flat ground under the Aiguillette.

Take a rising traverse westwards to reach the summit, which is the furthest peak to the right. Gentle curves can make this an extremely pleasant ascent in the shade, which should be enjoyed to the full as either the descent to Le Coupeau or the return to Le Brévent are both usually hot and sweaty experiences. From the summit either return by more or less the same route, or descend steep slopes then a forest track to Le Coupeau.

SNOW-SHOE WALK ESSENTIALS

ACCESS Start and finish at Le Brévent, or descend to Le Coupeau above Les Houches.

DISTANCE 3.5km (2¼ miles) from Le Brévent to the summit, 7-km (4½-mile) round trip, or 3.75km (2¼ miles) down to Le Coupeau from the summit.

HEIGHT GAIN 155m (508ft) to ascend the peak, then 380m (1246ft) if you return to Le Brévent.

APPROXIMATE TIME 2–3 hours from Le Brévent to the summit, 3 hours to return to Le Brévent, 1½ hours to descend to Le Coupeau.

DIFFICULTY 3.

TYPE OF WALK 1-day round trip.

INTERESTING FEATURES Views of the Chamonix valley, the Mont Blanc massif, Mont Buet, the Rochers des Fiz, the Aravis, the Chartreuse.

ADDITIONAL INFORMATION Conditions down from Le Brévent can be difficult if, for example, it hasn't snowed for a while. Care must be taken to find a feasible way through the complex terrain, and this can take a lot of time. If you plan to return to Le Brévent you must leave the summit of the Aiguillette by about 1pm as the last cable car down is at 4.30pm (check this on the day). To have to walk down from Le Brévent would not be good. The descent to Le Coupeau takes a steep south-facing slope and in hot weather avalanches are a major risk.

MAP 1:25 000: IGN Top 25 3630 ET Samoëns.

THE ALPENROSE (RHODODENDRON FERRUGINEUM)

This evergreen shrub, of the vast heather family, grows up to 1m (3ft) high and is to be found, often in dense thickets, throughout the Alps from 1500m to 3200m (4921–10499ft). Its generic name Rhododendron comes from the Greek *rhodon* or 'rose' and *dendron* or 'tree'. The pale-to-deep pinkish-red bell-shaped flowers grow in clusters and are in bloom from May until August, depending on the altitude.

Walking along paths bordered by alpenrose is a real joy, and anyone trekking in the Alps should come in July at least once for this experience alone. The mass of pink contrasts wonderfully with the shining high snowy summits and glaciers, and with the green of the pines and larches.

The alpenrose likes humidity, light and also the snow. It spends the winter covered by snow and this protects its leaves from freezing. Any buds that stick out from the snow-cover die, so this regulates the height to which the bushes grow, and you'll not usually find alpenrose of varying height in the same area.

In the past the local mountain people considered this plant to be a toxic parasite and tried unsuccessfully to kill it off by axe and by fire. The other threat to the alpenrose, and to several other alpine plants, is picking. It has been designated a protected species and should, therefore, be admired visually, but not taken home.

TREK 13: LA FOULY TO CHAMONIX

This glacier trek takes you from the Swiss Val Ferret, through some of the most impressive high mountain scenery in the massif, crossing seven glaciers, to descend into France at Le Tour at the head of the Chamonix valley. On the Swiss side there are no lifts, so a sense of wilderness is preserved, and this part of the trek contrasts with the final part when the Mont Blanc summit comes into sight and the whole of the Chamonix valley is spread out at your feet.

La Fouly is an old and traditional village, very popular nowadays with holidaymakers, since it is on the classic Tour du Mont Blanc. It has preserved its charm, however, and many of the visitors stay in the big campsite next to the river.

La Fouly to the Cabane de l'a Neuve

The trek starts just the far side of the campsite, in the forest, where you'll find signs directing you to the first hut of the tour, the Cabane de l'A Neuve. The well-marked, typically Swiss path begins gently, wandering up through the cool forest, leaving the civilisation of La Fouly behind, then gradually steepening, the roar of the torrents on either side increasing as they thunder down from the Glacier de l'A Neuve above. As the path leaves the shelter of the trees and the hot sun begins to make its presence felt, the ground becomes more stony underfoot.

Throughout this lower section of the walk you're constantly aware of the rock wall above, stretching from one side of the valley to the other, guarding access to the upper reaches. A series of chains provides an exciting solution to the apparent impasse, this part of the walk feeling particularly impressive as you sense the immense volume of water thundering over the rocky slabs, just a few feet away. At the top, the rocky promontory on the left provides a welcome resting place and gives the first really close view of the glacier.

The next task, however, is to cross the river. This is achieved, somewhat gingerly, a hundred metres

TREK ESSENTIALS

LENGTH 3-4 days.
ACCESS Start at La Fouly, finish at Le Tour.
HIGHEST POINT Col du Tour (3281m/10765).
MAPS 1:50 000: Carte Nationale de la Suisse 282S Martigny.
1:25 000: Carte Nationale de la Suisse 1345 Orsières, 1344 Col de Balme.
TREK STYLE Glaciated; mountain huts.
LANGUAGES French.
FURTHER OPTIONS Petit Darrey (3508m/11510ft), Aiguilles du Tour (3544m/1168ft and 3542m/11621ft).

(or yards) or so upstream, via a rather flimsy wooden bridge. The path now winds its way up the steep grassy slopes of Les Essettes, leading to the glacial moraine. Far quieter than most areas in the massif, this beautiful wild and rugged cwm has a real feeling of solitude. Far (but not so far) from the madding crowds, it retains a sense of secrecy and is absolutely unspoilt.

Marmots abound as you make your way towards the hut, perched on a rocky shelf high above. At the last moment, just when it looks like you'll have to resort to some technical rock climbing to reach the refuge, the path swings round to the left to traverse back higher up, finally approaching the building by a steep rocky chimney, again equipped with chains. Once at the hut, you are rewarded with a marvellous view: the steep north face of Mont Dolent (3823m/12543ft) not seen in its entirety from any-

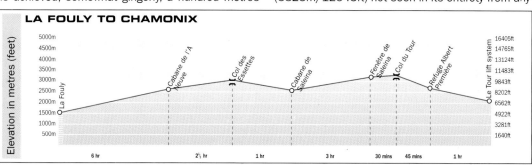

LA FOULY TO CHAMONIX

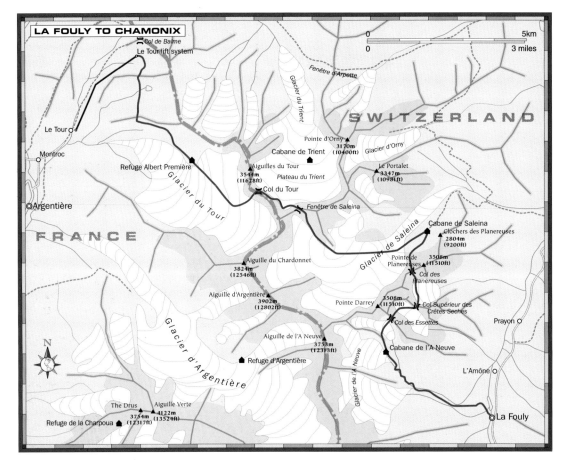

where else and, amazingly, skied down by Pierre Tardivel in 1990; the Aiguille Rouges de Dolent (3823m/12074ft) the Tour Noir (3835m/12583ft) the Aiguille de l'A Neuve (3753m/12313ft) the Grand Lui (3509m/1150ft) and the Grand Darrey (3514m/11529ft) provide an impressive backdrop.

Cabane de l'a Neuve to the Cabane de Saleina

This second day contrasts greatly with the first as you're now really in the mountains and, since much of this section is spent on glaciers, it feels more serious. From the refuge a steep path heads northwest, following the scree and moraine at the edge of the glacier, at first towards the Grand Lui then heading up right under a rock buttress to the base of a long couloir. This couloir can be snow, ice or rock, depending on conditions and leads to the first pass of the day, the Col Supérieur des Essettes (3113m/10214ft) at the base of the southeast ridge of the Grand Darrey.

It's now time to rope up, if you haven't already for the couloir, because for the next few hours the route is entirely on glaciers. As with all glacier

travel the general rule is 'rope up and cover up', so you can say goodbye to the overall suntan for a while. The next objective, the Col Supérieur des Crêtes Seches (3024m/9922ft), can be seen to the northwest across the Glacier de Treutse Bo. This col is unnamed on some maps but is situated on the ridge separating the Treutse Bo and Planereuses glaciers. Care must be taken not to lose too much height in gaining the glacier, which is then contoured to reach the col. The Glacier des Planereuses must next be dealt with in a similar manner – that is, by maintaining height to pass as close as possible under the rocky spur (500m/1640ft) to the north. From here, an optional extra for those seeking more adventure is the Petit Darrey, gained from the Glacier du Darrey and then the rocky northeast ridge to the summit.

The last of the cols for the day is the Col des Planereuses (3030m/9941ft) which is easily attained by a gentle rising traverse to the northwest. From the col a descending traverse, skirting under yet another rocky spur, gains easier snow and bouldery scree leading up to the refuge. The section under the spur is steep and often icy and should be treated with caution.

The Cabane de Saleina is a newly built, roomy hut. Perched high above the glacier on a rocky promontory, it commands a stunning view to the north of the Petit Clocher du Portalet, 200m (656ft) of soaring golden granite, smooth and sheer. Looking west from the Petit Clocher, its parent peak the Portalet (3347m/10981ft), the granite towers of the aptly named Aiguilles Dorées (3509m/ 11513ft), the Aiguille du Chardonnet (3824m/ 12546ft) and, lastly, the north and usually hidden east faces of the Aiguille d'Argentière (3902m/ 12802ft) dominate this remote postion.

This section takes about half a day, so you may be tempted to press on. There are, however, several good reasons for stopping at the hut. Firstly, glacier travel is, by its very nature, inherently dangerous, to a greater or lesser degree depending on conditions. Late in the season the glaciers become very open, making even popular routes extremely risky. The dangers can be reduced to a minimum by practising safe ropework, moving reasonably quickly, picking sensible ways across the glaciers and by crossing them as early in the day as possible. In this case, having walked for about four hours, (unless a very early start is made, in which case little may have been seen), by the time you reach the Saleina hut the sun will be hot and the snow soft. So it's wise to stop and make the most of the pleasures that the Saleina hut has to offer. Which brings me to the second reason for ending the second day here, for what could be better than sitting in the sun, surveying this beautiful tranquil side of the Argentière massif, whilst consuming copious cold drinks on the terrace?

Cabane de Saleina to Le Tour

The third section offers a number of options, all of which finally lead into the Chamonix valley, via more or less circuitous routes. Although the Col du Chardonnet, the Fenêtre du Tour or even the less than direct Col des Plines give equally spectacular and rewarding routes, my chosen itinerary is to join the well-known Three Cols Tour, taking in the Fenêtre de Saleina (3261m/11699ft) and the Col du Tour (3281m/10765ft) and finally arriving at the charming village of Le Tour at the head of the valley.

The Fenêtre de Saleina is at the top of the northerly branch of the Saleina glacier, defined by the granite spires of the Petite Fourche (3512m/ 11523ft) and the Aiguilles Dorées. A relatively easy pass, it claims such famous names as M. Charlet, J.D. Forbes and A. Balmat among its early climbers.

Its prestigious history and popularity are warranted since it gives access to the Plateau du Trient, impressively glaciated and dominated to the west by the double summits of the Aiguilles du Tour (3544m/11628ft and 3542m/ 11621ft). To the north, the Glacier du Trient, fed by the vast reservoir of the plateau, falls unseen in a chaotic fractured mass to the village of Trient.

Having gained the glacier by a gentle descending traverse from the hut, the route to the Fenêtre takes you to the right of the *rognon* (rock) at 2944m (9659ft). From here the final slope up to the col can be seen and you'll be able to determine whether it will be a straightforward snow slope or the loose rocky scree we have recently come to expect as a result of the Californian summers the Alps now boast.

From the Fenêtre it is possible to cross the plateau to the Cabane du Trient, stunningly situated under the Pointe d'Orny (3269m/10725ft). A night here would be an appropriate plan for those hardy souls who have survived the Petit Darray and who fancy another challenge in the shape of the Aiguilles du Tour which beckon directly opposite the hut.

To continue on to Le Tour, the route sneaks around under the small north face of the Tête Blanche (3429m/11250ft) and ascends the very short, though quite steep snow (or ice) slope leading to the Col du Tour – the Franco–Swiss border. The view from here is breathtaking: the whole of the Chamonix valley and the Aiguilles Rouges, hazy in the distance, giving the impression of endless space and freedom. Your destination is almost in sight and you leave behind the icy awe-inspiring mountains, heading for the mellower tones of the lower slopes. However, the way into France is blocked by an enormous wind hollow just the other side of the ridge. An easy scramble along the ridge in the direction of the Aiguilles du Tour leads in a few metres to a way down to the Glacier du Tour.

Don't relax too much though. You're not quite there yet, and despite the highway blazed courtesy of the local guides on their daily pilgrimage to the Aiguilles du Tour, this part of the descent is very crevassed and the route is intricate and dangerous.

The descent presents more wind hollows, guarding the golden rocky ridges and hiding glistening azure lakes, jewel-like in their depths. Eventually the rocky slopes at the edge of the glacier are gained, unfortunately adorned with the squalid litter of bivouackers who resist at all costs a night in the nearby Albert Première refuge. This marks the end of the glacier travel, so you can dispense with rope, harness, and crampons, and a quick ten minutes down the slopes brings you to the hut, named after Albert I of Belgium, who was a keen alpinist. If you're lucky the warden will serve you cold drinks while you rest awhile.

However, the valley beckons, so I expect you'll resist the temptation to stay, and press on down. If the call of the fleshpots is very strong it's possible to descend directly from the refuge to Le Tour in lit-

tle more than half an hour via the steep moraine ridge forming the right edge of the glacier. For those of you who value your knees, follow the path that, after a few minutes of descent on the moraine, traverses under the Pointes des Grandes and des Berons and down past the Lac de Charamillon to the north. At the junction, the right-hand path rises slightly to go towards the Col de Balme and the lift down to Le Tour.

PEAK: AIGUILLES DU TOUR

The western side of the Aiguilles du Tour group of peaks.

Situated on the Franco–Swiss border, the Aiguilles du Tour are two distinct peaks – the north summit (3544m/11628ft) and the south summit (3542m/11621ft) – which are very close together but separated by a deep cleft. Both command superb views of the Mont Blanc massif.

The normal route can be done from either the Trient or the Albert Première hut, the latter being a longer approach. From the Albert Première

refuge walk up behind the hut, you will set foot on the glacier after about 20 minutes – rope up here. Pass Signal Reilly and continue in a southeasterly direction until a steep slope gives access to the Col Supérieur du Tour (3289m/10787ft) and the Trient glacier. (It is possible to arrive here via the Col du Tour.) Now head north, past the Aiguille de Purtscheller, to a flattish area under the short, rocky east face of the south summit. (If coming from the Trient hut, this route is joined at the steep slope under the Aiguille de Purtscheller by descending from the hut to the Col d'Orny and continuing in a wide arc. Ascend the snow slope above, cross the small bergschrund and follow the east face over easy rocks to the south summit.

By descending the northeast ridge the north summit can be attained via a ledge going up to the right then easy rocks and snow to the top. Retrace your steps for the descent.

CLIMB ESSENTIALS

SUMMIT Aiguilles du Tour (3544m/11621ft and 3542m/11621ft).
PRINCIPAL HUTS Refuge Albert Premiére (2706m/8878ft).
GRADE F
HEIGHT GAIN 838m (2750ft).
APPROXIMATE TIME 3–4 hours.
MAP 1:25 000: IGN Top 25 3630 OT Chamonix.

TREK 14: AIGUILLE DU MIDI TO POINTE HELBRONNER

Trekking on glaciers is fabulous when it allows you to walk as close as possible to the high peaks without actually needing climbing skills and techniques. To be close to the ice and rock walls and the hanging glaciers and seracs, and to feel tiny amongst the grandeur of the mountains – this makes a trek unforgettable. Short though it is, the walk from Aiguille du Midi to Pointe Helbronner boasts some of the most spectacular scenery in the Alps and the beauty of the surroundings easily makes up for the trek's relative lack of difficulty.

TREK ESSENTIALS

LENGTH 1 day.
ACCESS Start and finish at the Aiguille du Midi cable car in Chamonix.
HIGHEST POINT The Aiguille du Midi (3842m/12606ft).
MAPS 1:50 000: Didier Richard 8 Mont Blanc.
1:25 000: IGN Top 25 3630 OT Chamonix.
TREK STYLE 1 day, glacier travel.
LANGUAGES French and Italian.
FURTHER OPTIONS Stay at the Torino hut and ascend the Tour Ronde; stay at the Cosmiques and ascend Mont Blanc du Tacul.

Look across to the Mont Blanc massif from anywhere in the Aiguilles Rouges and you'll quickly discern an odd rocket-shaped structure rearing up from the top of a rocky summit to the left of Mont Blanc du Tacul. This is the top station of the Aiguille du Midi cable car, which leads in two impressive stages to the summit of this pinnacle at 3842m (12598ft). The journey to the summit of the Aiguille du Midi is worthwhile for the view alone. Once there you're right in the heart of the high mountains. Mont Blanc's summit seems to be just a step away, and the views extend right over to the Grandes Jorasses and the Italian frontier, not to mention the precipitous drop back down to Chamonix, and the Arve valley beyond. It really is

superb – go on a rest day, if nothing else.

If you are equipped and experienced, or willing to take a guide, then the walk from the Aiguille du Midi cable car over to the Italian frontier is a fine glacier outing. It's certainly not long, nor is it arduous, but this is good since it leaves ample time to stop and absorb the unique scenery.

The construction of the impressive two-stage cable car was finished in 1955 and was an audacious feat of engineering. Film taken at the time

Descending the airy arête from the Aiguille du Midi cable car.

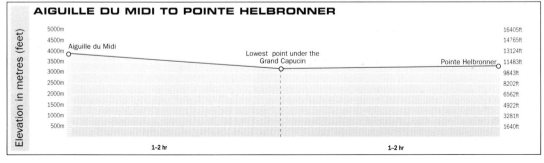

AIGUILLE DU MIDI TO POINTE HELBRONNER

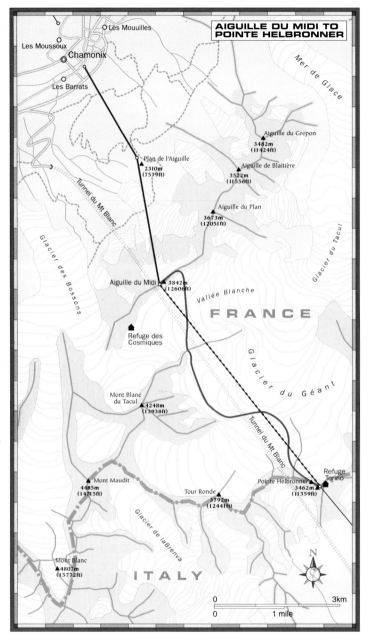

AIGUILLE DU MIDI TO POINTE HELBRONNER

there the problems began. After several months of closure the newly renovated lift didn't work properly and it required considerable adjustment to repair correctly, thus highlighting the exceptional achievement of the original.

Aiguille du Midi to Pointe Helbronner

Emerging from the cable car you follow the signs through the cold and dank tunnels to exit suddenly into an icy grotto. This is as far as you go if unequipped. It's time to put on glacier-walking gear – crampons, harness, rope and ice axe. The next bit is quite impressive as you descend the ridge leading down to the glacier. During the season this arête is very busy and you'll usually find it's an icy staircase. However, after fresh snow you could be making the track yourself.

Whatever the conditions, it's very exposed and not a place to discover you don't like heights. Falling off either side would be a bad idea. There are often people labouring up the ridge, having finished an alpine route, and ascending this after a long climb is hard work so don't be surprised if they seem reluctant to give way. If you like steep ground you'll appreciate this for what it is – a fine start to the walk. If you don't, just hang on in there – it doesn't last long and you'll soon be down. As you turn onto the glacier at the base of the arête you'll cross the bergschrund. This may or may not be visible but, be assured, it is there. Many folk walk over this unroped, oblivious to the deep, dark, gaping abyss beneath their feet.

Having arrived on the glacier, now's the time to really study those views. Rising up from the ice is the beautiful south face of the Aiguille du Midi, shining golden in the sun. Featuring some of the finest rock climbing routes in the massif, this cliff is justifiably popular and many teams camp on the glacier below the face to be assured of an early start on their chosen climb. Just beyond, perched

shows men climbing up the mountain, laden with masses of gear, to establish an initial line down to Plan de l'Aiguille, where the first car terminated. A cable car had existed nearby, at the Gare des Glaciers, since 1924, having been used for the first winter Olympics, which were held in Chamonix.

The section from Plan de l'Aiguille to the summit travels on a very long non-supported stretch of cable which, after much effort, became operational in 1955 and remained in service until 1991. It was then deemed necessary to refurbish the lift and

The Grandes Jorasses, the Dent du Géant and the Italian frontier, seen from the west.

on a bluff, is the Refuge des Cosmiques. This hut suffered significant damage several years ago, the warden waking in the morning to find that a large quantity of rock had fallen away from underneath the kitchen floor, which called for a hasty evacuation. This has since been well shored-up and stabilised, and it is a great place at which to spend a night under the huge northern slopes of Mont Blanc du Tacul (4248m/13938ft). The walk heads basically southwards down the glacier, past the east face of Mont Blanc du Tacul, home to many classic Alpine routes including the Gervasutti Pillar and the Supercouloir, to name just two.

In the distance, if the weather is clear (and if it isn't I don't recommend being here), you'll be able to spot your destination, the Helbronner lift station on Pointe Helbronner (3462m/11359ft) named after a famous Italian alpinist. Overhead are the cherry-like cabins, also known as cherries, that link the Aiguille du Midi to Helbronner. If

these aren't fairly regularly rolling by, you need to have another plan for returning to France at the end of the walk. They usually operate in high season until the end of the afternoon, but check the exact time before setting out – missing the last one would entail considerable extra expense, descending to Courmayeur then returning to Chamonix by bus. If you know in advance that the cherries aren't working, then you will have no option but to descend to Courmayeur, so be sure to buy a single ticket on the Aiguille du Midi, and don't miss the bus.

Butting up against the edge of the southeast face of Mont Blanc du Tacul is the spectacular Grand Capucin (3838m/12592ft), sporting many rocky test pieces and classics. Ahead to the south is the Tour Ronde (3792m/12441ft) with its popular north face. The Glacier du Géant falls away to the north, whilst the aptly named Dent du Géant (giant's tooth) shoots upwards just to the northeast. Beyond this is the Rochefort Arête, leading eventually to the Grandes Jorasses, known for its mighty north face.

The next section can be quite crevassed, depending on the season and may require a little route-finding. Generally there will be a good track, but if you are at all unsure go further down the glacier then back up to skirt around this obstacle.

The route up to Helbronner is now very obvious, straight ahead to the southeast. This slope used to be a summer skiing area until a nasty accident in the early 1990s, when a pisting machine fell into a crevasse killing the driver. So beware, there are some big holes under the snow.

On arrival at the lift station (3642m/11949ft) enjoy the wonderful views of the massif, as well as the distant vista of the Aosta valley and the Gran Paradiso range beyond. And of course it would be a sin to come to Italy and not sample the Italian hospitality – a cappuccino at the very least.

It may be tempting to contemplate returning on foot and this is possible if you havent lingered too long, but it is a long way, much of it in ascent, and you don't want to miss the last lift down. The cherries provide a very pleasant return journey and give a totally different perspective, as well as close-up views of the climbers on the south face of the Midi.

From the Refuge des Cosmiques, the north face of Mont Blanc du Tacul is spectacular.

THE MONT BLANC RANGE
REGIONAL DIRECTORY

GETTING THERE BY AIR

Geneva airport is the most convenient airport for the Mont Blanc region, whether you're going to the French or Italian side or into nearby Switzerland. The airport is served by many different airlines including Swissair, British Airways and Easyjet. Having landed, there are essentially four options for reaching the Mont Blanc area.

Car hire: Geneva airport is about one hour's drive from Chamonix and there are several car hire agencies operating out of the airport. As usual it's normally cheaper to book the car before you arrive.

Taxi transfer: To reach Chamonix there are several taxi services and in the ski season lots of minibuses transfer back and forth from Geneva to the resorts, but for year round, reliable service contact Air Transport Services. Booking ahead will get you the best price.

Bus: A public bus service (SAT voyages) runs from Geneva airport to Chamonix. To get to the Italian side of the Mont Blanc range there is a bus service linking Chamonix with Courmayeur (SAT voyages).

Train: There are two possible train routes to reach the Chamonix valley. Geneva airport has its own train station and the prettiest, most interesting, but slowest way is via Lausanne and Martigny, coming into France at the village of Vallorcine then heading over to Argentière and Chamonix. This journey takes about three hours. The alternative is a rather tortuous journey across Geneva and along the Arve valley to Chamonix – quicker, but not so scenic. To go to the Swiss region described in this chapter the train service from Geneva to Martigny is very good, from where regular Postbus services (PTT) run up the valley to La Fouly and Ferret. Bus timetables are available from local tourist offices .

If you choose not to fly, then it's possible to travel by train from many cities in Europe, linking up with the fast TGV service running through France to Saint Gervais le Fayet from where the local train runs up to the Chamonix valley.

GETTING THERE BY ROAD

Motorway and finally dual carriageway lead through France to Chamonix from where a mountain road goes over to Vallorcine and the Swiss frontier. Italy is accessible from Chamonix by the Mont Blanc tunnel or through Switzerland over the Grand Saint Bernard Pass. Friday evenings and Saturdays are very busy on the roads during the holidays, Sundays being noticeably quieter. In winter, snow tyres or chains are often necessary for the final ascent to Chamonix and from there onwards. The tourist offices will be able to advise locally.

Accommodation

In the main towns there are numerous choices of hotels or *gîtes*, as well as campsites in the summer. However, some of the smaller towns do not have many hotels and in high season booking in advance is essential. The best sources of information are the local tourist offices, where English is spoken.

Mountain Huts:

There are a lot of huts to choose from in parts of this region, many of which are noted in the trek texts. Since phone numbers change, individual numbers are not listed here. The best way to find out how to reserve a hut is to contact the local tourist office and they may even make the reservation for you. For well-known treks such as the Tour du Mont Blanc, the local tourist office can give you a list of hut numbers. If you want to make your reservation before the hut opens you'll need to contact the guardian at his private number, which the tourist offices should also provide. Huts owned by Alpine Clubs or by the National Parks can also be booked direct via the governing body.

DIRECTORY

For all telephone numbers the local numbers are noted – to telephone from abroad add the international code and drop the first 0, except for Italy where the entire number is dialled.

Geneva Airport: tel. 022 717 7111; www.gva.ch
Swissair: www.swissair.com
British Airways: www.britishairways.com
Easyjet: www.easyjet.com
SAT voyages: tel. 04 50 53 00 95; fax 04 50 53 68 14
Air Transport Services: tel. 04 50 53 63 97; email: andy@cham-ats.com; www.cham-ats.com
French Railways: tel UK. 08705 848 848; tel. France: 08 36 67 68 69; www.sncf.fr
Rail Europe: www.raileurope.com
Swiss rail: www.sbb.ch

French Tourist Offices for the Mont Blanc Range

For general information and all tourist office numbers: www.maison-de-la-france.com; www.tourisme.fr
Chamonix Tourist Office: tel. 0450 53 00 24; fax 0450 53 58 90; email: info@chamonix.com; www.chamonix.com
Argentière Tourist Office: tel. 04 50 54 02 14; fax 04 50 54 06 39
Vallorcine Tourist Office: tel. 04 50 54 60 71; fax 04 50 54 61 73
Les Houches Tourist Office: tel. 04 50 55 50 62; fax: 04 50 55 53 16; www.leshouches.com
Les Contamines-Montjoie Tourist Office: tel. 04 50 47 01 58; fax 04 50 47 09 54; www.lescontamines.com
Italian Tourist Office for the Mont Blanc Range
Courmayeur Tourist Office: tel. 0165 842060; fax 0165 842072
Swiss Tourist Offices for the Mont Blanc Range
For details of all tourist offices in the Valais region of Switzerland tel. 027 327 3570; fax 027 327 3571; email: info@valaistourism.ch; www.matterhornstate.com
Geneva Tourist Office: tel. 022 909 7000; fax 022 909 7075; email: info@geneva-tourism.ch; www.geneva-tourism.ch
Martigny Tourist Office: tel. 027 721 2220; fax 027 721 2224; email: info@martignytourism.ch; www.martignytourism.ch
Champex Tourist Office: tel. 027 783 1227; fax 027 783 3527; email: info@champex.ch
La Fouly Tourist Office: tel. 027 783 3303; fax 027 783 2717

7

THE PENNINE ALPS AND WESTERN OBERLAND

The Pennine range is a huge area of high summits, including such giants as Monte Rosa, the Weisshorn, the Matterhorn, the Grand Combin – the list goes on and on. Everywhere you look there are mighty peaks, snow covered and impressive. The area is bounded to the west by the Col Ferret and to the north by the Rhone valley, to the east by the Simplon pass, and many of the summits form the Swiss–Italian frontier ridge.

Monte Rosa is the highest and has several summits – the Dufourspitze (4634m/15204ft) being the loftiest. Also included here is a small section of the Western Oberland Alps.

Trek through this area and you will be treated to a visual extravaganza: glaciers and high peaks form the daily backdrop, whilst the walking terrain is no less entrancing, with great variety between the Swiss and Italian villages and valleys, many high, impressive passes and rocky plateaux and steep gushing rivers and waterfalls.

Zermatt, the best-known mountain town in this region, endowed as it is with the unique silhouette of the Matterhorn, has a wealth of fascinating history, whilst throughout the area traditional villages allow you to experience the Alpine way of life.

Approaching the summit of Castor, with the Weisshorn in the background.

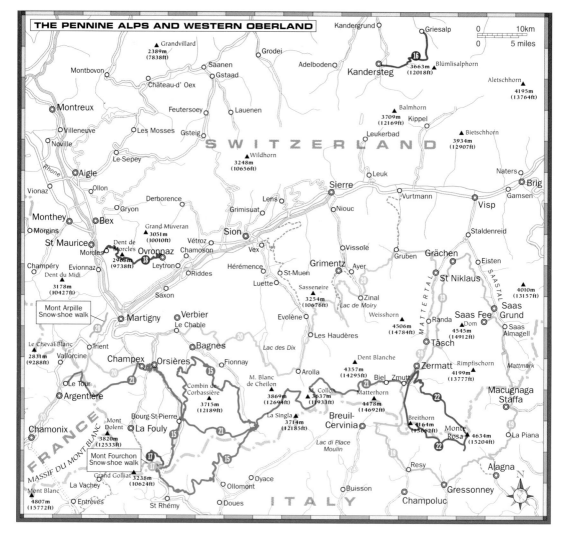

Like most Alpine villages, Zermatt existed in obscurity for many centuries. Between 1000 and 1300 the first hamlets were established – Blatten, Findeln, Zmutt and Winkelmatten. Mining and the breeding of cattle provided an income for the inhabitants. At this time the name 'Probornum' was used for the area, meaning 'prairie in the region of water'. For centuries the Comtes of Savoie reigned over the town, but that changed later when ownership was transferred to the Comtes of Haut Valais. By 1500 the name had changed to 'Zer Matt' meaning 'to the meadows'. The Col du Théodule, which had been crossed since Roman times and before, provided the main route between this part of Switzerland and what is now Italy, and Zmutt was the last staging post before the perilous crossing of the col.

The 17th century was particularly cold through-out Europe, and the glaciers advanced noticeably. The high passes remained snow-covered year round, and the harvests were very poor. The inhabitants of villages like Zermatt struggled to survive, living largely cut off from the rest of the region. However, when climatic conditions became more clement the first visitors arrived in the Alps. In 1780 the first foreigners came to Zermatt. The botanist Horace Bénédict de Saussure (see p86) made an appearance in 1792 and climbed the Kleine Matterhorn, concluding from his experiments that the Matterhorn itself was at a height of 4501m or 14768ft. Modern measurements record it as being 4478m (14692ft) so he wasn't far out.

In 1813, the first 4000-m (13124-ft) peak, the Breithorn, was climbed in the area, and from then on there was no stopping the growth of alpinism. The vicar of Zermatt set up a visitors' register in

1812, at first recording 10–12 people per year. However, this soon grew and hotels opened to accommodate the influx of tourists, who came to see the glaciers and to climb the peaks. In 1860, a carriage road was finished linking St Niklaus to Zermatt, and in 1865 Whymper and his team conquered the Matterhorn. It was only in 1891 however that Zermatt became accessible by train, and this was only in the summer.

Zermatt saw its first winter season in 1928 and its first ski lift, to Sunnegga, was constructed in 1947. Despite all the developments of the 20th century, making Zermatt a major Alpine town year-round, the town has kept road access limited to residents only. The streets remain car-free, leaving just pedestrians, cyclists and the silent electric taxis, which creep up unnervingly behind you.

The Matterhorn

Most people, it seems, have at some time seen a picture of the Matterhorn. The classic summit can be seen everywhere, from chocolate boxes to adverts. It's a mountain that inspires dreams, yet its history is a story of shattered ambitions and tragedy.

The Matterhorn was clearly going to be one of the harder summits, and some believed it to be impossible. Its Italian name, Monte Cervino, means Stag Mountain, with the idea of it being difficult and intimidating. It wasn't until 1858 that the Matterhorn was seriously attempted, the main protagonists being the Italian Jean Antoine Carrell and the famous British mountaineer Edward Whymper. The majority of the attempts were from the Italian side, from where it appears slightly more feasible, but all failed.

The ascent developed into a jingoistic race and by 1865 the two teams were ready to go all out for victory. In July, the Italian team led by Carrell set out for yet another try, while Whymper hurried back to Zermatt to find willing team mates. He joined up with Lord Francis Douglas, and as guides the two Peter Taugwalders, father and son. The group also included guide Michel Croz from Chamonix, the Reverend Charles Hudson and a novice climber Douglas Hadow. They decided to tackle the previously neglected Hörnli ridge from Zermatt.

On 14 July 1865 the people of Whymper's group were the first to stand on the summit of the Matterhorn (actually two summits joined by a narrow ridge). In a fit of excitement they threw rocks down onto the Italian team just below, who had ascended the Italian ridge, but hadn't yet reached the summit. Carrell and friends were so disgusted

and disappointed they turned around and descended without completing the climb, and Whymper's party set off down themselves.

Soon after starting the descent, on the steepest section, Hadow slipped and pulled Croz, Douglas and Hudson down with him, to fall the length of the north face. Whymper and the Taugwalders were saved by the rope breaking, and they descended to Zermatt to relate the tale which shocked the mountaineering world and beyond. The accident was minutely analysed for years to come, and many lessons were learned from it, one of the major accidents in the history of alpinism.

Carrell was persuaded to try again and three days later successfully completed the Italian ridge to the summit. It was immediately obvious to all concerned that the Matterhorn represented a potential goldmine. Huts were established and the guides of Cervinia and Zermatt now spend every summer taking people to the top. All the faces have been climbed, by numerous routes, and first ascents have been made in all sorts of manners by all types of people, with countless records being set. Nevertheless, there is no 'easy' route to the top, as they all involve climbing very steep and precarious ground.

Without doubt the Matterhorn is a unique mountain, the stuff of dreams, and to stand on its summits on a quiet day is a very special privilege.

The dramatic form of the Matterhorn makes a stunning backdrop.

TREK 15: TOUR DES COMBINS

The western end of the Pennine Alps is dominated by the huge glaciated peak of the Grand Combin (4314m/14154ft). This summit is seen from far and wide, on several of the treks in this book, and the tour of it and its satellite peaks is nothing short of spectacular. The landscape is extremely varied and many high peaks are to be seen, as well as interesting villages and ancient passes. The Grand Combin and the almost equally impressive Mont Velan (3731m/12241ft) are separated only by high ridges and glaciated peaks.

TREK ESSENTIALS

LENGTH 6 days.

ACCESS Anywhere along the route, but Bourg-St-Pierre is the most convenient start and finish point.

HIGHEST POINT If the TDC is done without extra summits, the Col des Otanes (2846m/9338ft).

MAPS 1:50 000: Carte Nationale de la Suisse 5003 Mont Blanc Grand Combin, or Association Valaisanne de Tourisme Pédestre Carte Nationale de la Suisse Grand Saint Bernard (this has the TDC labelled as such).
1:25 000: Carte Nationale de la Suisse 1345 Orsières, 1346 Chanrion, 1366 Mont Velan, 1365 Grand Saint Bernard.

TREK STYLE Mountain huts and small hotels.

LANGUAGES French and Italian.

FURTHER OPTIONS Ascents of Mont Rogneux and Mont Avril as described here; ascents of Pointe de Drône, and the Grand Saint Bernard circuit (described in Trek 17, see p132).

From Switzerland, in order to circumnavigate the Combin, a foray into Italy is necessary, coming back via the Roman road from Etroubles to the Grand Saint Bernard pass. Each day has its surprises and charms, and there is a marked contrast between the Swiss and the Italian valleys.

Bourg-St-Pierre to the Cabane du Col de Mille

Bourg-St-Pierre is the biggest village encountered on the Tour des Combins (TDC) so it's often chosen as the departure point for the trek, although clearly you could start anywhere along the length of

the hike. Be sure to take a look around the village before setting off, since it has many historical features that merit a visit. The village dates back to the 8th century when a hospice run by monks was founded, but it really developed in the 13th and 15th centuries. The church belltower, the oldest in the Valais, dates from the 10th century. A milestone stands at the northeast corner of the church with an inscription that translates as:

'To the pious, fortunate, invincible and noble Emperor Caesar Valerius Constantin, born for the good of Public Works. From Forum Claudii Vallense (Martigny) twenty-four thousand paces.'

The distance indicates the milestone was placed twenty-four Roman miles from Martigny. It dates from the reign of the Roman emperor, Constantine the Great (AD310), who had the road to the Grand Saint Bernard Pass repaired.

The village owes its position to the series of rocky outcrops, smoothed by the glaciers of the last Ice Age, which were easy to defend and which offer a certain amount of protection from the elements. For centuries this has been the last inhabited village on the way up to the pass, which was a vital link between Italy and Western Gaul. Many artefacts from Roman times have been discovered in and around the village.

This first stage is quite short, unless you aim to also ascend Mont Rogneux (3083m/10109ft), in which case an early start is essential. Walk out of town and cross the main road, to follow the small road to the chapel of Notre Dame de Lorette. A

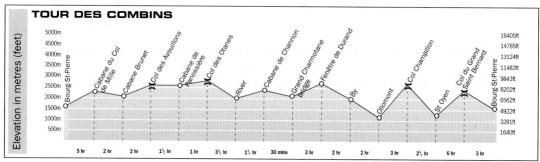

TOUR DES COMBINS

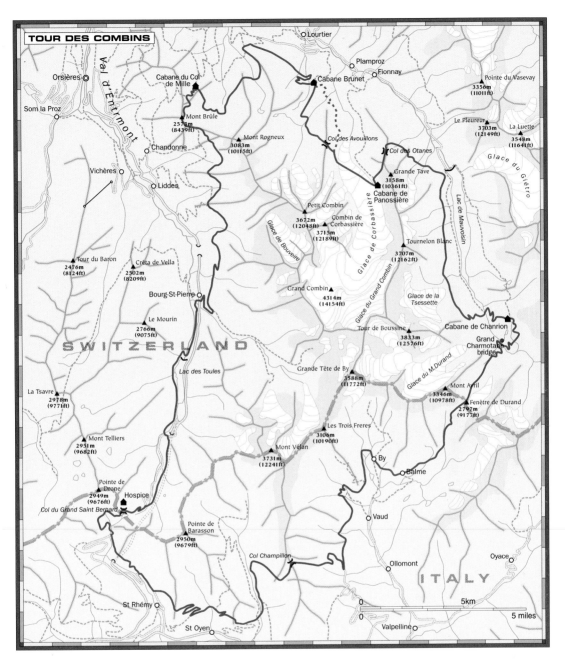

TOUR DES COMBINS

Lourtier
Plamproz
Fionnay
Cabane Brunet
Pointe du Vasevay
3356m
(11011ft)
Orsières
Cabane du Col
de Mille
Som la Proz
Mont Brûle
2578m
(8439ft)
Le Pleureur
3703m
(12149ft)
La Luette
3548m
(11641ft)
Chandonne
Mont Rogneux
3083m
(10115ft)
Col des Avouillons
Vichères
Liddes
Col des Otanes
Grande Tave
3158m
(10361ft)
Cabane de
Panossière
Glace du Giétro
Petit Combin
Combin de
Corbassière
3672m
(12048ft)
3715m
(12189ft)
Glace de Bouveire
Glace de Corbassière
Lac de Mauvoisin
Tournelon Blanc
3707m
(12162ft)
Tour du Baron
2476m
(8124ft)
Crêta de Vella
2502m
(8209ft)
Glace du Grand Combin
Bourg-St-Pierre
Grand Combin
4314m
(14154ft)
Glace de la
Tsessette
Cabane de Chanrion
Le Mourin
2766m
(9075ft)
SWITZERLAND
Tour de Boussine
3833m
(12576ft)
Grand
Charmotane
bridge
Lac des Toules
Glace du M.Durand
La Tsavre
2978m
(9771ft)
Grande Tête de By
3588m
(11772ft)
Mont Avril
3346m
(10978ft)
Fenêtre de Durand
2797m
(9177ft)
Mont Telliers
2951m
(9682ft)
Les Trois Freres
3106m
(10190ft)
Mont Vélan
3731m
(12241ft)
By
Balme
Pointe de
Drone
2949m
(9676ft)
Hospice
Col du Grand Saint Bernard
Vaud
Pointe de
Barasson
2950m
(9679ft)
Col Champillon
Ollomont
Oyace
St Rhémy
ITALY
0   5km
0   5 miles
St Oyen
Valpelline

gentle path leads up through forest, emerging into meadows at the *alpage* of Creux du Mâ. The way continues easily, past Bouveire d'en Bas and Le Coeur, contouring around the pastoral hillside, leaving you plenty of opportunity to drink in the splendid spectacle opening up to the west. Below is the Entremont valley, and further, beyond the foreground peaks of Le Mourin and the Crêta de Vella, are the northeasterly peaks of the Mont Blanc massif.

Having passed La Vuardette (2463m/8081ft) the ground becomes rockier and takes you under the western slopes of Mont Rogneux. Ahead is the Col de Mille (2472m/8111ft), also called the Col des Oujets de Mille, and just below is the Cabane du Col de Mille which was built in 1996. A possible diversion from here is Mont Rogneux, but it's no evening stroll and, unless you arrive early, if you want to do this summit it may be best to consider spending a second night here. The views are

The Grand Combin and its long snaking glacier. The Cabane de Panossière is on the moraine ridge of the true right bank of the glacier.

enough to make this an attractive option.

Mont Rogneux offers an even better belvédère and is reached by following the west ridge of the peak, which begins at the col. The path is obvious and straightforward to a rocky shoulder at 2850m (9351ft). From this point you need to keep your eyes open for the indistinct trail, marked occasionally by small cairns, that weaves its way round the rocks, staying mainly on or just left of the arête, to the western summit. (Be careful to avoid heading across the stony west face.) The main summit is then easily reached by the ridge.

The Cabane du Col de Mille provides a wonderful evening, taking in the fine views away to the west, and below to the lights of the valley.

Col de Mille to the Cabane de Panossière

Passing the Col de Mille you enter into the Commune of Bagnes, the biggest *commune* in Switzerland. Opposite is the huge ski area of Verbier, with the Pierre Avoi at its western end. From the col you need to head down a little way towards the Ecuries de Mille, then pick up the path that traverses round past the Plan d'Arolles to La Treutse from where you can look down at the scores of little villages making up this *commune* in the Bagnes valley. A good trail, bordered by bilberry bushes, takes you to the Cabane Brunet, a possible night stop if required, and certainly a good place for refreshments before tackling the main body of this day's walk.

A road leads to the Ecuries de Séry, then a footpath into the small gorge of Pron Séry, where the glacial waters gush down from the Petit Combin (3672m/12048ft) directly above. The Col des Avouillons (2647m/8685ft) takes you to the next valley, that of the Corbassière glacier, which issues from the Grand Combin and the Combin de Corbassière (3715m/12189ft). The path follows the glacial moraine of the left bank of the glacier, before crossing the glacier itself, at a very flat spot, to continue up the right bank of the glacier to the Cabane de Panossière.

This glacier crossing is safe without any crevasse danger, and just involves walking on gritty ice or snow. Nevertheless, if you want to avoid this final section you can make a detour from the Cabane de Brunet by descending into the Bagnes valley and then heading up from Plamproz, taking the right bank of the glacier all the way to the Cabane de Panossière (2638m/8658ft). The view of the Grand Combin, nobly guarding the head of the valley, is unbeatable and this refuge has to be a contender for best-positioned hut on the trek.

Cabane de Panossière to the Cabane de Chanrion

The day begins with a short but steep climb to the Col des Otanes (2846m/9338ft), the high point of the tour if you don't do any summit variations. If you haven't had enough of the views you'll get another dose from here, and the scenery is fascinating – a vast cirque of rocks and ice presided over by the grandiose Grand Combin.

The steep descent becomes increasingly gentle as you reach La Tseumette. Then having crossed the Pazagnou stream it's time to climb again, before contouring around the hillside above the huge Mauvoisin lake, with its curved dam, at 250m (820ft) apparently the tallest of its type in the world. Opposite are the attractive summits of Le Pleureur (3703m/12149ft) and La Ruinette (3875m/12714ft), contrasting dramatically with the barren and austere terrain of this traverse. This path is quite sombre in the afternoon, but early morning you'll be in the sun, which makes all the difference.

The east face of the Grand Combin towers above as you cut across under the snout of the Glace de la Tsessette, with the aptly named Jardin des Chamois on its left bank, and another quick descent takes you over the river, followed by a final series of switchbacks to reach the Cabane de Chanrion (2462m/8078ft). By now you'll be on intimate terms with the Grand Combin, discovering a different facet at every stop, and in the final rays of the evening sun you'll once again enjoy views of this summit.

Cabane de Chanrion to By

The previous section began and finished with ascents: this section is the opposite. The initial objective is very clear from Chanrion, and gentle slopes lead down once more to the river, which is crossed at the Grand Charmotane bridge. The steep ascent path soon eases and marmots and maybe even ptarmigan will greet you as you make your way to the Fenêtre de Durand (2797m/9177ft), which is flanked by the summits of Mont Avril (3346m/10978ft) and Mont Gelé (3518m/11542ft). The former would make a fine addition to the day, if you have the time, inclination and good weather. The summit is attained by its unmissable southeast arête. A small path follows the crest to the summit, with a few easy rocky slabs to cross. Whether you climb Mont Avril or not, the scenic rewards are once again stupendous, this time including the abrupt eastern slopes of Mont Velan.

The Fenêtre de Durand is the gateway to Italy, and to a change in scenery and ambience. The descent on south-facing meadows, is an experience to enjoy slowly, soaking up the sun and the sounds – the river, the birds, the marmots and the Italians. Hazy views of the valley below provide a welcome change from the impressive but harsh rock and ice of the previous days.

At the small hamlet of By a new hut is planned, but at the time of writing the hut was not finished; it would be best to descend to Ollomont to a hotel.

By to Saint Oyen

Although there is as usual a high pass to be crossed on this section, the majority of the walk seems different to the other days, since it doesn't have the big-mountain feel of previous stages. However, it has its own charms, and the contrast gives welcome variety to the trek.

A relatively flat drivable track takes you round the hillside to the Rifugio Giorgio e Renz, an Italian Alpine Club hut that is for private use only. The track continues to traverse, accompanied by a *bisse* (irrigation waterway), but you leave it to climb up to the Col Champillon (2708m/8885ft). To the west the panorama opens up to reveal the Mont

Many footpaths head out from Bourg-St-Pierre.

LE COMBAT DES REINES

In many Alpine areas, each year sees a traditional battle between the cows. Most cows are calm and placid creatures, content to spend the day munching grass and ruminating. A certain type, the Herens cow, however, has got a competitive streak, and one of these is destined to be the leaders of the herd. First though it must be decided which one is the strongest, so that for the rest of the season she'll lead the way whenever the herd changes grazing location.

It's difficult to find the origins of this custom which has existed for centuries, probably coming from the Valais region of Switzerland, where some historians claim to have traced such battles as far back as Celtic times. Others date it from Roman times.

The fights usually take place early in the summer season, before the cattle go up to the *alpages*. Only the cows with fighting tendencies take part, the others being content to continue grazing. After what can be a lengthy series of confrontations, one cow will emerge victorious, and she becomes the *reine des cornes* (Queen of the Horns) and the others will respect her authority for the season. These fighting cows tend to be poor milkers, and are easily recognised by their very heavy build, especially around the neck and shoulders. They do not, however, present any threat to people.

Nowadays the *combats des reines* have become big events in some areas, and yearly battles take place between cows of neighbouring herds to find the queen. Even in this age of tourism, the cow remains an extremely valuable commodity and if your cow is the strongest it means you have a valuable animal.

Blanc massif, whilst the Grand Combin is ever-present to the north.

As you descend into the Valle de Menouve you can look down towards Etroubles and ahead is the main road leading up to the Grand Saint Bernard pass. Civilisation is very close! From the village of Prailles you can choose whether to stay in Etroubles or St Oyen, or even St Rhémy just up the road. Take a look round the villages, where you'll find some beautiful examples, old and new, of the rustic traditional architecture of the northern Italian Alps.

Saint Oyen to Bourg-St-Pierre

Walk up the road to St Rhémy. Exit the village on the road, then, soon after, pick up the old Roman road (like a mule track) on the right. This takes you all the way to the Col du Grand Saint Bernard, crossing the main road twice on the way. Some people miss out this section, assuming it to be unworthwhile because of its proximity to the road, but the views are still good, and there's something special about following an old historic route.

It's fascinating to imagine how many thousands of feet have passed this way, in what conditions and for what reason. Apart from the Romans, numerous armies have crossed this pass, including Napoleon and his men. It's quite easy to conjure up images of the dangers faced by travellers in the mountains in the past, perils that led Saint Bernard to establish his hospice at the pass to provide safety, food and shelter for those forced to make this hazardous journey (see Trek 17: p132).

Arriving at the pass, prepare for crowds and cars, but don't panic, as you can quickly leave that behind. It would be a shame, however, to run away too soon. The Saint Bernard museum is a real delight for those keen to learn more about the history of the site, and the dogs, kept here in the summer, are of course gorgeous. Views too are wonderful, but you're used to those by now. Still, be sure to check out the fine pointed spire of the Pain de Sucre (2900m/9515ft) just west of the pass, and ahead the Pointe de Drône (2949m/9676ft).

From the col a path runs more or less parallel to the road, down the Combe des Morts, to L'Hospitalet. Take the trail into the Pierre *alpage*, then walk along the left bank of the Lac des Toules to regain Bourg-St-Pierre.

Typical Alpine church in Bourg-St-Pierre.

TREK 16: THE BLÜMLISALP TREK

Whilst the main part of the Bernese Alps falls outside the scope of this book, the western end of the range just about comes into the definition of the Western Alps that I've hesitantly applied. Technically, this is the Western Oberland. The Kiental and Kandertal valleys are formed by the division of the Kander valley at Reichenbach, south of the huge Thun lake. The rocky scenery of this area gives unique terrain for walking, and the treks here are spectacular and unusual. The Blümlisalp is situated way above the Oeschinensee, a picturesque blue lake, that is the pride of Kandersteg. The Blümlisalphütte commands a striking position, and can be visited by a fine two-day trek starting in the Kiental and finishing in Kandersteg. This trek offers stunning scenery, exciting terrain, and finishes at the famous lake.

Both Kiental and Kandertal valleys are delightful – Kiental is quieter and less frequented than Kandertal. Kandertal culminates at the pleasant town of Kandersteg. The head of the two valleys is barred by huge cliffs, forming an impenetrable boundary, and road traffic must go through the Goppenstein tunnel to reach the other side.

Before this tunnel was built by the Italians in the early 1900s, this really was the end of the road. The only ways over were via the Gemmi and Lötschen passes, both high and dangerous, yet they were for many centuries the major thoroughfares between the valleys. Much trading took place, goods often being paid for by peppercorns.

Sunrise on the Blümlisaplhorn.

TREK ESSENTIALS

LENGTH 2 days.
ACCESS Start in Griesalp and finish in Kandersteg, both accessible by bus from Reichenbach.
HIGHEST POINT The Blümlisalphütte (2834m/9298ft).
MAPS 1:50 000: Landeskarte der Schweiz 263 Gstaad-Lenk-Kandersteg, 264 Jungfrau.
1:25 000: Landeskarte der Schweiz 1248 Mürren.
TREK STYLE Mountain hut.
LANGUAGE German.
FURTHER OPTIONS: Fründenhütte, Kanderfirn glacier via Selden, Gemmi Pass.

Kandersteg was the last village before the passes, so travellers would spend the night there before embarking on the hazardous journey over to the other side.

Griesalp to Blümlisalphütte

There is a bus service up the Kiental valley, and it's advisable to take it as there is very little space to park in the tiny hamlet of Griesalp. This is a typical old Alpine village, complete with ancient chalets and barns and is justifiably a popular place to visit, so don't expect to be alone at the start of this walk.

The path begins by strolling through the shady

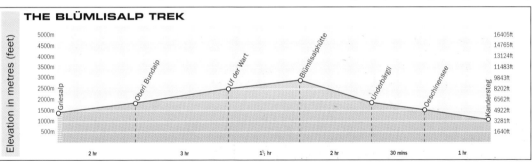

THE BLÜMLISALP TREK

Elevation in metres (feet)

Griesalp	Oberi Bundalp	Uf der Wart	Blümlisalphütte	Underbärgli	Oeschinensee	Kandersteg
2 hr	3 hr	1½ hr	2 hr	30 mins	1 hr	

5000m 16405ft
4500m 14765ft
4000m 13124ft
3500m 11483ft
3000m 9843ft
2500m 8202ft
2000m 6562ft
1500m 4922ft
1000m 3281ft
500m 1640ft

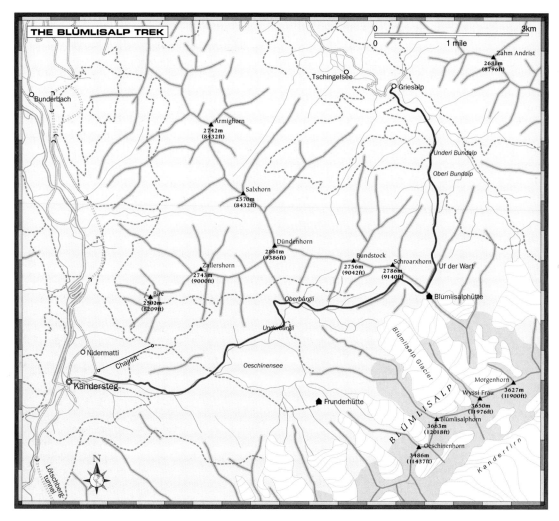

woods. You can either take the track or follow a path that stays near to the river then heads up steeply through the trees. Either way you'll come out of the forest at Underi Bundalp (1686m/ 5532ft). If you're here at the right time the meadows will be a mass of flowers, and as you make your way up to Oberi Bundalp you may feel you have inadvertently stepped onto the cover of a chocolate box! So far it's all very gentle, and you should make the most of this as it's about to steepen up.

Your direction is due south and ahead are the summits of the Oeschinengrat. Leaving the meadows behind you'll head into more and more barren terrain, although look closely and you will still find plenty of smaller alpines growing quite happily in apparently impossible ground.

When you pause for breath you're bound to notice that the way ahead looks just a touch unlike-

ly, and on getting closer, you are likely to be able to spot people descending what look like near-vertical cliffs. Don't worry though, as it's only when you get really close you see that the section up to and beyond the Uf der Wart (2508m/8229ft) is equipped with cables, which make it quite reasonable.

This is glacial moraine, left over from the last Ice Age when the glaciers forced their way down these valleys, pushing up ground and debris at the sides into the moraine ridges we see today. Moraine is always unstable and fairly unpleasant underfoot, but here you have plenty to hold on to to pull you up, so just keep going.

Just as you're probably thinking you've had enough you will emerge onto a col at the Hohtürli (2778m/9115ft) and just above you is the welcome sight of the Blümlisalphütte, against a backdrop of the Blümlisalp glacier coming down from the summits of the Morgenhorn (3627m/

11900ft), the Wyssi Frau (3650m/11976ft) and the Blümlisalphorn (3663m/12018ft). After you have taken a well-deserved break here, and begun to appreciate the superb situation of the night's lodgings, it's a very short jaunt up to the hut, which was quite recently renovated, in typically spick-and-span Swiss style.

Take the time later for an evening stroll up behind the hut, where you'll probably find chamois grazing at dusk. Looking north you can see the vast expanse of the Thun Lake far, far below and, nearer, to the east is the revolving restaurant of the Schilthorn ski lifts, famous amongst James Bond aficionados. Blümlisalp is an enchanting place to spend the evening, and certainly merits the effort you'll have put in to get there.

Blümlisalphütte to Kandersteg

The orange rays of an Alpine dawn will be catching the summits as you descend from the hut to the Hohtürli. Turn left instead of right and begin the descent under the Blümlisalp glacier, taking lots of stops to watch the sun rise on the mountains. This part of the walk should be savoured, being not only a visual but a sensual feast. The early mornings are the essence of alpine walking, when the chamois and ibex are grazing, the day walkers are still in the valleys and the air is crisp and fresh, with just a hint of the heat that will soon build up. You've got plenty of time, so linger, store up those images for the grey days of winter ahead, and just enjoy the feeling of being somewhere very special.

By the time you reach the *alpage* of Oberbärgli you'll probably be meeting other walkers heading up. This area is much frequented, but you'll soon see why. Oeschinensee is no overblown tourist attraction, it really is quite breathtakingly beautiful. Surrounded on three sides by steep grey and orange cliffs, it occupies an incredible position, with several towering waterfalls thundering into it. The lower slopes are carpeted with pink rhododendrons for much of the summer, providing an unexpected contrast with the forbidding grey of the cliffs.

At Underbägli you start to really sense that you've emerged from the rarefied atmosphere of the high mountains into a picture postcard, and the walk round the lake is just as charming in its way as the rest of the trek. Oeschinensee is Kandersteg's trump card, and no wonder. It is served by a chairlift, which rather surprisingly doesn't come right to the lake, so a short walk is involved for those coming up that way. It has a tasteful restaurant and a lot of benches, which

you'll probably be quite happy to make use of when you arrive. You could question the point of the wooden sculptures in the midst of so much natural beauty, but they're not too intrusive.

High above the cliffs on the eastern side of the lake you may spot the Fründerhütte, flying its flag proudly, another hut in a spectacular and improbable position. A long rest at the lake would seem to be a must, before heading off down to Kandersteg, either on foot by the well-marked trail or by lift.

EDELWEISS (*LEONTOPODIUM ALPINUM*)

This is the best-known alpine flower, symbol of the Alps. People are sometimes disappointed when they first see edelweiss as, compared to many other alpine plants, it's quite nondescript and dull at first glance, with no bright colours or scent. But take another look and you'll see that the edelweiss is very unusual and in full bloom, in the sunlight, it really is a unique flower.

Unfortunately too many people have thought the edelweiss would look better on their mantlepieces than in the mountains, so now it is a totally protected species.

You could walk for a week in the Alps and never come across the white star-shaped plant, its tiny yellow flowers hidden among large woolly silvery bracts, with its furry stem covered in hairs that trap air, discouraging evaporation and preventing the plant from drying out. Reputedly only found on inaccessible rock faces, the edelweiss is in fact present in many places in the Alps. However, it has a great preference for limestone terrain, so you'll be lucky to see it elsewhere. It grows between 1700–3400m (5578–11155ft) on grassy and rocky slopes and is in flower from July to September.

Edelweiss originally came from Asia, where there are many different types, some even forming small bushes. During the Ice Age the flower came to the Alps and eventually developed into the two species we have today. *Leontopodium* means 'lion's foot', but edelweiss is a Tyrolian name meaning 'white star'.

TREK 17: GRAND SAINT BERNARD CIRCUIT

The Grand Saint Bernard pass is not only a beautiful place to walk, but also a fascinating historical site, and a visit is highly recommended, either on foot in summer or on snow shoes in winter. The trek described here is just one day, but provides views in all directions, including the Mont Blanc massif, and the Grand Combin and Mont Velan. It is best to combine it with a visit to the hospice and museum to fully appreciate how life was in the Alps in times past. Just to walk here would be to miss out on a major part of the experience.

TREK ESSENTIALS

LENGTH 1 day.
ACCESS Start and finish at the Col du Grand Saint Bernard.
HIGHEST POINT Col du Bastillon (2757m/9046ft).
MAPS 1:50 000 Carte Nationale de la Suisse 292 Courmayeur.
1:25 000 Carte Nationale de la Suisse 1365 Gd St Bernard.
TREK STYLE 1 day, so no accommodation.
LANGUAGE French.
FURTHER OPTIONS Stay another day and ascend the Pointe de Drône (2949m/9676ft).

The Grand Saint Bernard pass now forms the boundary between Italy and Switzerland and has been used as a trans-Alpine route since prehistoric times. It has also been a very important local thoroughfare between the neighbouring valleys. As on all such routes, travellers were frequently in danger, not only from bad weather but also from attacks by highwaymen.

Since the 11th century there has been some sort of shelter or hospice for travellers in this place. The hospice was founded in 1025 by Saint Bernard, who came from what is now the Haute Savoie region of France. In the Middle Ages such religious gestures were usually made in the form of the foundation of abbeys or monasteries in episcopal cities, but in the Alps hospices were founded on the major communication routes.

Very quickly the name of Saint Bernard became synonymous with protection against the evil dangers of the mountains, and many images exist of the saint exorcising dragons attacking travellers. Saint Bernard thus became the protector of wayfarers in the Alps, and the patron saint of alpinists. There is a statue of Saint Bernard at the pass which can be reached along the old Roman road cut into the rock leading off the main road just on the Swiss side of the Italian customs post. At the base of the statue you can see the remains of a temple dedicated to Jupiter and for a long time this pass was known as Mon Jovis. The stones from the temple were re-used by the builders of the first hospice.

Today the Grand Saint Bernard Hospice is a monastery, with real monks and a hotel/*gîte*. It is also home to the Saint Bernard dogs. There is a museum that traces the history of the pass through the ages and has displays of natural history collections put together by earlier monks who were naturalists. The monks are trained in avalanche rescue, and the dogs were used for this for many years. However, with the increased use of helicopters in mountain rescue, the St Bernard dogs have been replaced by a smaller breed, although in the summers they are still bred here and can be visited in their kennels.

In winter the road over the pass is closed, and road traffic can only cross the frontier through a

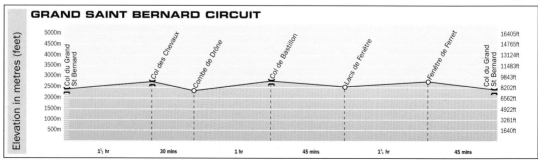

The Grandes Jorasses (its north face in profile) and Mont Blanc on the left, seen from the Col de Bastillon.

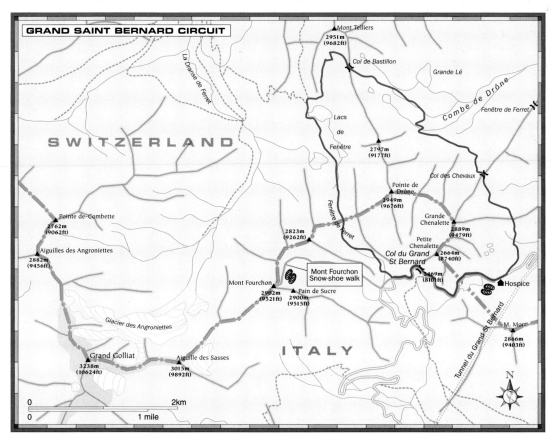

SNOW-SHOE WALK: MONT FOURCHON

In winter the road over the Saint Bernard pass is closed and access to the hospice is on foot – on skis or snow shoes. To do any of the summits in this area I recommend you stay the night at the hospice, in itself a very interesting experience. Mont Fourchon (2902m/9521ft) is a classic snow-shoe peak, and the views of the the Mont Blanc massif are superlative. It is also possible to combine this with an ascent of the neighbouring Pain de Sucre (2900m/9515ft). This latter looks like a miniature Matterhorn when viewed from the hospice, but is in fact very accessible.

A traverse around the hillside from the hospice, just above the iced-over lake, and through the snowed-up road tunnels leads to the western slopes of Mont Fourchon, and the ascent starts at the buildings of Montagna Baus. Head up the combe keeping to the north of the Tours des Fous, under the south slopes of the Fenêtre de Ferret. The angle steepens somewhat as you get higher and at about 2700m (8859ft) a long traverse should be made left, swinging back right just below the summit, where snow shoes are removed to climb the final few metres on foot. A thrilling panorama awaits you, and will probably keep you there for some time.

Most people descend from here, but if you have the time and energy, and if conditions permit, the Pain de Sucre is within easy reach. Descend from the summit and with snow shoes cross undulating ground southeastwards to the deep col between Mont Fourchon and the Pain de Sucre. This col is hidden from view when you're

---

SNOW-SHOE WALK ESSENTIALS

ACCESS Start and finish at Bourg Saint Bernard, the car park for the ski lifts.

DISTANCE 5.25km (3¼ miles) to the hospice; about an 8-km (5-mile) round trip to the summits.

HEIGHT GAIN 542m (1778ft) to the hospice; 550m (1804ft) to the summit of Mont Fourchon.

APPROXIMATE TIME 2 hours each way to the hospice – coming down doesn't tend to feel any easier than going up on snow shoes; 4–4½ hours from the hospice to the summit and back.

DIFFICULTY 3

TYPE OF WALK 2 day, round trip by same route, summits.

INTERESTING FEATURES The Grand Saint Bernard hospice and pass, spectacular views of the Mont Blanc massif.

ADDITIONAL INFORMATION From the hospice other possible snow-shoe treks include to the Fenêtre d'en Haut, the Pointe Barasson and, from the Bourg-St-Bernard car park, Mont Telliers.

MAP 1:25 000: Carte Nationale de la Suisse 1365 Gd St Bernard.

---

on the summit of Mont Fourchon. Leaving snow shoes here, climb a steep snow slope to the ridge, which is followed easily to the summit. Return, either by the same route, or from the base of the steep ground descend directly to join the ascent track lower down. This peak is only possible in suitable conditions, and if in doubt it is best not to attempt it – Mont Fourchon is a very satisfying achievement in its own right.

Monks setting off on skis from the Grand Saint Bernard Hospice.

THE CHAMOIS

The chamois is an animal of the forest and, in the past, is thought to have lived throughout Europe, especially in the valleys. Nowadays it is generally confined to mountain regions. A powerful but fragile animal of the antelope family, the typical adult measures 70–85cm (2^1/$_4$–2^3/$_4$ ft) high at the shoulders, and the males usually weigh between 40 and 60kg (90–134lb), the females being smaller. Compared to the ibex, the chamois has a more delicate body.

The fur changes colour according to the season, grey/beige to rusty red in summer, turning brown/black in winter. The chamois' horns are quite small, and those of the male are more turned back than those of the female. The hoof of the chamois is very distinctive. It has two toes that are linked by an elastic ligament, which allows the hoof to spread wide on snow, increasing the surface area, like a snow shoe.

The ideal habitat for the chamois is between 800 and 2500m (2625–8202ft) and they tend to stay at altitude during the summer. They spend the winters in the forest. They eat any vegetation they can find, standing on hind legs to get at bushes and small trees. Usually if you see one chamois, there will be others close by as they are not generally solitary animals, except for the older males. The main herd is led by an old sterile female, the males of one to four years forming a separate group.

The power of this apparently delicate creature can be seen in its ability to ascend steep slopes very quickly - they can climb 1000m (3281ft) in fifteen minutes. They live on average fifteen years, although 20-60 per cent of the young do not survive, succumbing to famine, avalanches or the consequences of late birth (which means the summer is too short for them to become hardy enough to endure the rigours of the winter). They don't have many enemies - foxes and eagles being the main threat to the young. The principal cause of death in adult chamois is parasites, and, of course, man.

long tunnel. Access to the hospice is – on skis or snow shoes. The hospice itself is very interesting, and spending the night there in winter allows some fine walks on snow shoes (see opposite).

From Col du Grand Saint Bernard
From the lake at the Col du Grand Saint Bernard (2469m/8101ft) a path leads north under the slopes of the Grande Chenalette (2888m/9475ft), making a rising traverse through rocky ground, climbing steadily high above the road to the Col des Chevaux (2714m/8905ft). This col ('pass of the horses') is testimony to the days when the hospice got its wood from the forests of the Val Ferret. Many horses were busy all summer transporting the wood supply up to the pass. The views of Mont Velan (3731m/12241ft) to the east are fabulous, whilst the Pointe de Drône (2949m/9676ft) is temptingly close.

A descent leads into the Combe de Drône, ornamented with attractive small lakes under the steep slopes of Mont Telliers (2951m/9682ft). The valley of the Combe de Drône looks tempting, but for this walk it's better to stay high as you're really just traversing around to go up to the next pass. The terrain is gentle past the lakes, which allows a pleasant interlude between the climbing and descents. The Col de Bastillon (2757m/9046ft) – also occasionally referred to as the Col des Chevaux, which can be confusing – is just below the rocky ridge of Mont Telliers and as you reach it the most breathtaking vista unfolds before your eyes. A long stop will definitely be in order to take in the panorama at this belvédère. The Grandes

Jorasses (4208m/13806ft) is dark, forbidding and huge. To its left is the steep snow-topped Italian face of Mont Blanc, whilst to the right of the Jorasses are the Aiguilles de Leschaux (3759m/12333ft), Talefre (3730m/12233ft), Triollet (3870m/12697ft) and the fine pointed summit of Mont Dolent (3823m/12543ft), the meeting point of France, Switzerland and Italy.

Below lie the Lacs de Fenêtre, nestling in the hollow of the La Chaux combe, adding a splash of colour to this barren spot. The high peaks provide a dramatic backdrop, and you can also admire the rocky folds of the Grand Golliat (3238m/10624ft) to the southwest, the spiky summits of the Aiguille des Angroniettes (2882m/9456ft) and the ridge that forms the boundary between Italy and Switzerland.

The initial descent from the Col de Bastillon is quite steep, but the path traverses to the right and to an easy passage through the rocks, where easier terrain leads to the Lacs de Fenêtre. Many birds frequent these lakes, such as the alpine accentor, the windchat and the wheatear.

The Fenêtre de Ferret (2698m/8852ft) leads you over the frontier into Italy for the final stage of this walk. This pass has been used since earliest times, frequently by smugglers, and offers you another superb view of the Italian side of Mont Blanc. The Col du Grand Saint Bernard is regained by a pleasant trail down the combe which is defined by Mont Fourchon (2902m/9521ft) and the Pain de Sucre (2900m/9515ft), and away down below are the misty depths of Etroubles and the Italian plains.

TREK 18: DENT DE MORCLES

From many high viewpoints in the Valais, two rocky peaks are prominent, flanking the Rhône just south of Lake Geneva. The western peak is the multi-summited Dents du Midi, well known for its surprisingly accessible highest point and for the Tour des Dents du Midi (see Trek 4, p65), but to the east is the much less frequented Dent de Morcles. At 2968m (9738ft) this peak presents a formidable rocky bastion on it west side, whilst its hidden east side rises gently above meadows, to a sloping summit plateau. There are two possible means of ascending the Dent de Morcles, and both are described to form a traverse of the peak, but for an easier trek you could go up and down by the route described here as the descent. This in itself gives a beautiful and spectacular trek.

From the top of Dent de Morcles the panorama is truly breathtaking, extending from Mont Blanc to the Matterhorn to the Gran Paradiso, with views encompassing a large part of the northwestern Alps, and for that reason alone this peak is a must.

The ascent takes a totally improbable route through the rocky southwest face, using a path made by the Swiss army. You won't be able to see the trail at all until you get there, but trust me, it's there. It follows an impressive and exposed ledge system, 'la Grande Vire', which takes a high traverse to finally scramble up a chimney to the summit. The traverse crosses several steep gullies which present no problem in dry and snow-free conditions late in the summer, but any remaining *nevé* in these gullies would make the way very dangerous. So this route should only be considered when you're sure that all the snow has gone. Needless to say, if the weather's bad, go somewhere else.

To reach the starting point at Morcles it's probably easiest to take the cable car from Dorenaz then walk along the track around the hillside to Morcles. This is quite a way so you will need to stay in the Cabane de La Tourche.

Morcles to the Cabane de Fenestral

Either walk or take the car up to Les Martinaux, from where the road is not really driveable. Follow the track up in a series of switchbacks, taking the footpath off to the left to the Cabane de la Tourche

at 2198m (7212ft). If you've had a late start then it would also be a good idea to stay here, and enjoy the fine views over the Rhône to the Dents du Midi. It is open in high season, but it is not usually wardened. Blankets and cooking facilities are provided. A good path leads horizontally from the refuge, traversing the steep hillside from under the Pointe des Martinets to the ridge coming down from Roc Champion, where you'll find the military buildings of Rionda.

The path continues in the same fashion, interspersed with ascending zigzags, to finally head out onto the true southwest face of the Dent de Morcles. Here the exposure is quite something, way above the valley, and you'll be either watching your feet or admiring the view, but probably not both at the same time. You cross numerous

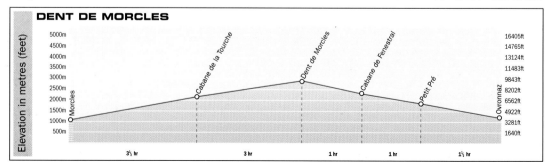

DENT DE MORCLES

The impressive west face of the Dent de Morcles towers above the Rhone valley and is visible from many places, here seen from Vallorcine.

couloirs that cleave this spectacular cliff, until you're right under the Grand Dent de Morcles. At this point you need to locate the old military path in the scree that goes up towards the summit. This footpath has become a little less than perfect over the years, but you can follow it without great difficulty as it leads comfortably almost to the top.

From a shoulder just below the summit, a rocky chimney provides an easy but exciting finale to this ascent, and you'll emerge to find a cross marking the end of the climb.

Look around – in all directions the view is stunning. It's difficult to know where to sit, since whatever you do you're bound to crick your neck straining to take it all in. Immediate views are to the north and west, respectively the Grand Muveran (3051m/10010ft) and the highest peak of the Dents du Midi (3257m/10686ft); to the south are the glistening snowcapped peaks of the Mont Blanc massif, seemingly just a stone's throw away; to the southeast is the huge Grand Combin, and further away the unmistakable Matterhorn, whilst far down the Rhône valley are the misty outlines of the Bernese Oberland summits.

Rarely do you have such a good view, and you'll certainly be reluctant to leave. However, don't stay

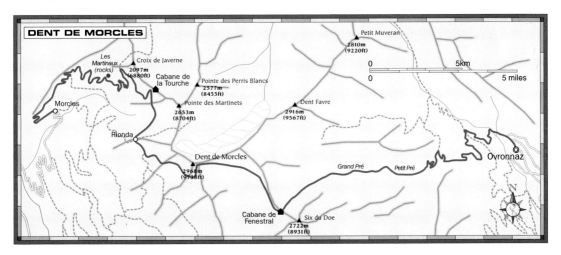

too long here as the way down from the summit is far from easy to find. This is a limestone plateau, with the usual crevasses associated with such terrain, so you need to keep your eyes open for man-eating holes. Occasional cairns mark the way, but if you haven't come up this way it can be rather disconcerting descending, and you may have to retrace your steps a couple of times if you come to an uncrossable void.

The general direction is east, heading for the lake at Grand Cor. It's necessary to descend a small rocky section before coming to easier ground. Traverse under the slopes of the Tête Noire (2876m/9436ft), then across flat and apparently barren terrain. Close inspection will reveal many different alpine flowers thriving in the rocks here, and also numerous fossils in the limestone, testifying to the marine origins of this ground.

From time to time red or orange arrows on the rocks confirm that you're going the right way and at around 2500m (8202ft) the ground ahead drops off steeply towards the Lac Supérieur de Fully, and at this point you take the path that skirts around the hillside to the Cabane de Fenestral. It is possible at 2500m (8202ft) to follow the ridge which descends southeast from Tita Seri, rather than traversing underneath, which gives a nice finish to the day.

From the Cabane you'll be able to enjoy lovely views down to the Fully lake and up towards the Dent de Morcles and its neighbour, the apparently more impressive Six Tremble (2701m/8862ft). You need to take food as there is rarely a warden at the hut, but cooking facilities are provided and so are blankets.

Cabane de Fenestral to Ovronnaz

This day is a lot gentler than the one preceding. Just above the Cabane is the Col de Fenestral (2453m/8048ft) and this gives access into the delightful Grand Pré. This beautiful combe is bounded by the limestone spire of the Dent Favre (2916m/9567ft) and the Tête Noire to the north, with the Six de Doe (2722m/8931ft) and the aptly named Grand Château (2497m/8188ft) to the south.

Nothing could be more unlike the rocky hike of yesterday than this pastoral paradise. The marshy flat meadows are home to cottongrass and orchids, lovers of wet ground. In high summer the cows will be grazing here, making the most of the rich grass before being taken down to the valley to spend the winter inside.

Grand Pré leads to Petit Pré, from where a well marked footpath goes to the Bougnone farm. The final part of the walk is through woods, either on the jeep track or down a steep path to the resort town of Ovronnaz.

HOUSELEEK (*SEMPERVIVUM*)

One of the principal characteristics of the houseleek is evoked by its generic name *Sempervivum*, meaning 'always alive'. These attractive plants are survivors and have adapted perfectly to the extremes of the alpine climate and the most difficult terrain. They are succulents, with a long stalk and a red or yellow star-shaped flower growing out of a greeny-purple rosette. They grow on rocks, on cliffs and on lichen – wherever there is only just a base layer of soil.

The main problem that all houseleeks have to resolve is the lack of water. They are obliged to save water and to economise. They do this in several ways: they have a thick waterproof outer skin, and to avoid evaporation their pores close when the sun shines. The cobweb houseleek (*Sempervivum arachnoideum*), has a network of hairs making a web between the leaves, which forms a pocket of water vapour around the plant. This variety lives in cracks in the rocks, where it uses its hairs to trap water by creating mini dams in the rocks.

The houseleeks are anchored only by slender roots to their chosen rocky sites, their water-saving properties rendering a deep root system unnecessary. Frequently uprooted by avalanches or land-slides, they hold together as a carpet or clump, and are only tem-porarily inconvenienced by such an event, re-establishing themselves rapidly wherever they end up. They can survive extremes of tempera-ture, more than 50°C (122°F) having been measured inside the rosettes, down to -20°C (-4°F) and less in winter.

In the Alps we can find more than ten species of houseleek, growing at altitudes ranging from less than 1000m (3281ft) in the valleys, where they can grow quite large, to above 3000m (9883ft)where they are proportionally smaller, with brighter flowers. Each rosette only flowers once, at the age of 3-5 years, but there are always new rosettes ready to take their turn.

TREK 19: TOUR OF MONTE ROSA

The Central and Eastern Pennine Alps are occupied by a great range of mountains of which the culminating point is Monte Rosa. A multi-summited peak, the Monte Rosa's highest point is the Dufourspitze, which reaches 4634m (15204ft), second in height in the Alps only to Mont Blanc. The average height of the summits in the Monte Rosa group considerably exceeds that of the Mont Blanc massif, with several summits over 4500m (14765ft), and many of the neighbouring peaks, such as the Weisshorn, Matterhorn and the Dom, also tower above the 4000-m (13124-ft) mark.

The Tour of Monte Rosa circumnavigates the massif, taking old trade paths over high passes, and descending into deep forested valleys, only to climb back up through meadows and ancient glacial boulder fields to discover new views of the spectacular summits of this region. A marked contrast is to be found between the Italian and Swiss sides of the massif, which enhances this superb trek.

The Tour of Monte Rosa (TMR) has only recently been established as an official long-distance trek, similar to the French *Grands Randonnées*, although clearly the paths have existed for years, some for centuries. There are several variations, but here I will describe the logical TMR as it is shown on local maps, staying reasonably close to the massif, rather than heading off way down into the main valleys of the Rhône on the Swiss side and the Valsesia in Italy.

The tour is circular so can be started anywhere and done in either direction. However, I prefer clockwise and I suggest a Swiss starting point because of ease of access with the efficient Swiss train and bus services. I have suggested stages, but in some parts, particularly around Cervinia and Zermatt, there are lots of accommodation possibilities, so look carefully at the maps and choose your own days according to time considerations and viewing priorities.

Saas Fee to Monte Moro

From the village of Saas Fee take one of the signed footpaths down through the forest to Saas Almagell and then continue up the the valley to Mattmark. This is pleasant enough alongside the river, under the steep slopes of the Stellihorn, but it's a long day to Monte Moro. There is a postbus service to Mattmark dam which allows energy to be saved for the main part of this section, the ascent to Monte Moro.

Strolling along the eastern bank of the Stausee Mattmark, a surprising number of flowers – stonewort, saxifrage and campanulas among others

TREK ESSENTIALS

LENGTH 7-10 days.
ACCESS Start and finish in the same place: Saas Fee, Cervinia, Zermatt or anywhere else on the route.
HIGHEST POINT Théodule Pass (3317m/10876ft) or Testa Grigia (3479m/11408ft).
MAPS 1:50 000: the best is the Kümmerly & Frey Tour Monte Rosa.
1:25 000: Instituto Geografico Centrale (IGC) 109 Monte Rosa, 108 Cervono Matterhorn; Landeskarte der Schweiz 1348 Zermatt, 1328 Randa, 1308 St Niklaus, 1329 Saas; Swiss Tour Monte Rosa Hiking Map (available in Zermatt).
TREK STYLE Mountain huts and small hotels; glacial walking.
LANGUAGES Italian and German.
FURTHER OPTIONS Any of the peaks seen from the trek, some of which are detailed here.

– are to be found tucked in the rocks at eye level. Numerous marmots will be spotted, scurrying among the boulders, and you could spend considerable time here, but don't linger too long as this is the Alps and the flat part doesn't last long.

At the end of the lake the climb begins. A pleasant trail leads up through meadows, and looking back you'll already be able to see the Weissmies (4023m/13199ft) and the Lagginhorn (4010m/13157ft) to the north, with the glaciers of the Strahlhorn (4128m/13544ft) and the Rimpfischorn (4198m/13774ft) nearer to hand just up above. At times you can see remains of the old medieval track that goes over the Monte Moro Pass (2868m/9410ft), your objective on this ascent. This has been a frequently walked pass for centuries, allowing access from Italy to the Valais, and was much used in the 15th and 16th centuries for taking goods and animals from one valley to the other. Although it is a popular route, a keen eye is still needed to spot the red-and-white flashes marking the way, and when you reach the lovely pastures of Tälli be sure to follow the Tälliboden not the Stafelbach.

Coming over the Colle Supérieur della Cime Blanche, the view is dominated by Monte Cervino.

be captured, awestruck, by the fantastic sight of the east face of the Monte Rosa. From here it is at its most spectacular, of Himalayan proportions— it is as high again from the pass as it is from the valley – and the intricacies of its gigantic mass will hold your gaze time and again.

If you're going to stay at the Rifugio Citta di Malnate, just below, you'll probably have time to ascend the Joderhorn (3035m/9958ft), just east of the col. This provides extensive views over the Italian plains, but can't improve on the Monte Rosa backdrop. I first came to this pass on a misty day and despite tantalising breaks in the cloud, Monte Rosa did not see fit to make an appearance. However, on the descent the weather obliged and suddenly there it was, huge and unbelievable, dominating the skyline.

The hut is just below the pass at the top of the cable car which comes up from Macugnaga Staffa. I can't pretend that this is an attractive place on the outside, being surrounded by the debris of a building site and old lift cables. However, the views are fabulous and the sunrise on the east face must be quite something. This day can be combined with the next day if the bus is taken to Mattmark, but it does make for a long and arduous day.

Monte Moro to Macugnaga Staffa

From the pass the descent to Macugnaga Staffa is given as two-and-a-half hours. Take this with a pinch of salt – it's a long and tortuous descent,

The way becomes rocky, winding improbably through boulders and up granite slabs. This will certainly test those leg muscles on the first day and you'll doubtless be relieved to finally spot the glinting gold figure of the Madonna of the Snows perched up on the pass. This is the border with Italy, and the views stretch down to the Valsesia far below. However, on a fine day you'll neither be looking down there nor at the Madonna. Rather you will

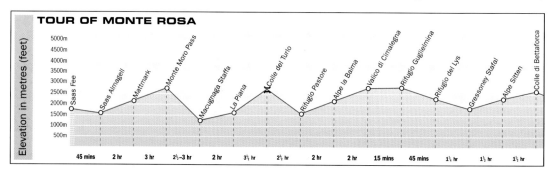

TOUR OF MONTE ROSA

which takes its toll on tired knees. Monte Rosa continues to tower over you as you make your way down through rocks and scree, then meadows and finally into the larch forest above the town. The way is not always very clear at the beginning, so keep your eyes open for those flashes. Directly opposite is the Colle del Turlo (2738m/8983ft), the next high pass, and you'll be able to see that it's just as challenging as the one you've just done.

Macugnaga Staffa is a charming town, the hamlet of Staffa forming the central part, and is well worth taking the time to look around, with attractive buildings set against the ever-present backdrop of Monte Rosa. Hotels and all other facilites are to be found here.

Macugnaga Staffa to Rifugio Pastore

This is a long day, with no real possibility for shortening it. It begins gently enough, though, ambling out of town to follow the raging Anza torrent. At Quarazza you'll doubtless be tempted to stop and spend the day there next to the lake, but unfortunately there's a long way to go so continue on up through shady spruce forest to emerge into sunny meadows at the Alpe Piana. This is a delightful place to stop and picnic, and to savour the splendour of this typical alp, encircled as it is by tiers of rocks alternating with green slopes, and here and there interspersed with impressive waterfalls.

Turlo Pass has a history equally as long as the Monte Moro, and has seen the passage of travellers and tradesmen, with their mules, for many centuries. The track has been rebuilt on several occasions, the last major renovations being in 1918, the work of the 4th Alpini. The military influence is unmistakable in the precision of the zigzags which lead at a perfect gradient through steep woodland to the Alpe Schena, then more gently to a final long climb up through glaciated rocks to the pass. Here a large stone table and benches give a rather surreal air to the whole thing. Although Monte Rosa is no longer visible, other peaks take its place: far away, beyond

The newly constructed Europahütte, with the Weisshorn behind.

the Monte Moro, is the Weissmies, whilst down to the south are the misty depths of the Valsesia and to the west is the continuation of the TMR via the Colle d'Olen (2881m/9452ft).

The descent is similarly well constructed and you'll feel the weight of history as you tread in the footsteps of ancient travellers. It's a long, long way down, and added to the previous day's descent those legs will probably start to complain. At the Faller *alpage* the trail steepens noticeably and heads through forest to eventually come out at the much-welcome grassy meadow where the Rifugio Pastore is situated. Once again Monte Rosa makes an appearance, and the lights of the Regina Margherita refuge can be seen at night on the summit of the Signalkuppe (4554m/14942ft).

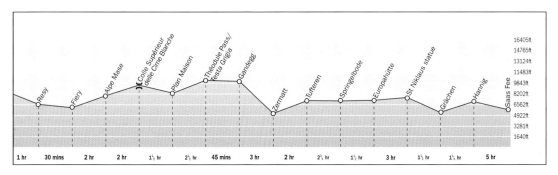

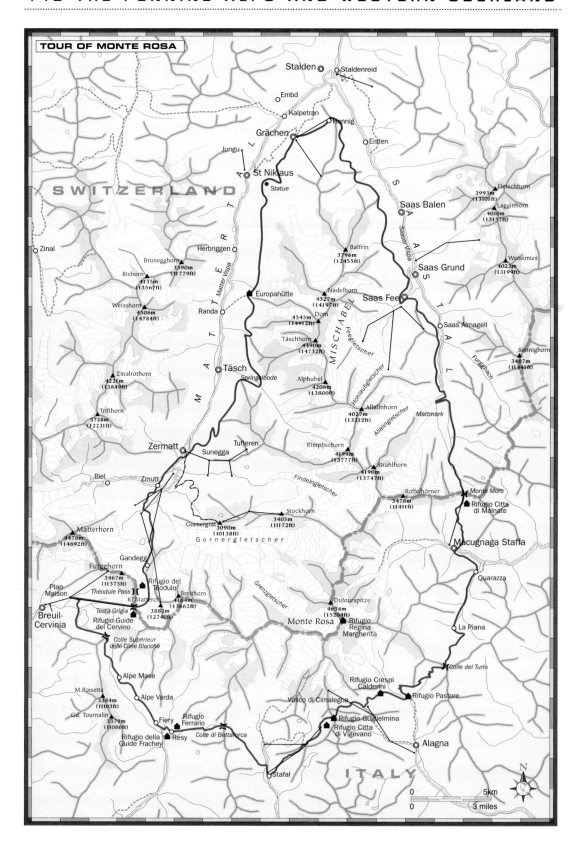

TOUR OF MONTE ROSA

Rifugio Pastore to Rifugio Guglielmina

The Rifugio Crespi Calderini is reached by a steep climb up into the descriptively named Vallon delle Pisse. This is classic meadow terrain, and ahead is the impressive Cascade delle Pisse, which you climb alongside. It's very sunny here in the morning, and amongst the bushes it can get rather humid, but as height is gained so the air gets drier. You're right under the glaciers of the Piramide Vincent, at 4215m (13829ft) one of the smaller summits of the Monte Rosa. From the old cable-car station at Alpe la Balma (2207m/7241ft) a choice must be taken. In good weather the path numbered 10c past Mullini is to be recommended, but in bad conditions it would be prudent to take path 10 over the Bocetta delle Pisse down to Seiwji and Alpe Pianlunga and then walk up the Valle d'Olen to the Colle d'Olen.

Path 10c leads into the high glacial basin of the Conca delle Pisse, dominated at its head by the Stolemberg (3202m/10506ft). This wonderful cwm is so pretty that you're not even aware that there's a cable car overhead. Cottongrass grows by the small lake, and tiny toadflax and other intensely coloured alpines are to be found thriving in the rocks.

The path changes to 10b and gains height quickly through the steep rocky slopes to the Valico di Cimalegna at about 2832m (9292ft). This unlikely passage is well marked, but in bad weather it would be a different proposition altogether and should then be avoided. From this high point the views are superb, with the Piramide Vincent, Liskamm (4527m/14853ft) and Castor (4228m/13872ft) forming the northern horizon. Looking at the map you'll be able to see clearly how you're progressing as you circle around the Monte Rosa and these new views reinforce the impression of being very close to this huge massif. The Colle d'Olen is easily reached and far away in the distance the Gran Paradiso and Mont Blanc can be seen. The Rifugio Guglielmina is a fantastic place to stay, having preserved its old style, affording a feeling of the pioneering spirit of a bygone age. There is also the Rifugio Citta di Vigevano close by.

The Europaweg traverses the hillside opposite the beautiful, snowy Weisshorn.

Rifugio Guglielmina to Resy

This section takes you through the ski resort of Gressoney Stafal and consequently there are some possibilities of taking lifts if you so desire. From the Colle d'Olen the footpath is well marked and easy down to the old Rifugio del Lys, at the middle station of the main cable-car route. The Lago Gabiet would make a pleasant detour. Onwards, the trail goes down the Vallone di Mos, to the village of Stafal. If you need shops or accommodation head down the road into Gressoney Stafal. Otherwise the route continues in the same direction to the top of the short cable-car ride that terminates at Alpe Sitten. If it's working I recommend you take this ride up, as it saves walking out of the valley in the heat of the day.

The path continues up to the Colle di Bettaforca which can be a bit of a grind, with not a lot to recommend it, but it doesn't take too long, and at the pass you follow an easy track to the hamlet of Resy. This is a charming place, perched high above Ayas valley, and enjoys sunshine until the very end of the day. There are two *rifugios* here, and both are quite popular.

Resy to Zermatt

This is a long section and most people will want to split it, but there are various possibilities so I'll leave it up to you to decide how you tackle this. For once the day starts with a descent (don't miss the right turn five minutes from the hut), but of course this means there'll be plenty of ascent later. Shady forest as far as Fiery gives way to the high meadows of the Alpe Varda and Alpe Mase. This area is one of the gems of this trek. I have always been there early in the morning, when the sun has just arrived to warm up the air, and the huge glacier tumbling down from the Breithorn (4164m/ 13662ft) towers above. The path meanders around hummocks and over small streams before beginning the climb to the Colle Supérieur delle Cime Blanche (2982m/9781ft) above the jade waters of the Gran Lago.

From the col you'll be greeted with your first view of the Matterhorn (4478m/14692ft), known as Monte Cervino (Stag Mountain) in Italian. The path snakes around the hillside quite circuitously to reach Plan Maison, which is in the lift system of the Cervinia ski area. There is accommodation here.

The next objective is the Colle del Teodulo or Théodule Pass (3290m/10795ft) which is one of the oldest routes out from the Valle d'Aosta. It is named after St Théodule, the first bishop of Sion and the patron saint of the Valais. There is a path

to reach this col, but it seems more popular nowadays to take one of the area's lifts, and it has to be said that it takes a particular type of mindset to enjoy walking uphill under functioning lifts! However, the lift is not always working to the Théodule Pass, and it usually seems to be the Testa Grigia cable car that functions in the summer, going up to the summit at 3480m (11418ft). There are *rifugios* at the Théodule and at the Testa Grigia passes.

However you get there, what counts is the view. This section is a visual feast and is to be savoured to the full. The Matterhorn is absolutely stunning from these high points, and it's exciting also to have the views of the Monte Rosa massif to the east and to realise how far around it you've come. Ahead to the north on the eastern side of the Mattertal are the peaks of the Strahlhorn, Rimpfischorn, Alphubel (4206m/13800ft), Täschhorn (4490m/14732ft) and Dom (4545m/ 14912ft), to name just some, whilst on the western side are the Ober Gabelhorn (4063m/13331ft), Zinalrothorn (4221m/13849ft) and the Weisshorn (4506m/14784ft). You won't want to leave here, but rest assured that the view doesn't disappear for some time as you descend. The Théodule glacier is quite flat and has got summer ski pistes on it, but this doesn't change the fact that it's a glacier and glaciers have crevasses in them. You're less likely to hurt yourself if you fall into a crevasse roped up to other people, and if you do fall in it's important that those people know what to do. So, be warned, this isn't a normal summer path and should be treated with respect.

At Gandegg you leave the ice for glacial moraine and will soon arrive at the Gandegg restaurant. A lunch break is strongly recommended here, as it would be a great shame to rush away from this unique spectacle and it's a good opportunity to reflect on the Italian part of the route that you've now completed, before getting embroiled in the pleasures of Zermatt. There are various possibilities for descending to Zermatt – take your pick.

Zermatt to the Europahütte

The Europaweg is a relatively new path that has been established to make a high-level route above the Mattertal valley. It is not normally marked as such on the current maps, but a special map covering it and the continuation – the Höhenweg to Saas Fee – can be bought in Zermatt.

Either take the Sunegga lift out of town, or walk up to Tufteren (2215m/7267ft). The well-marked path then starts its interminable traverse round the hillside, always staying around the 2000-m (6562-ft) mark. Needless to say views are fantastic, totally dominated by the Weisshorn. The idea of traversing for the next two days, with only one major change of scenery may seem a little dull, but this couldn't be further from the truth. After days of climbing up and down high passes, it is a welcome change to stay at the same altitude, and this walk is so spectacular that you'll probably have difficulty moving on. Be sure to take plenty of film, since you'll be snapping away. Don't be fooled though – this is no flat stroll; the Europaweg and the Höhenweg are both surprisingly arduous, with a lot of undulating terrain.

A long diversion has to be taken above Täsch to cross the Täschbach, followed by some quite tiring climbing around Springelbode, leading to the junction with the path coming up from Randa, after which it's just a short distance to the newly built Europahütte. From here you can admire the impressive sculpted east ridge of the Weisshorn, which descends in one mighty sweep right down to Täsch, as you enjoy a well deserved cold beer on the hut balcony.

Europahütte to Grächen
The well made path is an impressive feat, but for how long it will last in places is questionable. Worrying signs advise you to 'Walk quickly through the danger zone', and looking up you'll see rocks poised precariously overhead. It seems that they've created a never-ending job, since every winter avalanches and storms will destroy the more exposed sections of the trail. However, it certainly provides superlative walking in unbeatable surroundings. Look back occasionally to take in the panorama stretching from the Breithorn, past the Matterhorn to the Weisshorn. Above are the long glaciated slopes of the Dom, occasionally visible, and further along the Balfrin.

Finally, just before you start your descent into Grächen, you'll come across the statue of Saint Niklaus. The history and legends surrounding St Niklaus are quite fascinating. Originally from Asia Minor, he was a bishop in the 4th century in what is now Turkey. He survived various persecutions and torture, finally dying in 350. In 1087, the relics of Niklaus were transferred to Italy, and the cult of this figure, already widespread in the Orient, became popular in the West. Various incredible stories were told: as a baby Niklaus was said to have fasted twice a week of his own volition; later as bishop, he supposedly stopped one day at an inn where three small children had had their throats

slit and been cut into pieces and put in the salting room. Our hero revived them, sent them off to school and then set about converting the innkeeper to Christianity!

Ahead the Riedgletscher blocks the way, so the path descends. You'll see Grächen a long time before you arrive there, so be prepared for a lengthy section at the end through the woods. There is accommodation in the town itself, or try the beautifully situated hotel at Zum See.

Grächen to Saas Fee
An early morning climb or cable-car ride takes you to Hannigalp, where you change hillsides, and head around the ridge to pick up the Höhenweg. This route has existed for some time as a high-level path above the Saastal. Lusher and greener than the Europaweg, it's gentler, but can still feel quite tiring. It features some exposed sections, and care should be taken in bad weather. Keep your eyes open as ibex and chamois are to be found on these slopes. Ahead is the beautiful snowy summit of the Weissmies, and next to it the rocky Lagginhorn. These will dominate your view as you complete this final section of the trek back to Saas Fee.

Clear signposts direct trekkers on the Europaweg.

PEAK: ALLALINHORN

CLIMB ESSENTIALS

SUMMIT Allalinhorn (4027m/13212ft).
GRADE F
HEIGHT GAIN FROM MITTEL ALLALIN 573m (1880ft).
APPROXIMATE TIME 2–3 hours.
MAP 1:25 000: Landeskarte der Schweiz 1328 Randa.

The Saas Fee metro lift makes the ascent of this peak by the northwest ridge a relatively easy proposition, making it one of the most accessible 4000-m (13124-ft) summits in the Alps. Of course this means there will always be lots of people here, but that doesn't change the fact that the views are superb and that it is a high-altitude snowy summit, which is good for a first high peak and for acclimatisation. It should also be remembered that this is a glaciated peak and although it may be near the ski lifts it still has crevasses. Its name is said to come from the Latin meaning 'little eagle'.

From the top of the metro lift walk out onto Mittel Allalin (3460m/11352ft) and cross the ski pistes heading southwest of the prominent spur. A steeper, crevassed section of glacier leads to the Feejoch (3826m/12553ft). From here climb the summit slopes to reach the summit ridge, then follow this to the top.

The descent is by the same route. After this ascent it would be a shame not to have lunch at the Mittel Allalin Restaurant, the highest revolving restaurant in Europe. If you take an hour over your meal you will complete 360°!

The Rimpfischorn (on the left) and the Allalinhorn seen from the northeast.

ARNICA (ARNICA MONTANA)

Known throughout the Alps for its medicinal uses, it seems that the curative properties of arnica were only discovered in the Middle Ages. Since then, these attractive yellow flowers have been sought for their tincture, formed by the lengthy soaking of the flowers in alcohol. This potion is said to cure many problems and is particularly effective for bringing out bruises and easing the pain of sprains and bumps. Arnica also has roots that are similar to tobacco, hence its popular French name of *tabac des Savoyards*. It has also been used in the past as a colorant and as a cleaning agent.

As with several other flowers, such as the marguerite, the vanilla orchid and the dandelion, the flowerhead of the arnica plant is actually made up of a cluster of flowers. The large yellow petals are just there to attract insects to the flowers, which would otherwise be too small to be conspicuous. This also protects the flowers from wind damage and they save energy by being so small and presenting very little surface area to the elements. Twenty flowers altogether also create a much better landing platform for insects than one tiny flower would alone.

Easily confused with the widespread leopardsbane (*Doronicum*), arnica can be recognised by its leaves, which grow opposite each other on the stem and form a rosette at the bottom, whereas the leopardsbane's grow alternately. Arnica is, of course, protected and grows in meadows and open woods up to 2850m (9345ft), flowering from May to August.

Reaching the top of the southeast ridge of the Weissmies. Part of the descent (the west face can be seen) is shown on the left.

PEAK: THE WEISSMIES

This is an extremely beautiful summit. Its glaciated northwest face contrasts with the steep, rocky south and east sides, so a traverse of the peak inevitably involves different types of climbing. The traverse is the route described here (south-southeast ridge, west face), and whilst this isn't the easiest route up the mountain it is the most interesting and varied. For the normal route you would ascend and descend by the west-face route described here as the descent.

From Saas Almagell follow the well-signed path to the Almageller Hütte (2894m/9495ft). The next day take the indistinct path up to the Zwischbergenpass (3268m/10722ft), between the Portjengrat and the Weissmies. At this stage the sun should just be rising and you'll be treated to a wonderful sunrise beyond the pass, with Lago Maggiore in the distance if you're lucky. To the south is the Monte Rosa massif.

The southeast ridge is reached by the snowslope on its right, and then followed by easy scrambling to about 3960m (12993ft). Here a snow arête gives an exposed finish to the summit. Views are fabulous in all directions, and it seems you can see every summit of the Western Alps.

The descent takes the Trift Glacier, which in

CLIMB ESSENTIALS

SUMMIT Weissmies (4023m/13195t).
PRINCIPAL HUT Almageller Hütte 2894m (9495ft).
GRADE PD
HEIGHT GAIN 1129m (3704ft).
APPROXIMATE TIME 2–3 hours.
MAP 1:25 000: Landeskarte der Schweiz 1329 Saas.

places is very crevassed, so care should be taken as you make your way down, surrounded by spectacular ice scenery. Initially follow the southwest ridge to about 3800m (12468ft), then go northwest down the left bank of the glacier. At about 3400m (11155ft) start to head north to traverse diagonally down the right bank of the glacier and continue on down here until you pick up the path at around 3000m (9843ft) across the moraine to the Hohsaas restaurant and skilift.

If you choose to do the normal route up and down the glacier, Hohsaas has dormitory accommodation and makes for a better starting point than the Weissmies hut which is several hundred metres lower.

PEAK: MONTE ROSA

CLIMB ESSENTIALS

SUMMIT Monte Rosa Dufourspitze (4634m/15195ft); Signalkuppe (4554m/14933ft).
PRINCIPAL HUT Monta Rosa Hütte 2795m (9170ft).
GRADE Dufourspitze PD+ (involves rock scrambling); Signalkuppe PD (a long snow plod).
HEIGHT GAIN 1839m (6034ft).
APPROXIMATE TIME 6-8 hours.
MAP Landeskarte der Schweiz 1348 Zermatt.
ADDITIONAL INFORMATION Whilst neither of these climbs is difficult, the altitude will doubtless make itself felt and you're likely to feel unduly tired.

The Monte Rosa is a series of ten summits that culminate in the Dufourspitze. Although Mont Blanc is higher, Monte Rosa has a greater area and is the highest massif (ie it has the most ground above 4000m/13124ft) in Western Europe. It marks the frontier between Italy and Switzerland and whilst the Swiss side is similar to many other Alpine faces, the Italian side falls away in massive precipitous faces of Himalayan proportions, with a drop of over 2500m (8202ft) down to Macugnaga.

The best way to climb all the summits of Monte Rosa is to combine them with a multi-day traverse of the Zermatt skyline peaks (see p164). For those who don't have the time or energy to do this, the Dufourspitze and the more straightforward summit of Signalkuppe (4556m/ 14939ft) are described here from the Monte Rosa hut. However, this hut gets very busy and is relatively low down so the climb from here is long. Descent is by the same route as the ascents for both climbs.

The ascent of the Dufourspitze is made more demanding by the fact that the main difficulties occur on the summit ridge, where the effects of the altitude will certainly make themselves felt. The Signalkuppe, whilst also being a long

climb, doesn't have the same technical difficulty as the Dufourspitze and there is the reassuring presence of the Rifugio Regina Margherita on the summit (the highest hut in Western Europe), which could be useful if you are late or very tired.

The Monte Rosa hut is reached from Zermatt by taking the Gornergrat railway to Rotenboden, then following the diagonal path down the grassy hillside, which forms the right bank of the Gornergletscher, to get onto the glacier. The way across the glacier to the hut is marked by a variety of poles and oil cans.

To climb the Dufourspitze, follow a cairned route along the lateral moraine and up to Obere Plattje (3200m/10499ft). Gain the Monte Rosa glacier trending left then to the right of the rock island at 3827m (12556ft). Climb steeply up the Scholle to the Satteltole, from where a final steep section leads to the west ridge of the Dufourspitze at Sattell at 4359m (14302ft). Follow the narrowing snow slope up leftwards onto the ridge proper and continue along this. The terrain is mixed at first then more rocky, so after moving over or around various obstacles you finish with a final chimney and a few easy rocks to the summit. Note that all the rock sections can be icy depending on conditions.

To climb the Signalkuppe, follow the route described above to the Obere Plattje. Join the Grenzgletscher here and stay on its right bank. Late in the season, and sometimes throughout the season, the middle section of the glacier can be impassable and you have to take to the steep snow slopes on the right bank. Skirt under the southwest ridge of the Dufourspitze heading southeast. Traverse under the northern slopes of the Parrotspitze and the Seserjoch to the cwm below the Colle Gnifetti. Instead of going up to the col, head right up the western flank of the Signalkuppe to finish on the west ridge.

The Dufourspitze route up the glaciated northwest side of Monte Rosa.

TREK 20: CHAMONIX TO ZERMATT – THE WALKER'S ROUTE

Imagine a trek where you start in the shadow of the Mont Blanc massif, and every high pass you cross brings a new panorama of 4000-m (13124-ft) peaks, until finally you arrive at the foot of what must be the best known summit of them all, the Matterhorn. Well, this is that trek. Not only does it allow you to see more high peaks than any other trek in the Alps, but also it has lots of other attributes: constantly changing scenery, plentiful and varied accommodation, and the added interest of passing through contrasting areas of Switzerland, both French- and German-speaking.

TREK ESSENTIALS

LENGTH 10–14 days.
ACCESS Start in Chamonix and finish in Zermatt.
HIGHEST POINT Col de Prafleuri (2965m/9728ft).
MAPS 1:50 000: Carte Nationale de la Suisse 5003 Mont Blanc Grand Combin, Landeskarte des Schweiz 5006 Matterhorn-Mischabel. You'd need to carry an extra rucksack to take all the 1:25 000 maps that cover this route!
TREK STYLE Mountain refuges and small hotels.
LANGUAGES French and German.
FURTHER OPTIONS Extend the trek to Saas Fee, or even to Simplon.

Traditionally the Haute Route from Chamonix to Zermatt was done as a glacier traverse, wending its way around the high peaks, for the most part following glaciers. That route (see p158) was pioneered by various British alpinists, with local guides, in the 1860s and has since become an extremely popular ski-mountaineering route.

The Walker's Route is different in that it makes its way between the mountaineering Meccas of Chamonix and Zermatt by means of non-glaciated passes. These often-ancient trails were used previously for moving between valleys, for trade or grazing, and so the route doesn't hug the Alpine massif quite so closely. It consequently gives a great variety of walking terrain, and excellent views of the summits.

Chamonix to Trient

The Chamonix valley has several footpaths that parallel the road on each side, at different altitudes – the Petit and Grand Balcon Nord and the Petit and Grand Balcon Sud. They are well marked on the map and on the ground, so choose whichever takes your fancy to reach Argentière and on to the village of Le Tour at the head of the Chamonix valley. The

Col de Balme (2191m/7189ft) is the gateway into Switzerland and can be reached in several ways – by footpath directly up from the village, by the far nicer path up the ridge of Les Frettes and over the Aiguillette des Posettes, or of course by lift, if it's open.

From the col make the most of the stunning views of the Mont Blanc massif, because you're about to leave these summits behind. The descent is straightforward, past shepherds' summer buildings and through the woods on well made switchbacks to the very quiet village of Trient. There is accommodation here.

The Matterhorn dominates the view around Zermatt.

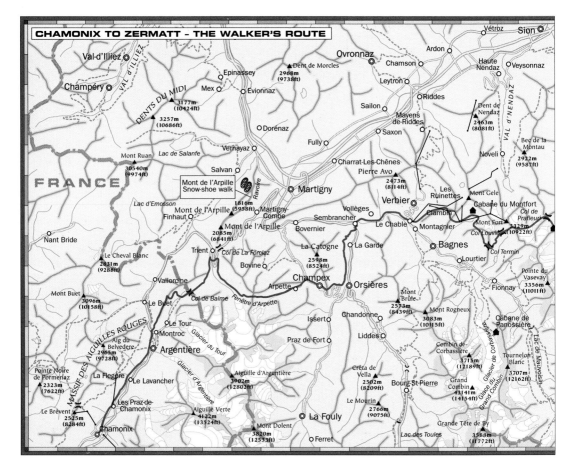

CHAMONIX TO ZERMATT – THE WALKER'S ROUTE

Trient to Champex

At present the trek is following the Tour du Mont Blanc and at this point there is a choice, either of the normal route via Bovine (1987m/6515ft), or of the high variant of the Tour du Mont Blanc, via the Fenêtre d'Arpette (2665m/8744ft). Your decision should take into account the weather, your energy levels, and whether or not you've already done the TMB by one way or the other. Bovine is a lovely route, very pastoral, climbing up though forest to Portalo (2049m/6723ft) from where the views of the Rhône valley stretch away to the Bernese

Oberland. From Bovine the trail descends quite steeply through flower-strewn meadows and boulder fields to reach a farm track that leads via back roads into Champex.

The Fenêtre d'Arpette is completely different. The climb up from Trient is long, steep and hot in the sun. The final section is steep and stony, but all this effort is more than amply rewarded by the spectacular Trient glacier, so close that you feel you could reach out and touch it. The myriad shapes and colours of this tumbling chaos of ice keep your mind off aching muscles as you plod upwards. The

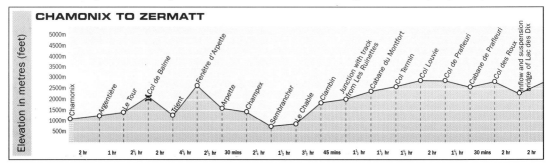

CHAMONIX TO ZERMATT

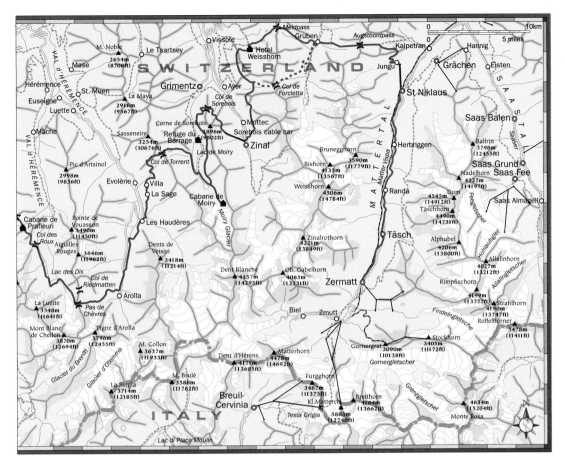

Fenêtre is in fact a small notch in the rocky ridge, from where the descent to the Arpette valley is equally steep, but at least then gravity is on your side. Things ease up gradually and you stroll through pastures to arrive at the Relais d'Arpette, a hotel, *gîte* and restaurant.

The path signposted 'Petit Ruisseau' is by far the nicest way onwards to reach Champex. This small resort is rather upmarket, but manages to cater to all types of visitor, including you, the tired and grubby trekker. There is the full range of accommodation available, from dormitories to smart hotels, and the most picturesque lake, with the Grand Combin perfectly reflected in its crystal-clear waters. Look, but don't swim!

Champex to the Cabane du Montfort

This stage may be divided into two days, and if you don't like taking lifts then it will have to be. However, I'm not at all averse to the odd section of mechanical uplift. Having once walked the stage from Le Chable to the top of Les Ruinettes lift system I can see no great reason to recommend it, but decide for yourself having looked at the map.

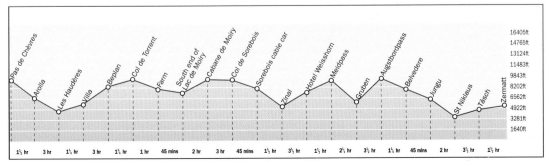

It would help to have eyes in the back of your head in order to be able to appreciate the fantastic view behind you on the section from Col Termin to Col de Louvie.

There are plenty of hotels to choose from in Le Chable if you do decide to stop there.

The meadows down from Champex are delightful, and offer different flora and fauna since the altitude is lower. Snakes and fat green lizards are often to be found sunning themselves on the hot tracks, sliding lazily away at your approach, whilst the villages passed through give an insight into rural life in these parts – farming is still largely traditional. You'll even see old people scything the grass by hand – whether this is quaint or not is debatable.

Sembrancher is a pleasant town, with sunny squares and several hotels. The route to Le Chable strolls along the Val de Bagnes. If you're planning to walk up to Verbier and then via Clambin to the Cabane du Montfort, the route is waymarked with local yellow paint flashes and takes a series of tracks and footpaths through little villages and shady forest to emerge on the track which leads to Montfort. Alternatively the cable car in Le Chable is all too obvious, and will take you in two stages to Les Ruinettes. It is only open from early July to early September, and may close for lunch.

From Les Ruinettes the views are superb, but take a minute to distance yourself from the lift station. This new vista is dominated by the Grand Combin (4314m/14154ft), a huge monster of a peak, all the more impressive for the absence of an 'easy' route to the summit. Views of this wonderful glaciated giant will accompany you for the next day's walk. To the southwest are the spectacular steep faces of the Argentière peaks: the Aiguille d'Argentière (3902m/12802ft), the Tour Noir (3835m/12583ft) and Mont Dolent (3820m/12533ft), this latter being the summit where Italy, France and Switzerland meet.

The Montfort refuge is a short walk from the lift station, firstly along the track, then following a water leat, or *bisse*, which irrigates farming land. The clear waters provide a refreshing change, and are bordered by many different flowers. You'll see the refuge on a bluff ahead, with its Swiss flag flying proudly. This is a great hut – a warm welcome, superb views (including the already far-off Mont Blanc if you're lucky) and the most plentiful hut food in the Alps.

Cabane du Montfort to the Cabane de Prafleuri

To begin this marvellous day take the slightly exposed path that traverses the hillside under the Bec des Rosses. Named the 'Chemin des Chamois', this area is known for its wildlife. I've actually seen as many ibex here as chamois, and it is a treat to come across groups of young males practising their horn-butting in preparation for the real thing when they prove their superiority before the winter breeding season. The Col Termin (2648m/8688ft) provides a new view, this time over towards the Rosablanche (3336m/10945ft), although the Grand Combin will remain the backdrop for much of the day. There are often herds of chamois or ibex grazing in the morning in this area, so approach quietly and you've a good chance of spotting them before they decide you're not desirable company.

The Lac de Louvie looks most tempting below, but you remain high, traversing towards the Col de Louvie (2921m/9584ft), which is reached by a final steep pull amongst boulders. Here you enter a barren and quite desolate scene, with the Grand Désert glacier the next obstacle. The state of this very flat and short glacier crossing varies immensely according to the time of year and quantities of snow. It's usually an easy if slightly soggy twenty-minute walk from one side to the other, with no crevasse danger. However, in a dry year, late in the season, it can be ice, with gravel on top; this can be quite difficult to walk on, a slide potentially causing nasty grazes. If it's warm and ice is melting then you'll be slopping through puddles, but this is preferable to solid ice. Head for the red-and-white marker on the other side – possibly a contender for the biggest paint flash in the world? In fog cross on a bearing of 72° – it's important not to veer off too low or to head up the glacier.

The rest of the route up to the Col de Prafleuri (2965m/9728ft) is well indicated by flashes and cairns. A short steep descent can be interesting just before the final slopes up to the col. An unexpected scene awaits you at this pass since the area below has been somewhat ravaged by quarrying to construct the Dix dam, and the remains of the works and old buildings are rather unsightly. Still, the ibex don't seem to mind, and while staying at the Prafleuri hut be sure to look out at dusk for the huge-horned males that normally gather to graze in the vicinity.

Cabane de Prafleuri to Arolla

You're heading for new views on this stage, those of the Arolla peaks. The Col des Roux (2804m/9200ft) puts you in the early morning sunshine for a lovely amble down through interesting yellow boulders and meadows. The Dix lake looks immense, and beyond you will be able to almost make out the second col of this section, the Pas de Chèvres (2855m/9367ft). The most impressive

peak here is the Mont Blanc de Cheilon, with its beautiful, steep north face. To the east is the contrasting rounded snowy dome of the Pigne d'Arolla (3796m/12455ft), and later you'll see Mont Collon (3637m/11933ft) further to the east, which dominates the tiny village of Arolla.

A flat track above the Dix lake allows a rest and time to drink in the postcard views up ahead. The shores of the lake provide many desirable residences for marmots and you're sure to spot the odd round beige furry bottom perched on a sun-baked rock, its owner gazing out over the lake. Named after a group of ten outlaws who lived in the valley many years before it was flooded, and who used to regularly descend to nearby towns for a bit of pillage, the Lac des Dix is impressively large. It's possible to have a guided visit of the dam, which is very interesting for a rest day. The inflow to the lake is enormous, coming through tunnels from many neighbouring glaciers, and you'll be able to get a close-up view as you cross the bouncy suspension bridge at the far end.

The climbing begins again, with a long ascent to the Pas de Chèvres. Look out for the edelweiss here on the ascent from the lake. The Pas de Chèvres provides a bit of excitement with a rather conveniently placed ladder for the final few metres of rock guarding this pass. This is no problem, but if you hesitate to clean the outside of the upstairs

The Cabane de Moiry.

windows at home you may wish to take the neighbouring Col de Riedmatten (2919m/9577ft), which hasn't got a ladder and doesn't need one.

The ladder's not the only exciting part of this day – the best is that from the pass you get your first view of the Matterhorn (4478m/14692ft), far away, but definitely there. The descent to Arolla is relatively gentle, and there are plenty of tempting places to sit and enjoy. Mont Collon and its tumbling glacier are spectacular, and you'll soon arrive at Arolla, which has a disproportionate number of hotels for such a small village.

Arolla to La Sage
This is quite a short section but needs to be done as a day, or avoided by bus, since after La Sage there is no accommodation for some way. It does not need a lot of description, suffice to say that the walking is very pleasant, through forest and past typical alpine chalets. Les Haudères is a fascinating old village, all higgledy-piggledy back streets and ancient chalets leaning at crazy angles, adorned with masses of vibrant geraniums. From Les Haudères to La Sage a good trail avoids the road.

La Sage to the Cabane de Moiry
Today's big objective is the Col de Torrent (2919m/9577ft), which is a climb of more than 1200m (3937ft) from La Sage, but what a wonderful ascent! The views are spectacular, back towards the Arolla peaks and away to the Dent Blanche (4357m/14295ft) in the south, and the path is well graded, winding up through meadows, with the occasional flat section enabling you to catch your breath and look around.

The rather muddy lake at Beplan marks the end of the pastures and is a convenient lunch stop, before tackling the zigzags up to the pass. You'll soon forget all the pain when you see the grand panorama before you. To the south are the peaks you've come to know – the Pigne d'Arolla, Mont Blanc de Cheilon, Grand Combin and even Mont Blanc if you've got good eyesight. To the east is the mighty Weisshorn (4506m/14784ft), which you'll get to know quite well by the end of the trek. Below,

Another col, yet another stupendous view – the bright blue glacial waters of Lac de Moiry are just visible.

Late *nevé* en route to Jungu.

here a good path traverses the western slopes of the Aiguilles de la Lé and the Garde de Bordon, to meet up with the path ascending from the dam towards the Col de Sorebois (2835m/ 9302ft). This traverse is not marked on the map, but affords a good morning's walk and chamois are often to be found grazing.

The path to the col is obvious and not too difficult, culminating in the now familiar zigzags which always mean you're about to get a new view. This is no exception. This time the Weisshorn appears considerably closer, joined by the Schalihorn (3974m/13039ft) and the Zinalrothorn (4221m/13849ft). You've arrived at the top of Zinal's ski area, and the pistes lead to the cable-car station. If you like knee-jarring descents follow the signed footpaths into the town, otherwise take the lift. Zinal is attractive, with a particularly fascinating old sector. There are several hotels and a *gîte*.

and much nearer, are the amazingly blue waters of the Lac de Moiry.

It's difficult to move on from here, but needs must and finally you'll set off towards the lake. At the farm buildings at 2481m (8140ft) a decision must be made. There is accommodation at the restaurant above the Moiry dam at the northern end of the lake, but if time and energy allow, the best place to stay is the Cabane de Moiry. However, it does require another 600m (1969ft) of ascent. To go to the *cabane* from the farm follow the path along the western side of the lake. There are two options: the main track above the lake which hits the road at the far end of the lake, or a path signed 'Tour du Lac' which stays much higher and approaches the Moiry hut across the flat snout of the Moiry glacier. This avoids the final climb, but the path is undulating and quite tiring.

Rising up from the end of the the lake is the path normally taken to the Cabane de Moiry and it is equipped with chains and ropes for a short section, then takes a series of interminable switchbacks up to the hut, which is perched above the glacier. The best way to dispense with this section is to concentrate on the wonders of the glacier, just next to the path. It's worth the effort because once at the hut you'll be able to sit on the terrace, beer in hand, and watch the sun go down on the Grand Cornier (3961m/12996ft) and the Pointe de Bricola (3658m/12002ft).

Cabane de Moiry to Zinal

From the hut you need to descend the zigzags and continue to a junction marked 'Tour du Lac'. From

Zinal to Gruben

There is a fabulous high traverse from Zinal towards St Luc. The Walker's Route takes this but unfortunately in the wrong direction – that is to say all the best views are behind you. However, what better reason for frequent stops? Visible are the Dent Blanche, Zinalrothorn, Ober Gabelhorn and even the Matterhorn, just reminding you it's still there. This trail leads to the Hotel Weisshorn, which is a superb renovated building from the 19th century, perched high above the valley, commanding fantastic views of the Diablerets glacier. Hotel Weisshorn is a great place to stay if you have time.

The Meidpass (2790m/9154ft) leads over to Gruben, but if you don't intend to stay at the Hotel Weisshorn, a shorter version of this section is to turn off the main trail at the ruined buildings of Tsahelet and take the path to the Forcletta pass (2874m/9430ft). For either pass the path weaves up through increasingly barren ground, and at both cols the Weisshorn is again seen along with the neighbouring Bishorn (4135m/1367ft) and Brunegghorn (3590m/11779ft).

Below lies the Turtmantal, which has to rank as one of the most attractive and peaceful alpine valleys that I know. Descend the initially stony slopes that transform into typical meadows and

Contemplating the continuation of the trek from the Col de Sorebois.

finally larch forest to discover the hamlet of Gruben, with its gleaming white church. I arrived here one summer's afternoon to find a wedding in full swing, the church decked out with bouquets of wildflowers and everyone dancing in the street. Normally things are not so lively, but take the time to wander around here and discover the charms of the Turtmantal.

Gruben to Zermatt

Some people will want to split this day into two, to allow time to walk from St Niklaus up to Zermatt. To do it as one section you have to take the train from St Niklaus to Täsch, just walking the final part into Zermatt.

The Augstbordpass (2894m/9495ft) is the final col on the trek, but it's one of the best. The climb up is continually interesting, firstly in the forest, with glimpses of Gruben catching the early morning sun, then higher up you enter the meadows of Grüobtälli, and will be able to discern the shady slopes of the pass up ahead. Scree and boulders make for tough going, but the path is always good right to the top. The views from here are fine, but the best is to come.

After descending a little way, the path curves around to the southeast, traversing round the Troara ridge. After rounding the crest you begin to see the mountains, and a huge cairn marks the best viewpoint. The Dom (4545m/14912ft), the highest peak entirely in Switzerland, and the Täschhorn (4490m/14732ft) are true giants, towering above the Mattertal far below. The head of the valley is bounded by the chain of Liskamm (4527m/14853ft), Castor (4228m/13872ft), Pollux (4092m/13426ft) and the massive summit of the Breithorn (4164m/13662ft). The Matterhorn remains stubbornly out of sight and won't be seen again until the last minute. This view makes the whole trek worthwhile, and arriving here is very exciting and moving.

But it's not over yet, and the view remains with you as you make your way to the amazing hamlet of Jungu, perched way above the valley. Jungu is served by a rather old and intimidating cable car, which is great fun to ride down. For those with extra time a night spent in the tiny *gîte* here would be a real treat, but otherwise head on down to St Niklaus. There is a path down, but I have to say I wouldn't miss the lift for anything.

From St Niklaus there are paths leading along the valley past Randa, scene of an immense rockfall and landslide in 1991 which temporarily cut off the upper Mattertal and caused the river to flood.

Tracks and paths continue on along the valley to Täsch. If time is short or you don't fancy the valley walk, the train can be used to avoid this section and to prepare for the final stage into Zermatt.

A footpath through the woods above the railway line contrasts pleasantly with the rest of this day, although by this stage you'll be so excited about arriving at Zermatt you may not want to linger and enjoy this stroll. Every time you crest a rise you'll be wondering if you're going to see the Matterhorn and finally, all of a sudden, it's there, enormous and unlike any other peak. Photos are obligatory, and from this point it's just a short continuation before you arrive on the main street of Zermatt, probably feeling a little like an alien among the crowds of tourists and souvenir shops. Walk proudly along the main street, happy in the knowledge that you walked there, more or less!

BISSES

A *bisse* is the name given to an artificial irrigation channel in the Alps. Such waterways can be either carved out of rock or made out of wood, and often date back centuries. With the decline in mountain agriculture *bisses* have largely fallen into disuse, but they are true historical monuments. In some parts of Switzerland widespread campaigns have been undertaken to try and save as many of them as possible, and there are several in the Western Alps that feature in the treks described here. Paths often go alongside them and the clear bubbling water provides welcome freshness on hot afternoons.

SNOW-SHOE WALK: MONT DE L'ARPILLE

Perched high above the Rhône valley, the Mont de l'Arpille is a great outing in winter, both for first timers on snow shoes and for those who have already walked in winter in the Alps. There are exceptional views of the flat-bottomed Rhône valley, and the Roman town of Martigny, and even on days when clouds obscure the high summits this walk is worthwhile since the views below are as good as those above. However, on a clear sunny day, the Mont Blanc massif, the Trient peaks and the summits around Emosson are all seen from here.

The walk isn't long, but is nevertheless quite varied. The starting point is just above the village of Ravoire, at a point called Chez Pillet. This is well-signed from the village. The way is quite easy to follow, heading up into the trees behind the houses. In typical Swiss style there are frequent footpath signs and even in heavy snow conditions I've found most of these to be visible. As is often the case, it's possible to feel a bit confused in the forest, and there are several forest tracks, not all of which are marked on the map. The path tends to cross these, but if you're puzzled the general direction is southwest to emerge from the trees, after about an hour, into the Arpille *alpage*.

From the *alpage* chalets carry on in the same direction, up towards another forested area. Here you need to be careful not to traverse the steep east slopes of the peak, as these can be avalanche-prone. It's better to head up onto the rounded ridge then go south towards the top. The final stage is beautiful, winding in and out of the trees, through gently rolling slopes, to finish on the flat summit.

It's possible to descend directly to the Col de la Forclaz, by taking the western slopes of the peak and then down steeply through the forest to the south. Or return by the same route to Chez Pillet.

SNOW-SHOE WALK ESSENTIALS

ACCESS Start at Chez Pillet, Ravoire, and either finish here or at the Col de la Forclaz.
DISTANCE 8-km (5-mile) round trip from Chez Pillet.
HEIGHT GAIN 750m (2461ft).
APPROXIMATE TIME 4–5 hours round trip.
DIFFICULTY 2
TYPE OF WALK 1-day circuit.
INTERESTING FEATURES The valley and mountain views, the contrast between the forest and the open terrain.
ADDITIONAL INFORMATION Chez Pillet is a permanently inhabited hamlet and parking is limited. If there are no places park further down and walk up the road to here, or take one of the signed paths that head up the hill further down the road. They all lead to Arpille.
MAP 1:25 000: Carte Nationale de la Suisse 1325 Sembrancher, 1324 Barberine.

TREK 21: CHAMONIX TO ZERMATT – THE GLACIER ROUTE

Chamonix and Zermatt, two names that inspire dreams and ideas. To walk from one to the other through the high mountains is one of the most beautiful glacier walks in the Alps. This route was first done in the Victorian era, 1861 to be precise, by British mountaineers with local guides. Nowadays the route is very often skied in the spring, but it is still popular as a walk in the summer, and justifiably so. It passes close to many of the high peaks of the Pennine Alps, with the opportunity to ascend a couple en route. Views are stunning, from Mont Blanc to the Matterhorn, with many fabulous summits inbetween.

TREK ESSENTIALS

LENGTH 8 days.
ACCESS Start in Le Tour at the head of the Chamonix valley and finish at Zermatt.
HIGHEST POINT Pigne d'Arolla (3796m/12455ft).
MAPS 1:50 000: Carte Nationale de la Suisse 5003 Mont Blanc Grand Combin, 5006 Matterhorn Mischabel.
1:25 000: Carte Nationale de la Suisse 1344 Col de Balme, 1345 Orsières, 1346 Chanrion, 1347 Matterhorn, 1348 Zermatt.
TREK STYLE Glacier trek with high mountain huts.
LANGUAGES French and German.
FURTHER OPTIONS: Ascend Mont Blanc de Cheilon from the Vignettes; ascend any of the Zermatt peaks on arrival, such as the Breithorn, Monte Rosa or the Matterhorn.

Since the Haute Route, as it's known, was first done the recession of the glaciers has changed some cols and glaciers, and nowadays you're likely to encounter some ice and rockfall danger, especially late in the season. So care should be taken in route choice, and early starts are always

to be recommended for glacier travel.

There are several variations to the route, but here I describe what seems to be the most popular way, both in terms of route and direction. There's no real reason why you shouldn't go from Zermatt to Chamonix, but tradition and force of habit mean that this is rarely done.

Le Tour to the Cabane du Trient

Although known as the Chamonix to Zermatt trek, it really starts at the head of the Chamonix valley. Some people insist on walking up from Le Tour itself, but as you'll have realised by now I don't see any reason to walk under functioning cable cars, so take the cable car and then the chairlift from Le Tour to just below the Col de Balme.

The path to the Albert Première Refuge takes a rising traverse around the hillside first south and then east, to pick up the path on the glacial moraine which leads to the hut. The Glacier du Tour is just below and the views are great, but this hut must be one of the most popular in the Alps so expect it to be busy. If you're planning on ascend-

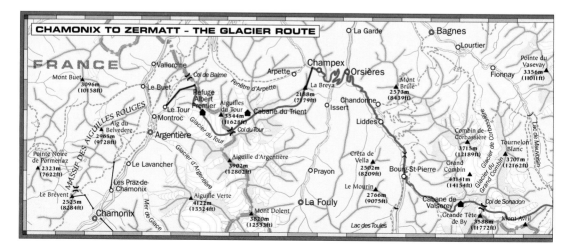

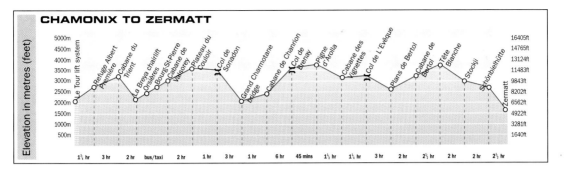

ing the Aiguilles du Tour, then it would be wise to stay the night at the hut. If not then I recommend you press on, unless you've made a late start, or want to take it easy on the first day.

About twenty minutes beyond the hut you'll set foot on a glacier for the first time on this trek. Your objective, the Col du Tour (3281m/ 10765ft), is just before the small summit of the Tête Blanche, and this gives access to the Trient glacier, which forms a huge plateau where it would be quite easy to get lost in bad weather. It is interesting to note here, for anyone using the French 1:25000 map 3430 OT, that the contour interval changes on the border from 10m to 20m.

Take the Trient glacier in a wide arc in the direction of the Cabane du Trient, which is to be found under the Pointe d'Orny at 3170m (10400ft). Be careful in bad visibility as there is an enormous wind hollow directly in front of the hut, and it would definitely spoil your day to fall into this. Pass the hollow on the right to locate the short path in through rocks leading up and left of the hut.

For your first night in the mountains you won't be disappointed – the Cabane du Trient enjoys great views of the northern side of the Aiguilles du Tour and the Aiguilles Dorées.

Cabane du Trient to Bourg-St-Pierre

Walk down the left bank of the Orny glacier, gaining the moraine path a few hundred metres (or yards) before the Cabane d'Orny. From here you can admire the spectacular profile of the rock spire of the Clochers du Portalet, before continuing down the pleasant, well-worn path that eventually leads to the chairlift of La Breya, having traversed high around the northern slopes of the Combe d'Orny. The lift takes you to the outskirts of Champex, and works regularly, closing for an hour or so at lunchtime.

Champex is a fine place to enjoy a break, before taking the bus (via Orsières) or taxi to Bourg-St-Pierre. This small town has several possibilities for accommodation, and is also very interesting historically, being on the route to the Grand Saint Bernard Pass (see p132).

(Note that if you are late in the season it is advisable to check in Champex about the conditions of the crucial passage from the Cabane de Valsorey to the Plateau du Couloir. Phone the

warden and, if in doubt, consider changing your route to avoid this section by going directly to the Chanrion hut via Mauvoisin – take the bus/taxi from Champex to the Mauvoisin lake.)

Bourg-St-Pierre to the Cabane de Valsorey.

No glacier travel today, but a good steep climb up to the Valsorey hut. Outside the village the path is signed, but as with all these walks, the hardest part is often finding the way out of town.

The walk starts off relatively gently up the Valsorey valley, pleasantly following the river. At the Chalets d'Amont (2197m/7208ft) the path heads southeast, and a steep section is equipped with chains and cables. The path then continues up to the hut, which is perched at (3030m/9941ft), under the southwestern slopes of the huge bulk of the Grand Combin.

Cabane de Valsorey to the Cabane de Chanrion

This stage is serious and should not be attempted in bad weather. If conditions aren't right, retreat carefully from the Valsorey and take transport round to Mauvoisin.

Climb up northeast behind the hut for about 600m (1969ft) and make a traverse rightwards

to the Plateau du Couloir (3664m/12021ft). This can vary dramatically from easy snow early in the season to ice and scree later. From the Plateau, which is immediately under the Grand Combin, you head down onto the Glacier de Sonadon, quite flat at this point. The Col de Sonadon (3504m/11497ft) is directly ahead to the east, and is crossed easily to reach the Durand Glacier.

The climbing is over for a while, and you must descend the glacier to the valley above the Mauvoisin lake. The descent of the Durand Glacier will vary from year to year, but generally takes the left bank briefly before traversing right (south), at about (3300m/10827ft), to pass between two serac bands. The going becomes easier and you leave the glacier at around 2700m (8859ft) to pass point 2735.7 and descend to the bridge at 2182m (7159ft) via the Grand Charmotane, or leave the glacier a little further down at 2500m (8202ft) at Tsé Burgo, and go on down to the bridge.

The glacier walking is all done for the day and you can relax and enjoy the wonderful views. Up to the west are the steep glaciated slopes of La Tsessette (4141m/13587ft), next to the Grand

Dawn from the Col de Charmotane.

Combin. To the northeast is La Ruinette (3875m/12714ft) and, down the valley, the Mauvoisin lake formed by what is reputedly the biggest dam of its kind in the world.

The Cabane de Chanrion is 280m (918ft) above, so take it nice and easy and you'll be there in no time, and if you haven't had enough of the scenery by now, prepare to spend a great evening in the shadow of the Grand Combin.

Cabane de Chanrion to the Cabane des Vignettes

Two options present themselves for this day, and the decision about which one to take depends largely on the weather. The first possibility, taking the Otemma glacier, involves no technical difficulties and stays relatively low, making it a good choice in less-than-perfect weather. The second, up the Brenay glacier, involves a section of steeper ground to pass a serac barrier and also allows for the ascent of the Pigne d'Arolla (3796m/12455ft).

For the Otemma glacier route take the road south-southeast past Les Pintas and around into the Otemma valley, then follow the glacier northeast towards the Col de Charmotane between the Pigne d'Arolla and the Petit Mont Collon. Although the glacier is quite long and rather flat, the peaks all around are fine, and as you gain height so the views become more beautiful.

Just before reaching the col bear slightly left to climb more steeply, leaving the glacier via the little col just a few metres left of point 3162m (10374ft). The southeast slopes of the Pigne d'Arolla are directly above, but you follow the flat snow terrace which leads to the Col des Vignettes. The Cabane des Vignettes is situated a couple of hundred metres to the east, on a rocky promontory at the end of a rocky ridge. People seem to find the toilet situation here quite memorable!

The Brenay glacier route is approached by following the path north from the Chanrion hut, then northeast onto the glacier. The steep slopes of La Ruinette (3875m/12714ft) and Mont Blanc de Cheilon (3870m/12697ft) provide an impressive view ahead. The glacier steepens between the rocky buttress of La Serpentine and the Seracs du Brenay. This can prove a slightly difficult section, before the going becomes easier and, keeping right of point 3434m (11267ft), you reach the Col de Brenay (3639m/11939ft). From here you easily gain the flat col of the Pigne d'Arolla, and the summit is just a few minutes to the north. The views are splendid, with Mont Blanc de Cheilon to

the west and Mont Collon (3637m/11933ft) to the east. High peaks are to be seen further away in all directions, and this is certainly one of the highlights of the trek.

When you can tear yourself away from the summit, return to the col then descend the southeast-facing slope of the Pigne, more or less following the fall-line. At 3320m (10893ft) turn left to make a descending traverse of a steep slope, between seracs, which leads to the Col des Vignettes. Alternatively, if this traverse is too icy, go south at this point and skirt underneath the rocks at about 3120m (10237ft) to reach the little col to the west of 3162m (10374ft) on the Otemma route. Continue as for that route.

A night spent at the Vignettes hut will be unforgettable, perched high above the Arolla valley, with the rocky summits of the Aiguille de la Tsa, the Dents de Bertol and the Bouquetins right opposite.

Cabane des Vignettes to the Cabane de Bertol

From the hut you need to reverse the Otemma route as far as the Col de la Charmotane (3053m/10017ft), then continue southeast, south and southeast again up the Glacier du Mont Collon to the Col de l'Evêque (3392m/11129ft). Having passed the western side of Mont Collon you're now going to go under the eastern face. This is achieved by descending to the east, on the right bank of the glacier, to pass a steep area between 3300m (10827ft) and 3180m (10433ft).

The angle then eases and you continue down the Haut Glacier d'Arolla until it's possible to leave it at about 2550m (8366ft) to pick up the path to the Plans de Bertol. Time for a rest here, before tackling the steep, but well marked trail, then the snow of the Bertol glacier to the Col de Bertol at 3279m (10758ft). The hut is just above, to the north of the pass, high on the rocks, and is accessed by chains and ladders and surrounded by a sea of glaciers.

Cabane de Bertol to the Schönbielhütte

This is a fabulous day, when you'll want the camera at the ready. Not only do you get to see the Matterhorn in all its magnificence, but you also pass into German-speaking Switzerland. In good weather the traverse of the flat upper section of the Glacier du Mont Miné will cause no problems. Take a generally southeasterly direction to gain the fantastic viewpoint of the Tête Blanche (3724m/12218ft). In bad visibility, if there is no track, it can be difficult to find the way to here.

The long-awaited view of the Matterhorn fron the top of the Stockjigletcher, below the Tête Blanche.

The Tête Blanche gives you the views you've dreamed of: the Matterhorn and the Dent Blanche are suddenly really close while further away are all the Zermatt peaks. This is a place to linger, and hopefully you'll have brought enough film to last the day.

Force yourself to continue on down onto the Stockjigletcher, via the Col de la Tête Blanche at about (3580m/11746ft). This glacier is heavily crevassed, so you'll need to tear your gaze away from the visual delights of the peaks and watch out for holes. Get to the rocky lump of the Stockji, and from point 3141m (10306ft) descend a steep zigzag path roughly southeast to gain moraines leading northeast to point 2624m (8609ft). Now cross the Schönbiel glacier in the same direction to pick up the hut approach path, which climbs improbably through steep ground to reach the hut.

(Note that from the top of the Stockji there is an early-season short-cut down the wide north-facing couloir which starts just east of point 3091.8m (10144ft), but this should only be considered when full of snow. From its foot go up north-north-east across the glacier to gain the path leading southeast to the hut under point 2738m/ 18983ft.)

Staying at the Schönbielhütte is an experience you don't want to miss. A fit party could certainly continue on to Zermatt, and if it's nightlife and shops you're yearning for then go for it, but this hut occupies such a marvellous position with the north face of the Matterhorn right opposite the front door that I can't imagine how anyone could want to miss it. The Matterhorn is such a unique summit that it's totally absorbing to study the different faces and ridges. Its neighbour, the Dent d'Herens (4171m/13685ft) is equally spectacular, and so this last night in the mountains will definitely be one to remember.

Schönbielhütte to Zermatt

Plenty of time for a leisurely stroll down to the real world. A good trail goes above the left bank of the Zmutt glacier, eventually passing through the charming hamlet of Zmutt. It's worth stopping for refreshments here, and exploring the traditional houses. Zmutt is one of the area's oldest settlements. Its importance dates back to Roman times when it was the last staging post before the long climb up to the Théodule Pass, which was the route used to travel over to Italy.

Stroll down into Zermatt past numerous old chalets and flower-filled meadows – a welcome contrast after days of snow and ice. Then celebrate!

PEAK: MONT BLANC DE CHEILON

The beautiful sculpted north face of this peak will certainly have caught your eye if you've done Trek 20 (Chamonix to Zermatt – The Walker's Route). It can also be included by a strong and fit party on the fifth day of the Haute Route (Trek 21), and without adding an extra day, the Glacier de la Serpentine can be followed, instead of the Seracs du Brenay, to the Col de la Serpentine. Leaving excess baggage here you can climb and reverse the east ridge of the mountain, then head east to surmount the Mur de la Serpentine to rejoin the normal route at the Col du Brenay.

Whilst the north face can be climbed, the normal route goes up the much more amenable southwest face of the mountain. It is most conveniently climbed from the Cabane des Dix, but I've also given several variants to allow it to be included in a trek.

From the Dix hut follow moraines and the short glacial slope southwest to the Col de Cheilon (3243m/10640ft). This point can also be gained from the Chanrion hut via the Col Lire Rose (3115m/10220ft) and the Col Mont Rouge (3325m/10909ft) but this is much longer.

Just on the south side of the col follow the steepening snow slope eastwards for a short while until it's possible to cut leftwards onto the rocky ridge (there are several possible places). This is followed, either on the ridge or more easily on its right, until a steep snow slope appears

CLIMB ESSENTIALS
SUMMIT Mont Blanc de Cheilon (3869m/12694ft).
PRINCIPAL HUT Cabane des Dix 2928m (9607ft).
GRADE PD
HEIGHT GAIN 941m (3087ft).
APPROXIMATE TIME 3-4 hours.
MAP Carte Nationale de la Suisse 1346 Chanrion.

on its left (north) side. Continue on the ridge a short while longer, to avoid the steepest snow, then trend east up the snow to gain the final rocky summit ridge around 3785m (12418ft). Gain the summit by this ridge, with just one slightly difficult step.

Once again views are marvellous, extending in all directions. To the west is the Grand Combin and to the east the sharp summit of the Dent d'Herens. To descend you can continue the traverse with slightly more difficulty to the Col de la Serpentine (3547m/11638ft) and from there descend to either the Dix or the Vignettes hut (the latter via the Pigne d'Arolla). Or reverse the summit ridge to 3785m (12418ft) then continue in the same direction up to 3827m (12556ft). Now descend in an arc, first south then westwards under the steep slopes of La Ruinette to gain the flat of the Gietro Glacier midway between points 3361m (11027ft) and 3359m (11021ft). From there the Col de Cheilon is easily regained.

The superb sculpted north face of the Mont Blanc de Cheilon, as seen from the Cabane des Dix.

TREK 22: THE ZERMATT FRONTIER PEAKS – THE GLACIER ROUTE

This is the glacier trek to beat them all. It provides the opportunity to climb a large number of 4000-m (13124-ft) summits, but these are not all obligatory, and just undertaking this challenging trek takes you into scenery that is outstanding. Some of the summits are very close to each other, the glaciers immense, and the views, of course, breathtaking.

TREK ESSENTIALS

LENGTH 4 days – more if combined with the main Monte Rosa summits.
ACCESS Start and finish in Zermatt.
HIGHEST POINT This depends on peaks climbed. If only Castor is climbed then the Lisjoch passage (4246m/13931ft) is the highest point.
MAPS 1:50 000: Landeskarte der Schweiz 284 Mischabel, 294 Gressoney.
1:25 000: Landeskarte der Schweiz 1348 Zermatt, IGC 109 Monte Rosa.
TREK STYLE Multi-day glacier trek, with summit possibilities, staying in high mountain huts.
LANGUAGES German and Italian.
FURTHER OPTIONS Covered in the text.

Zermatt to the Rifugio delle Guide Valle d'Ayas

Take the Klein Matterhorn cable car from Zermatt and at the top of the lift walk through the tunnel and halfway along the ski tow, then follow a well-beaten track left to the Breithorn Pass at 3824m (12547ft). Here the obvious choice is to ascend the Breithorn (see p167). This peak is a glacier walk. After descending the Breithorn, traverse under the south slopes of the mountain, just under the new Rossi Volante bivouac hut to beneath the Schwarztor, the col between the Breithorn and Pollux.

Now walk up to the foot of the rocky south ridge of Pollux. Passing just next to it, gain the Verra glacier which you descend to reach the Rifugio delle Guide Valle d'Ayas (Rifugio Ayas), situated at 3420m (11221ft) on the rocky promontory of Lambronecca. The hut is not marked on older maps, on which just the Rifugio Mezzalama is shown further down the same ridge. The Ayas hut is sometimes known as the Nuova Mezzalama hut. Its grid reference on the Swiss map is 6525 0855.

(Note the alternative ski route shown on some maps, which avoids the climb up to Pollux by short-cutting through the seracs, cannot usually be passed in summer.)

Rifugio Ayas to Rifugio Quintino Sella

The summits of Pollux (4092m/13426ft) and Castor (4228m/13872ft) – in Greek mythology the sons of the goddess Leda – are feasible from the Ayas refuge as part of the route to the next hut, and indeed Castor provides the best route over. There are various possible routes up Pollux, the best being the west-southwest ridge, which involves some scrambling and climbing up steep fixed ropes. From the rop of the rock, where there is a Madonna, an exposed snow or ice ridge leads to the summit. Descent is by the same route, so you could leave your rucksacks at the bottom while climbing this.

Castor is best ascended by its west face, to exit left onto the northwest ridge for the final airy arête

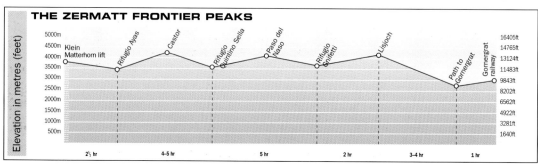

THE ZERMATT FRONTIER PEAKS

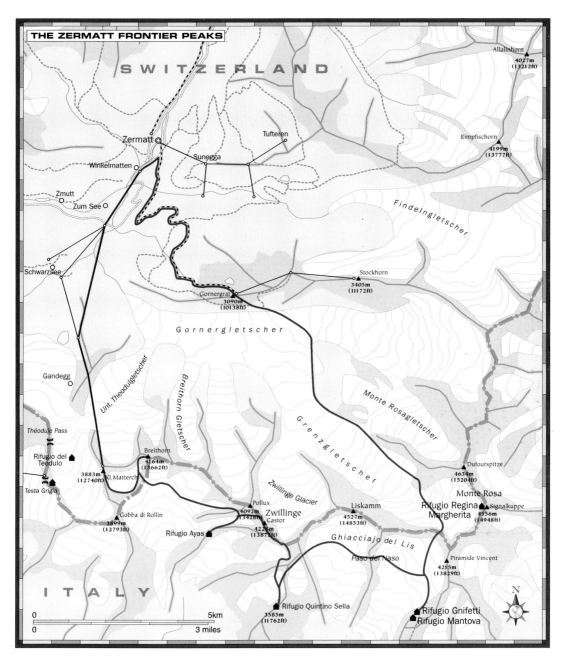

that leads to its beautiful summit. Views from both Castor and Pollux are extensive, with Liskamm and the Monte Rosa summits close by; the Dom, Täschhorn and the Alphubel above the Mattertal, and the Matterhorn and the Dent d'Herens on the Italian frontier above Cervinia. Far away are Mont Blanc and the Gran Paradiso. This view is to be seen in varying forms from all the summits in this area so I won't describe it each time. Suffice it to say that this trek provides superb views both near

and far and the only thing you'll probably miss is the greenery of the valleys which you'll appreciate all the more afterwards.

From the summit of Castor follow the undulating ridge southeast to its very end at point 4093m (13429ft) – don't try to turn right before this. Now turn south and descend, steeply at first, on the ridge, then head rightwards onto easier slopes and continue south-southeast to reach the Quintino Sella hut at 3585m (11762ft).

The impressive northeast face of Liskamm, from the Parrotspitze.

Rifugio Quintino Sella to Rifugio Gnifetti/Rifugio Mantova

This section involves the crossing of the rather impressive Paso del Naso, under the steep ice and rock of the south face of Liskamm. Ascend the Felik Glacier passing right of the base of the rocky ridge coming down from the Felikjoch. Cross the Lis Glacier in an arc at the easiest angle. The slopes of the Paso del Naso are steep and you must be very careful here. You can't see what's beneath you until after it's finished, but you wouldn't want to fall. The pass is in fact a shoulder above the Cresta del Naso buttress which forms the south ridge of the summit of Liskamm.

The Naso is ascended diagonally from left to right and can vary from straightforward snow to hard ice. Pass around the nose at about 4150m (13614ft), not going over the summit of the Naso, and then descend the steep snow/ice slope eastwards. If this is too icy late in the season then another way is possible by taking the broken rocks just on the right (south), sometimes marked by a pole, then traverse back left to the foot of the steep slope. From here ascend gently east then southeast to meet the well-worn track from Gnifetti to Monte Rosa in the vicinity of the Balmenhorn.

Descend now easily to the Gnifetti hut or the Mantova just below. Choose whichever is more to your taste. Both enjoy great views away down to the Gressoney valley far below. To the northeast are the southern peaks of Monte Rosa: Ludswighöhe, Corno Nero, the Balmenhorn and Piramide Vincent. Further down is the Punta Giordani, the most southerly and insignificant summit. To the north is the huge whaleback summit of Liskamm.

Rifugio Gnifetti/ Rifugio Mantova to Zermatt or the Rifugio Regina Margherita

Today's objective is to return to Switzerland. This can be achieved by simply heading up the Lis Glacier to the Lisjoch which is passed further east at 4246m (13931ft) just above the col, at a place sometimes marked with a pole (as the north side of the Lisjoch proper is in fact a steep serac face). It is possible to climb Liskamm, but that ascent goes beyond the scope of this guide as it is exposed and quite difficult.

Alternatively you could take in as many of the southern Monte Rosa summits as you wish – there are plenty to choose from. The Pyramid Vincent (4215m/13821ft), Balmenhorn (4167m/ 13672ft), Ludwigshöhe (4341m/14243ft) and Parrotspitze (4432m/14533ft) are straightforward snow slopes and ridges, whilst the Corno Nero (4321m/14177ft) is very short but steep (on all sides). There is a charming little hut on the Balmenhorn, which could provide a haven in cold weather.

Whatever you decide to do, you'll arrive at the top of the Grenzgletscher, back in Switzerland, under the main Monte Rosa summits. This is a mountaineer's playground – so many high summits and so close together. Both the Signalkuppe (4554m/14942ft) and the Dufourspitze (4634m/ 15204ft) are easily climbed from here (see p148). If you've followed this trek and wish to climb these peaks, it's probably best to stay in the Rifugio Regina Margherita rather than descend all the way to the Monte Rosa hut only to have to climb up again. From the Margherita hut it's a short descent to the Colle Gnifetti and then traversing the Zumsteinspitze (4563m/14971ft) and the Grenzsattel (4453m/14610ft) onwards to the summit of the Dufourspitze.

To descend to Zermatt follow the tortuous Grenzgletscher, normally on its right side, to exit onto the moraine somewhere between 3100m (10171ft) and 2960m (9712ft), depending on the snow cover. Go past the Monte Rosa hut to the Gornergletscher, which is traversed without difficulty to gain a rising footpath leading to the Gornergrat railway at Rotenboden. Descend by train to Zermatt.

PEAK: THE BREITHORN

From the Mattertal valley the Breithorn appears as a huge complex mass of rock and ice, dominating the western end of the Monte Rosa group of peaks. Dwarfed beside this summit is the insignificant-looking Klein Matterhorn (3883m/ 12740ft), summit of the cable car out of Zermatt. This lift allows the Breithorn summit to claim its place as probably the most accessible 4000-m (13124-ft) peak in the Alps, challenged only by the Allalinhorn near Saas Fee.

Easy it may be, but this doesn't mean it isn't worthwhile. It's a good first experience at this altitude, and if you haven't previously been to 4000m (13116ft) you will doubtless feel the effects of the thinner air. This climb also takes you up into the high mountains with the inevitable wonderful views.

You won't be alone here, but don't let the

CLIMB ESSENTIALS

SUMMIT Breithorn (4164m/13662ft).
GRADE PD
HEIGHT GAIN FROM COL 368m (1207ft).
APPROXIMATE TIME 2–3 hours.
MAP 1:25 000: Carte Nationale de la Suisse 1348 Zermatt.

large numbers of people make you think there are no dangers – the area is glaciated and there is at least one bergschrund waiting for unsuspecting unroped climbers.

From the Klein Matterhorn lift station walk through the tunnel and up the increasingly steep southwest summit slopes, to reach the broad southwest ridge. This leads easily to the summit, but beware of the steep drop-off down the south face. Return by the same route.

The Breithorn's south face is a gentle glaciated slope that allows a relatively easy ascent compared to its impressive north face.

THE PENNINE ALPS REGIONAL DIRECTORY

GETTING THERE BY AIR

Geneva and Zurich are the most convenient airports for the Pennine Alps. Both airports are served by many different airlines, including Swissair, British Airways and Easyjet. From the airport you need to either hire a car or use the extremely efficient Swiss public transport system to reach the starting points for the treks in this guide. Trains will take you along the major valleys and up to Zermatt for example. For towns not on the train lines there are Postbuses which leave from the post offices in town. These distinctive yellow buses also carry the mail from the village post offices to the main sorting offices. They are always on time and the service is regular. During office hours you buy your ticket in the Post Office, otherwise pay the driver direct. Timetables can be found at the post offices and at the local tourist office.

GETTING THERE BY TRAIN

It's easy to access the region by train from many cities in Europe, and if you book in advance you may get a Swiss railcard giving reductions on your journey.

GETTING THERE BY ROAD

Driving out, you'll need to buy a 'vignette' to use the Swiss motorways, which can be obtained at the frontier. Italian motorways have tolls and credit cards are not always accepted so be sure to have cash – Swiss or Italian.

ACCOMMODATION

In the main towns there are plenty of hotels or *gîtes*, as well as campsites in the summer. However, some of the smaller towns do not have many hotels and in high season booking in advance is essential.

Mountain huts

There is an enormous number of huts to choose from in this region. Since phone numbers change, individual hut numbers are not listed here. The best way to find out how to reserve a hut is to contact the local tourist office and they may well make the reservation for you. For well known treks the local tourist office can give you a list of hut numbers. If you want to visit a hut out of season or make your reservation before the hut opens you'll need to contact the guardian at his private number, which the tourist office can provide. Huts owned by Alpine Clubs or by the National Parks can also be booked via the relevant governing body.
For all accommodation the best sources of information are the tourist offices, where English is spoken.

DIRECTORY

For all telephone numbers the local numbers are noted – to telephone from abroad add the international code and drop the first 0, except for Italy where the entire number is dialled.
Geneva Airport: tel: 022 717 7111, www.gva.ch
Zurich airport: tel: 01 157 1060, www.zurich-airport.com
Swissair: www.swissair.com
British Airways: www.britishairways.com
Easyjet: www.easyjet.com
Swiss rail: www.sbb.ch
Rail Europe: www.raileurope.com
Italian rail: www.itwg.com

Swiss Tourist Offices for Pennine Alps treks

For contact numbers for all tourist offices in the Valais/Wallis region of Switzerland: tel. 027 327 3570; fax 027 327 3571; email: info@valaistourism.ch; www.matterhornstate.com
For the whole of Switzerland: www.myswitzerland.com
Geneva Tourist Office: tel. 022 909 7000; fax 022 909 7075; email: info@geneva-tourism.ch; www.geneva-tourism.ch
Zurich Tourist Office: tel. 01 215 40 00; fax 01 215 40 44; email: information@zurichtourism.ch; www.zurichtourism.ch
Zermatt Tourist Office: tel. 027 967 0181; fax 027 967 0185; email: zermatt@wallis.ch; www.zermatt.ch
Täsch Tourist Office: tel. 027 967 1689; fax 027 967 2118; email: info@taesch.ch; www.taesch.ch
Saas Fee Tourist Office: tel. 027 958 1858; fax 027 958 1860; email: to@saas-fee.ch; www.saas-fee.com
St Niklaus Tourist Office: tel. 027 956 3663; fax 027 956 2939; email: info@st-niklaus.ch; www.st-niklaus.ch
Grächen Tourist Office: tel. 027 955 6060; fax 027 955 6066; email: info@graechen.ch; www.graechen.ch
Verbier Tourist Office: tel. 027 775 3888; fax 027 775 3889; email: verbiertourism@verbier.ch; www.verbier.ch
Val de Bagnes Tourist Office: tel. 027 776 1682; fax 027 776 1541
Martigny Tourist Office: tel. 027 721 2220; fax 027 721 2224; email: info@martignytourism.ch; www.martignytourism.ch
Sion Tourist Office: tel. 027 322 8586; fax 027 322 1882; email: info@siontourism.ch; www.siontourism.ch
Zinal Tourist Office: tel. 027 475 1370; fax 027 475 2977; email: zinal@vsinfo.ch; www.zinal.ch
Turtmann Tourist Office: tel. 027 934 2443; email: info@eischoll.ch; www.eischoll.ch
Les Haudères Tourist Office: tel. 027 283 1015; fax 027 283 3315; email: leshauderes@evoleneregion.ch
Arolla Tourist Office: tel. 027 283 1083; fax 027 283 2270; email: arolla@span.ch; www.arolla.com
Bourg-St-Pierre Tourist Office: tel. 027 787 1200; email: info@saint-bernard.ch; www.saint-bernard.ch
Ovronnaz Tourist Office: tel. 027 306 4293; fax 027 306 8141; email: info@ovronnaz.ch; www.ovronnaz.ch
Kandersteg Tourist Office: tel. 033 675 8080; fax 033 675 8081
Kiental Tourist Office: tel: 033 676 1010; fax 033 676 1354; email: vvkiental@datacomm.ch
Frutigen Tourist Office: tel. 033 671 1421; fax 033 671 5421; email: frutigen-tourismus@bluewin.ch; www.frutigen-tourismus.ch

Italian Tourist Offices for Pennine Alps treks

Aosta Tourist Office: tel. 0165 33352
Cervinia Tourist Office: tel. 0166 949136; fax 0166 949731
Macugnaga Tourist Office: tel. 0324 65119; fax 0324 65775; email: sviva@libero.it; www.macugnaga-online.it
Gressonney Saint Trinité Tourist Office: tel. 0125 355185/366143
Gran Saint Bernard Tourist Office: tel. 0165 78559

French Tourist Offices for Pennine Alps treks

For general information and French tourist offices: www.maison-de-la-france.com
Chamonix Tourist Office: tel. 04 50 53 00 24; fax 04 50 53 58 90; email: info@chamonix.com; www.chamonix.com
Reservations: tel. 04 50 53 23 33; fax 04 50 53 87 42

THE ALPS AT RISK

Most Alpine areas feature national parks or reserves that are protected to a greater or lesser degree. Construction of buildings and ski resorts is limited and controlled and road development is strictly regimented, all with the aim of conserving the region in as natural a state as possible, whilst allowing the local economies to develop. The one major exception to this is the Mont Blanc massif which benefits from no official protection at all, despite the fact that the Chamonix valley is one of the most-visited tourist sites in the world. The massif already has several ski areas, and a tunnel beneath it, and remains at risk from burgeoning development which in turn is responding to an ever-growing tourist trade.

The Mont Blanc region is now at the forefront of a problem that threatens all European mountain regions, protected or not: that of air pollution. This is largely the result of a rapid growth in heavy-goods transport over the last few decades, with the Alps providing the main transit routes for trucks moving between European countries. This pollution is widely considered to have catastrophic consequences: the modification of the mountains by roads and tunnels, the over-use of certain routes,

the consequent noise, and the possible climatic changes caused by carbon emissions.

Several environmental groups are active in the Alps, trying to restrain the growth of transport and also to change the form it takes. To get an idea of the dramatic recent changes, consider the Mont Blanc tunnel. Completed in 1966, the tunnel saw 48,000 lorries in its first year. In 1998, 770,000 lorries passed through. This is an increase of 1,700 per cent, and added to this is the fact that the tunnel has not been modifed, and that modern trucks are generally much longer and heavier than they were thirty years ago.

General statistics show that heavy-goods traffic across the Alps has increased by 30 per cent since 1970. It is thought that this has polluted the air in the narrow mountain valleys, damaging the trees and natural habitats, and affecting the quality of life in these areas. Eleven million people live in the Alps, most of them in narrow valleys where living space is limited and at an altitude where air pollution is more noticeable and more damaging to health and habitat. In short, never in this region's history has there been such a shock to the environment as in the last thirty years.

Climbers making their way up the Signalküppe (4554m/14942ft); the Rifugio Regina Margherita can be seen on the summit.

In March 1999 a fire broke out in a truck travelling through the Mont Blanc tunnel. The load of margarine and flour proved to be extremely flammable, and the fire quickly got out of control. At least 38 people died as a result of the fumes and fire in the tunnel. That tragedy resulted in a renewed demand for the prohibition of lorry traffic in the Chamonix valley. Prior to the accident 2300 lorries were going through the tunnel every day. The air-pollution levels in Chamonix (6,000 inhabitants) were believed to be the equal of those of Grenoble (165,000 inhabitants). Added to this was noise pollution: the law allows 60 dba (Decibel A) at night and 65 dba in the day, but 74.4 dba were measured in the day and 65.6 at night.

Groups such as Mountain Wilderness, the Association Pour Respect du Site du Mont Blanc, and the Iniziativa de las Alpas (Alpine Initiative) are all calling for trucks to be carried by rail across the Alps. Several railway tunnels already exist in Switzerland, and whether more will be built elsewhere is the crucial issue of the next few years.

In a referendum in 1994 the people of Switzerland voted in favour of the Alpine Initiative, whose main policies are to limit trans-Alpine traffic by transferring goods onto rail within ten years, and to forbid any increase in route capacity in the alpine regions. As a consequence an article for the protection of the Alps has now become part of the Swiss constitution. It remains to be seen how the Swiss government will translate this article into action, and whether other countries will follow suit.

The regulation of freight traffic is just the first step in trying to restore the Alps to the state they were in before 1970. It can only be hoped that further environmental-protection measures will be applied throughout the Alps so that future generations can enjoy their spectacular natural beauty.

FURTHER INFORMATION
Iniziativa de las Alpas (Alpine Initiative),
Case Postale 29, CH 3900 Brig
www.initiative-des-alpes.ch

Association pour Respect du Site du Mont Blanc,
Maison de la Montagne,
F 74000 Chamonix
www.chamonix.org/arsmb

Mountain Wilderness,
5 Place Bir Hakeim,
F 38000 Grenoble
www.mountainwilderness.org

WINTER CODE OF GOOD CONDUCT

The following code of conduct has been drawn up by the French association of trekking guides (the *Accompagnateurs en Montagne*). Whilst it's clearly desirable to avoid rules in the mountains, there are certain guidelines that should be followed. This is to ensure that everyone has a safe and enjoyable time in the mountains, and that at the same time the natural world remains relatively undisturbed by our passing through. Although drawn up with winter trekking in mind, the ideas expressed here are equally relevant for summer trekking and mountaineering.

How to have fun walking, while remaining safe and respectful of nature:

Be conscious of the dangers
Fog, hard icy slopes, stream beds, lakes, avalanches, the cold, summer paths impassable in winter, wind, intense sun, hidden rocks and fences... there are many dangers to be aware of.

Be well-equipped
Use clothes and equipment that are made for winter conditions. Be sure to take enough food and drink. Be sure to have appropriate safety equipment – map, first-aid kit, survival bag, rope, avalanche transceiver, shovel, probe – depending on the nature of the walk.

Be respectful and aware of nature
Find out about any areas that have restricted access. Try to avoid disturbing any animals, which are already in a fragile state in the winter. Don't leave the route just to get a close up view of a creature – binoculars are sufficient. Respect the peace of the mountains and take care with young trees and plants.

Be respectful of others
The ski pistes are primarily for skiers, and the cross-country trails are easily broken down by snow shoers and walkers. Many people go to the mountains for the peace and silence.

Be aware of your tracks
One track in virgin snow is beautiful, ten different ones are not so fine.

Be well-informed
Take note of the conditions, and the weather forecast. Speak to the experts – mountain leaders and guides, ski pisteurs, park and hut wardens, etc.

FIRST AID IN THE ALPS

If you have a serious accident in the Alps you can generally expect to get help fairly rapidly. However, some first-aid knowledge is essential for any mountain venture as accidents can happen at any time, in any place, not just in the mountains. Anyone, in any walk of life, can benefit from taking a standard first-aid course.

The most common health problems encountered in the mountains, and the first aid required in such situations, are listed below.

Injuries to limbs caused by falls or stumbles
In the case of limb injuries it is not always necessary to call for help. If the limb is the only injury and the casualty is willing, then a slow descent to the nearest village may be possible. However, help should be called if there are possible associated injuries, such as possible internal damage or a compound fracture; trying to move the casualty could cause further damage.

Head injuries due to rockfall
Head injuries, unless very superficial, should be treated seriously, and any loss of consciousness dictates a rescue call as allowing a person who has been unconscious to walk without medical supervision could incur concussion. Concussion is caused by the shaking of the brain, leading to initial unconsciousness often followed by a sometimes brief period of consciousness. Later the brain can swell which may lead to serious cerebral compression. Whilst waiting for rescue keep the victim warm, comfortable and reassured. Insulate the casualty from underneath well. If the casualty is unconscious keep a regular check on the breathing and pulse and keep the airway clear of obstruction.

Illness as a result of heat, fatigue or altitude
These problems can usually be treated with food, rest, drink and a reassessment of the day's objective. For further information on acclimatisation and Acute Mountain Sickness (see box on page 280).

Cold injuries, most commonly hypothermia or frostbite
In the case of hypothermia and frostbite, prevention is the best cure. Be aware of your body in the cold – any numb parts should be a cause for immediate concern. When frostbite or hypothermia are already established it's far more serious. Frozen extremities should be rewarmed as soon as possible, but not refrozen. A person with severe hypothermia is very ill and needs emergency care urgently.

Stomach problems caused by bad food or water or poor hygiene
Stomach problems can usually be treated with pharmacy drugs, which it's wise to carry on any multi-day trek. The main danger of these conditions is dehydration resulting from the loss of fluids.

Heart problems
These problems are very serious and require an immediate change of plan. Everyone should have a working knowledge of resuscitation techniques, and these can't be learnt from books – a course is needed, and regularly, since hopefully you'll never have to perform in earnest.

FIRST-AID KIT LIST

Below is a suggested list for a first-aid kit for a multi-day trek in the mountains. The aim is to carry only the lightest essentials, which means throwing away extra packaging, and trying to get small containers for pills etc. Being resourceful allows you to avoid carrying too many bulky articles - for example a scarf can be used as a sling.

Blister kit
Pencil and paper
Antiseptic cream
Betadine
Sterile dressings (small and big)
Cottonwool swabs
Roll of adhesive tape
Dextrose tablets
Diarrhoea tablets
Aspirin (for circulation problems such as frostbite or heart attacks)
Painkillers (eg paracetamol)
Anti-inflammatories
Antihistamine cream
Crêpe bandage
Scissors
Tweezers
Needle

Bibliography

Trekking and Climbing
English Language
Cliff, Peter: *The Haute Route Chamonix Zermatt* (1993), Cordee, UK. A practical guide to the route, both on foot and on skis.

Dumler, Helmut and Burkhardt, Willi: *The High Mountains of the Alps* (1993), Diadem, UK. The bible for the 4000-m (13124-ft) peaks, describing the main routes to the summits, often with a historical account of the first ascent of the peak.

Goedeke, Richard: *The Alpine 4000-m Peaks* (1993), Diadem, UK. A concise guide to the normal routes on these peaks.

Lieberman, Marcia: *Walking the Alpine Parks of France and Northwest Italy* (1994), The Mountaineers, USA. Useful for its information about the parks, and its suggestions for non-glaciated walks of varying levels of difficulty.

Rebuffat, Gaston: *The Mont Blanc Massif* (1991), Diadem, UK. The English translation of the popular book by one of France's most revered Alpinists. Cannot fail to inspire.

Reynolds, Kev: *Walking in the Alps* (1998), Cicerone, UK. A modern version of Hubert Walker's *Walking in the Alps*, describing areas rather than detailed walks.

French Language
Cassany, Didier: *Rando-Raquettes* (1996), Editions Olizane, Switzerland. Offers a variety of snow-shoe walks in the Chamonix region and French-speaking Switzerland.

Lamory, Jean Marc: *Raquette à Neige – La Haute Savoie* (1999), Didier Richard, France. A guidebook describing a large number of snow-shoe walks in La Haute Savoie.

Lamory, Jean Marc: *Raquette à Neige – La Savoie* (1998), Didier Richard, France. A guidebook describing snow-shoe walks in La Savoie.

Millon, Pierre: *Les Grands Sommets du Randonneur* (1997), Glénat, France. An inspiring book describing the ascension of non-glaciated peaks – almost all by a walking route or a route with easy scrambling – in the French Alps, the Pyrenees and Corsica.

Piola, Michel: *Le Topo du Mont Blanc Massif Tomes 1 and 2* (1988, 1993), Editions Equinoxe, Switzerland. The definitive guides to rock routes of all grades in the Mont Blanc massif.

History
French Language
Ballu, Yves: *À la Conquête de Mont Blanc*, Découvertes Gallimard, France. A guide to the history of Mont Blanc and associated summits since the 18th century.

Payot, Paul: *Au Royaume du Mont Blanc* (1978), Denoël, France. A wonderful history of the Mont Blanc region.

Pillet, Jean-Marc: *Au Pays du Grand Saint Bernard*, Valais Guides, Switzerland. Full of interesting facts about the region.

Nature
English Language
Flegg, Jim and Sterry, Paul: *Photographic Guide to Birds of Britain and Europe* (2001), New Holland, UK. Good photos enable relatively easy identification of birds encountered on treks – provided the birds stay still for long enough.

Goodden, Rosemary and Robert, Bee Joyce: *Green Guide to Butterflies of Britain and Europe* (2001), New Holland, UK.

Grey Wilson, Christopher and Blamey, Marjorie: *Alpine Flowers of Britain and Europe* (1992), Collins, UK. A well-presented guide to the flowers of the Alps, ideal for people who are willing to take the time to search for flowers by family.

Jaitner, Christine: *Alpine Animals* (1991), Kompass, Austria. Simple photographic guide to the most common animals found in the Alps. Small and easy to carry.

Murie, Olaus J and Peterson, Roger Tory: *Animal Tracks* (1998) Peterson Field Guide, USA. Although aimed at the American mountains, this book covers many of the animal tracks encountered in the European Alps.

Sterry, Paul: *Photographic Guide to Mushrooms of Britain and Europe* (2001), New Holland, UK.

Sutton, David and Emberson, Colin: *Green Guide to Wild Flowers of Britain and Europe* (2001), New Holland, UK. A simple guide to the flowers of the Alps.

French Language
Bang, Preben and Dahlström, Preben: *Guide des Traces d'Animaux* (1996), Delachaux and Niestlé, Switzerland. The definitive guide to the animal tracks you may encounter in the Alps.

Dragesco, Eric: *La Vie Sauvage dans les Alpes* (1995), Delachaux and Niestlé, Switzerland. This book is a joy for anyone with a real interest in wildlife. It offers amazing photos and lots of information.

Acknowledgements

I'd like to thank the following people for their help and advice with this book:

Jean-François Rouge, Tim Brewton, Mike Cable, Gilles Brunot, Luisa Dusi, Jean Mappelli, Bernard Marsigny, Christine Jucker and Hermann Inäbnit, Alan Poxon, Hugh Clarke, Steve Jones, Wil Hurford, the Museums of Chamonix and Zermatt, and Victor Saunders (for asking me to write the book). Also to the various editors of New Holland who trusted me to come up with the goods. Also, and especially, my thanks to Jon de Montjoye, who provided information, especially for the glacier treks and alpine peaks, proofread, and shared me with this project for many late nights and early mornings.

I'd also like to thank all those people who have trekked with me in the Alps, and who have let me use them in my photos.

All photos by Hilary Sharp, except those by Jon de Montjoye (pages 1, 4, 33, 40, 67, 120–121, 123, 140, 160, 166); Mike Cable (pages 2–3); Bernard Marsigny (page 38); Wil Hurford (pages 56, 60, 169); Mario Colonel (pages 59, 114, 148); George Jackman (page 149); Tim Brewton (back cover).

Glossary

The following terms may need some explanation. They are used throughout the book.

Alpage
A summer farm usually above the treeline. The cattle are brought up here for the months of July and August to graze.

Bergschrund
A crevasse which forms at the junction of a mountain and glacier. The glacier is, by gravity, pulling away from the mountain, which cannot move, and therefore cracks, leaving this crevasse. The term 'bergschrund' is German.

Col
This is a pass or a saddle. In German it is usually 'joch' and in Italian 'colle' or 'bocca'.

Couloir
The French term for a gully, This word is becoming more and more common in English now.

Cwm/corrie/combe
This is a basin formed around three sides by hills or mountains. It can be steep sided, like a cirque, or more gently rounded. Often there is a lake in the basin and a stream flows out of the unenclosed side, down into the valley. It is the result of previous glaciation.

Glissade
From the French word *glisser*, meaning to slide. Glissading can be a very fast, efficient means of descending snow slopes, but it should be approached with caution and common sense. To glissade you can either slide down on two feet, using arms, trekking poles or ice axes to balance; or, and this is easier but wetter, slide from a sitting position, using your feet to control yourself and possibly trailing your ice axe in the snow behind. Care should be taken to check the run out of the slope – boulders or a step cliff present dangers, and it's very difficult to glissade in crampons. If in doubt, walk down.

Nevé
Old snow remaining from the winter. It is usually hard and icy and can remain in gullies and on north-facing slopes until well into the summer season, making passage difficult or dangerous.

Rognon
A rock or buttress, standing alone in a glacier. These are often landmarks for glacier travel, and can be crucial in the fog.

Serac
This describes a hanging or overhanging ice or snow cliff, formed by the glacier.

Index